Octobe

October 1917
workers in power

PAUL LE BLANC, ERNEST MANDEL
DAVID MANDEL, LEON TROTSKY
ROSA LUXEMBURG, LENIN

Resistance Books
IIRE
MERLIN PRESS

This collection first published in 2016 by
The Merlin Press Ltd
Central Books Building
Freshwater Road
London
RM8 1RX
www.merlinpress.co.uk

in association with Resistance Books and
the International Institute for Research and Education
www.resistancebooks.org
www.iire.org

October 1917: Workers in Power is issue number 60
of the IIRE Notebooks for Study and Research

Edited by Fred Leplat and Alex de Jong

ISBN 978-0-85036-727-0

Cover photo: Petrograd Soviet Assembly 1917

Printed in the EU on behalf of Stanton Book Services, Wellingborough,
Northants

CONTENTS

PREFACE

The Russian revolution of 1917 turned the country upside down: the Tsar was deposed in February and in October the workers took power. Ten decades after this momentous event, the debate still rages about its meaning. Was it a dangerous utopian experiment brought about by a coup d'état organised by an elitist Bolshevik party? Or was it the result of a mass movement of workers and peasants who no longer wanted to be ruled in the old ways and who initially just sought 'bread, peace and land'?

The bureaucratic and brutal dictatorship of Stalin, which lasted nearly three decades following Lenin's death, has enabled the right to portray the October Revolution and the early years of the Soviet Union as a failure. Moreover, they argue, any popular uprising for a social justice, like the French Revolution of 1789 or the Russian Revolution of 1917, will necessarily lead to a totalitarian outcome.

This book is intended to provide a critical examination of the achievements of the Russian Revolution and to refute the argument that it was a utopian experiment doomed to failure.

The introduction by Paul Le Blanc, 'Making sense of October 1917', evaluates the events one century on – discussing recent scholarship and debates, new ways of comprehending class, the centrality of women and that of ethnicity, race and national identity. Le Blanc considers 'what went right' with this revolution, and 'what went wrong'. Were the Bolsheviks elitists, sectarian and authoritarian? What is still relevant today and what is not?

The short historical introduction by Francois Vercammen, 'The stages of the 1917 Revolution', along with the chronology and list of people, places and events, should be useful to readers who are not so familiar with the events of the period.

Was October 1917 a coup d'état or a social revolution? Writing as both a historian and political activist, Ernest Mandel sets out to analyse the events and vigorously reassert the deep legitimacy of the Russian Revolution. He considers the gains of the revolution, discusses the mistakes made by the Bolshevik leadership in 1917-21, and sets out lessons for revolutionary Marxists today.

David Mandel's 'Economic power and factory committees in the Russian Revolution' draws on Russian-language archives to tell the story from below. Petrograd workers did not dream at first of 'socialist experiments'. Factory committees met fierce resistance from owners; they were driven to take management into their own hands and to seek the nationalisation of industries. Common conceptions about the 'utopian' and 'anarchistic' impulses supposedly behind the October Revolution are reassessed and refuted. In a further text, David Mandel reasserts the legitimacy of the October Revolution, like the other authors in this book.

The short texts by Lenin, Rosa Luxemburg and Leon Trotsky are included to give a flavour of the times by contemporary leading members of the communist movement. The speech by Leon Trotsky, 'In Defence of October', given on 27 November 1932 while he was in exile, is also a reminder that the fight for the spirit and the legitimacy of the Russian revolution is not new.

The book contains an extensive bibliography to help readers who may wish to study further the Russian revolution and its legacy.

I am extremely grateful for the advice that Paul Le Blanc provided in selecting the texts by Lenin, Rosa Luxemburg and Leon Trotsky, in making suggestions for the bibliography, and pointing out inaccuracies in Ernest Mandel's text. Without his help, this book would not be so useful and stimulating.

I wish to express my gratitude to Tony Zurbrugg at Merlin Press for his help and patience in ensuring that I provided a manuscript in the right format and with as few errors as possible. Adrian Howe at Merlin Press should be congratulated in finding the dramatic photograph of the Petrograd Soviet featuring on the cover.

Resistance Books and the IIRE are grateful to the Marxist Internet Archive for placing in the public domain 'To the Population' and 'Letter to American Workers' by Lenin, and 'In Defence of October' by Trotsky. These texts from the Marxist Internet Archive have been included in this book.

Fred Leplat
Resistance Books, London
July 2016

AUTHORS' BIOGRAPHIES

Paul Le Blanc is Professor of History at La Roche College (USA) and author of internationally acclaimed works on the labour and socialist movements, including *Lenin and the Revolutionary Party, From Marx to Gramsci,* and *Leon Trotsky.* An editor of the eight-volume *International Encyclopaedia of Revolution and Protest,* he is currently helping to oversee the Verso Books edition of *The Complete Works of Rosa Luxemburg.*

David Mandel is a Canadian scholar, union and political activist. He teaches political science at the Université du Québec à Montréal and has been active in labour education in the Russia, Ukraine and Belarus for many years. He has written extensively on the labour movement in the Russian Revolution and also in the post-Soviet period, including *The Petrograd Workers in the Russian Revolution - February 1917-June 1918* (a revised and enlarged edition to appear in 2017, Brill and Haymarket Press) and *Labour after Communism* (Black Rose Press).

Ernest Mandel (1923-1995) was a Marxist economist, activist and a leading member of the Fourth International. Ernest Mandel published many articles and around 30 books during his life, which were translated into many languages. Among his most important publications are *Marxist Economic Theory* (1962) and *Late Capitalism* (1972). He was central to the founding of the International Institute for Research and Education.

François Vercammen (1944-2015) was a leading member of the Belgian section and of the Fourth International. He was instrumental in establishing the International Institute for Research and Education. During his last active years he worked on the analysis of what he called the 'European despotic proto-state' and building links among the European anti-capitalist left.

ABBREVIATIONS

CC: Central Committee

CI: Communist International

CP: Communist Party

CPSU: Communist Party of the Soviet Union

CS: Soviet of Factory Committees

Kadets: Constitutional Democrats

NEP: New Economic Policy

RSDLP: Russian Social Democrat and Labour Party

RSFSR: Russian Soviet Federal Socialist Republic

SPD: (German) Social-Democratic Party

SR: Social Revolutionaries

SS: Nazi paramilitary forces

TsIK: Central Executive Committee of Soviets of Workers' and Soldiers' Deputies.

USSR: Union of Soviet Socialist Republics

USPD: (German) Independent Social Democrat Party

CHRONOLOGY OF THE RUSSIAN REVOLUTION

May–June 1896
General textile strike in St. Petersburg, which was renamed Petrograd at the start of World War I. The first large-scale coordinated labour action, which resulted in legislation shortening the working day. This was the first time any social group had been able to force the hand of the autocratic state through direct confrontation.

9 January 1905
Bloody Sunday when government massacre a peaceful demonstration of workers petitioning the Tsar for economic and democratic reforms. Workers all over the country responded in a massive strike wave that opened the Revolution of 1905, during which soviets made their first appearance.

November 1905
Petrograd workers launched a strike for the immediate introduction of the eight-hour day. The state and capital co-operated in a lockout of more than 100,000 workers. This was the beginning of the defeat of the revolution, which was assisted by the arrival of loyal troops from the Far East as the war with Japan ended, and by the start of a severe economic depression.

April 1912
Massacre of striking workers in the Lena Goldfields in Siberia, which coincides with the end of the depression. Workers all over Russia, and especially in Petrograd, responded with a massive strike wave, in which political and economic demands were inextricably combined.

1912–August 1914
Major labour upsurge, following the 1907–11 period of reaction, directed equally against the Tsarist state and against capital. The Bolsheviks became the dominant political force in the labour movement. On the eve of the war, Petrograd was the scene of pitched battles, complete with barricades, between workers and police. Many observers found the atmosphere reminiscent of 1905, except that now the polarization between the workers and the bourgeoisie was much deeper.

August 1914

Outbreak of World War I. An initial patriotic upsurge in society (much less among industrial workers), military mobilizations, and severe repression cut short the revolutionary movement.

August 1915–February 1917

Continued growth of the increasingly politicized strike movement. This was encouraged by the deteriorating economic conditions due to a war that was viewed as imperialistic, as well as by the severely repressive political and factory regimes.

February 1917

The strike movement culminated in a spontaneous general strike of Petrograd workers who won over the garrison. The revolution spreads rapidly, practically without bloodshed, to the rest of the country. Officially, power was in the hand of a Provisional Government formed by liberal politicians, representatives of the propertied classes, who had reluctantly rallied to the revolution once it had been accomplished. But the Petrograd Soviet, an elected assembly of worker and soldier delegates, dictated the government's official programme. The moderate socialist leaders of the Soviet were instructed by the Soviet to 'control' the bourgeois government. Real power was in the hands of the Soviet, which alone enjoyed the confidence of the soldiers. The programme of the Soviet was the immediate proposal of a democratic peace, free distribution of the landed estates to the peasantry, an eight-hour workday, and a democratic republic.

April Days, 1917

Publication of a secret government note to the Allies promising that Russia would respect all (imperialist) treaties and pursue the war to a victorious conclusion sparked off demonstrations in Petrograd against the government, causing the first limited armed clashes of the revolution. To bolster the government, the moderate socialist leaders of the Soviet formed a coalition government with the liberals. Workers initially supported this, believing that it would make more effective the control by the Soviet of the liberals. But they soon realized that the moderate socialists were prisoners of the liberals who were hostile to the programme of the Soviet, and the workers began to demand the direct transfer of power to the soviets. At the same time, economic dislocation deepened in the face of inactivity and sabotage by the government and owners, giving rise to the movement for workers' control. By early June, the Bolsheviks were a majority in the workers' section of the Petrograd Soviet.

July Days, 1917

On 3–4 July, workers and soldiers demonstrated to pressure the moderate leaders of the Central Executive Committee of Soviets to take power. The government, supported by some of the moderate socialists, responded with repression against the labour movement and the Bolsheviks. A period of reaction set in for several weeks.

27–31 August 1917

General Kornilov, supported by the liberals, marched on Petrograd in a coup attempt aimed at crushing the soviets and other organizations of workers. But his troops melted away en route, as the workers of Petrograd mobilized to defend the revolution.

September 1917

New elections to the soviets yielded Bolshevik majorities in the soviets of workers' and soldiers' deputies of almost all industrial centres. The Bolsheviks were the only party advocating soviet power. Peasants were seizing the land, not waiting for an agrarian reform that was constantly postponed by the coalition government, and the soldiers were beginning to desert en masse from the front.

25 October 1917

The Petrograd Soviet seizes power. The next day, the All-Russian Congress of Soviets of Workers' and Peasants' Deputies, endorsing the insurrection, took power and adopted decrees on land, peace and workers' control. Negotiations between the Bolsheviks and the moderate socialists on the formation of a coalition socialist government failed, as the moderates rejected the principle of soviet power, i.e. of a government without representation of the 'progressive bourgeoisie'. Only the Left Social Revolutionaries, a mainly peasant-based party close to the Bolsheviks, agreed to join a coalition.

12–14 November 1917

After three postponements by the Provisional Government, the Soviet government held elections to the Constituent Assembly. The Bolsheviks won 23.6 per cent of the overall vote and an overwhelming majority among workers. The populist Social Revolutionaries were the largest party with 40.9 per cent (the Mensheviks received 3 per cent, the liberals and rightist parties 8.4 per cent, and the national and Muslim parties 20.1 per cent), but a significant part of the Social Revolutionary vote (more than half) was actually cast for Left Social Revolutionaries, who were unable to run a separate list because their formal split with Right Social Revolutionaries had occurred only in September.

5 January 1918

The Constituent Assembly is dissolved once it became obvious that the moderate majority returned in the elections would reject soviet power and opt again for coalition government with the liberals.

May 1918

The number of employed industrial workers in Petrograd dropped to 143,000, from 406,000 at the start of 1917 and 340,000 at the start of 1918, as the economic collapse gathered force. By September 1918, only 120,000 factory workers were still employed in Petrograd. Hunger was becoming chronic in the cities. An uprising of Czech troops in transit through Russia marked the start of foreign intervention. The civil war lasted until the end of 1920 and made impossible any serious attempts to resolve the economic crisis.

INTRODUCTION
MAKING SENSE OF OCTOBER 1917

Paul Le Blanc

A hundred years on, the Russian Revolution of 1917 continues to be as much of a political battlefield as ever it was. Its meaning in this volume is suggested by documents from three revolutionary partisans of that time – Lenin, Luxemburg, and Trotsky – but also by two more recent discussions of the revolution. A rich general overview is provided by the late Ernest Mandel, one of the most prominent Marxist intellectuals of the twentieth century, and additional light is shed on the revolution's dynamics by present-day social historian David Mandel. This introduction discusses divergent interpretations of the Russian Revolution over the past century, touching on continuing controversies and new understandings among sympathetic but critical-minded interpreters, which may suggest its continuing relevance for problems and questions we face in our own time.[1]

Long-dead friends reaching out to us

An arduous voyage in 1917 brought four close friends, idealistic young journalists from the United States, to the shores of Russia. In the midst of a horrific World War, the centuries-old tyranny of monarchist autocracy had been overthrown. The revolutionary process was continuing, and the four wanted to understand what was going on.

The revolution began with International Women's Day rallies on March 8 (February 23 according to the old Tsarist calendar) that 'got out of hand'. They sparked momentous insurgencies among the common working people of Petrograd, with the military's rank-and-file refusing to repress the people's uprising and instead joining it. Masses of workers and soldiers (the latter mostly peasants in uniform) organized a growing and increasingly substantial network of democratic councils – the Russian word was *soviets* – to coordinate their efforts. In addition to liberty (freedom of speech and organization, equal rights for all, the right of workers to form trade unions, etc.), they demanded peace and bread, also calling for land to the country's impoverished peasant majority. In the wake of the monarchy's sudden collapse, conservative and liberal and moderate socialist politicians scurried to form a Provisional Government that would contain the revolutionary process and consider how 'best' to address the demands for peace, bread, land. The most militant faction of the Russian socialist movement – the Bolsheviks (majority-ites) led by Vladimir Ilyich Lenin – insisted that peace, bread and land would only be achieved by overthrowing the Provisional Government and giving all political power to the soviets. This, they believed, would spark a world process of workers' revolutions that would end war and imperialism, overturning all tyrannies, and bringing a transition from capitalism to socialism. After several months of intensive activity and experience, the Bolsheviks and their allies won majorities in the soviets and went on to make the second revolution of 1917 – a popularly supported insurrection on 7 November (24 October according to the old calendar).

The first of the four friends to get their books out (in October 1918) were Louise Bryant and Bessie Beatty. The freshness of their astute observations and vibrant impressions continues to reward the reader after ten decades.

With *Six Months in Red Russia*, Louise Bryant is visibly wrestling toward an understanding of the vast and complex swirl of experience. 'I who saw the dawn of a new world can only present my fragmentary and scattered evidence to you with a good deal of awe,' she tells us. 'I feel as one who went forth to gather pebbles and found pearls.' Reaching for generalization, she writes: 'The great war could not leave an unchanged world in its wake – certain movements of society were bound to be pushed forward, others retarded. ... Socialism is here, whether we like it or not – just as woman suffrage is here, and it spreads with the years. In Russia the socialist state is an accomplished fact.'[2]

'Revolution is the blind protest of the mass against their own ignorant state,' writes her friend Bessie Beatty in *The Red Heart of Russia*. 'It is as important to Time as the first awkward struggle of the amoeba. It is man in the act of making himself.' Obviously still trying to comprehend what she had seen, she muses: 'Time will give to the world war, the political revolution, and the social revolution their true values. We cannot do it. We are too close to the facts to see the truth.' But she immediately adds: 'To have failed to see the hope in the Russian Revolution is to be a blind man looking at the sun rise.'[3]

The last of the books to appear (in 1921), Albert Rhys Williams's *Through the Russian Revolution*, reaches for the interplay of cause and effect, objective and subjective factors:

It was not the revolutionists who made the Russian Revolution. ... For a century gifted men and women of Russia had been agitated over the cruel oppression of the people. So they became agitators. ... But the people did not rise. ... Then came the supreme agitator – Hunger. Hunger, rising out of economic collapse and war, goaded the sluggish masses into action. Moving out against the old worm-eaten structure they brought it down. ... The revolutionists, however, had their part. They did not make the Revolution. But they made the Revolution a success. By their efforts they had prepared a body of men and women with minds trained to see facts, with a program to fit the facts and with fighting energy to drive it thru.[4]

The 'middle' book – appearing on January 1919 – was the one destined to become the classic eyewitness account, John Reed's magnificent *Ten Days That Shook the World*. A fierce partisan of the Bolsheviks, he quickly joined the world Communist movement that the Bolsheviks established in the same year that his book was published. But no one of any political persuasion can disagree with this generalization: 'No matter what one thinks of Bolshevism, it is undeniable that the Russian Revolution is one of the great events of human history, and the rise of the Bolsheviki a phenomenon of worldwide importance.'[5]

In more than one sense, these friends continue to reach out to us. Of course, they offer their own lived experience and eyewitness impressions of what happened in one of the great events in human history. But also, while they and all who they knew have long-since died, the patterns and dynamics and urgent issues of their own time have in multiple ways continued down through history, to our own time. The experience, ideas, and urgent questions they are wrestling with continue to have resonance and relevance for many of us today, and this will most likely be the case for others tomorrow.

Corroboration and contrasts

In the 1930s three particularly significant accounts appeared. Leon Trotsky's three-volume *History of the Russian Revolution* of 1932-33 was followed by William H. Chamberlin's two-volume *The Russian Revolution 1917-1921* – both published outside of the Soviet Union. From within the USSR, in 1938, came the most authoritative account, embedded in the seventh chapter of *History of the Communist Party of the Soviet Union (Bolsheviks) Short Course* – composed by a commission of that organization's Central Committee, with the very active participation of Joseph Stalin.

'Trotsky's writing was absorbing, and the translator, Max Eastman … did him justice,' recalled Carl Marzani, one of many radicalizing intellectuals in the United States during the 1930s. 'The details, from the revolutionary insider, were fascinating, but the volume excited me most as a sample of Marxist writing and methodology. Trotsky set the revolution within a historical context, and treated the Tsarist Empire as a whole, a society rich with contradictions.' High praise indeed from someone who would soon become a Communist Party organizer in the Age of Stalin. More recently the decidedly non-Trotskyist scholar Ian Thatcher has chimed in: 'Trotsky's summary of the factors he had highlighted to account for 1917 still forms the research agenda. … Measured against *The History of the Russian Revolution* most 'modern' research does not seem so modern after all. … It is essential reading.' Chamberlin, a highly respected correspondent of the *Christian Science Monitor* with twelve years of journalistic experience in Soviet Russia, was evolving from radical supporter to conservative critic of the Soviet regime but sought to provide a balanced account that later scholars have viewed – in the recent words of Sheila Fitzpatrick – as 'still the best general work on the Revolution and Civil War.' Both Trotsky's and Chamberlin's accounts drew from primary source materials and reminiscences of participants, and both were consistent with what John Reed, Louise Bryant, Albert Rhys Williams, and Bessie Beatty had reported years before.[6]

In stark contrast, the account from Stalin and his collaborators contained major elements that were missing from the accounts of the four American friends. While none of them had even mentioned Stalin, the *Short Course* volume reported that in 1917 Lenin was especially reliant on 'his close colleagues and disciples in Petrograd: Stalin, Sverdlov, Molotov, Ordjonikidze,' and that the Bolshevik Central Committee 'elected a Party Centre, headed by Comrade Stalin, to direct the uprising.' More than this, it was claimed that people who they had seen as among Lenin's closest comrades were in fact his enemies, and that 'the Bolsheviks defeated the attempts of the capitulators within the Party – Zinoviev, Kamenev, Rykov, Bukharin, Trotsky and Pyatakov – to deflect that Party from the path of Socialist revolution.' In the same period, General Secretary of the Communist International George Dimitrov explained to Communists and others throughout the world the need to 'enlighten the masses … in a genuinely Marxist, a Leninist-Marxist, a Leninist-Stalinist spirit,' mobilizing 'international proletarian unity … against the Trotskyite agents of fascism,' and recognizing that a 'historical dividing line' in world politics was represented by one's 'attitude to the Soviet Union, which has been carrying on a real existence for twenty years already, with its untiring struggle against enemies, with its dictatorship of the working class and the Stalin Constitution, with the leading role of the Party of Lenin and Stalin.' The *Short Course* was designed to facilitate this task.[7]

No less divergent from the early accounts of John Reed and his friends, and similarly inclined to stress the unity of Lenin and Stalin, were a proliferation of works, from the late 1940s to the 1960s, by Cold War anti-Communist scholars. The bitter ex-Communist working for the US Department of State, Bertram D. Wolfe, pioneered in a distinctive development of the continuity thesis. 'When Stalin died in 1953, Bolshevism was fifty years old. Its distinctive views on the significance of organization, of centralization and of the guardianship or dictatorship of a vanguard or elite date from Lenin's programmatic wirings of 1902,' Wolfe wrote. 'His separate machine and his authoritarian control of it dates from … 1903.' In that half century, Wolfe insisted, 'Bolshevism had had only two authoritative leaders' – Lenin and Stalin. There were many who followed this lead. 'Stalinism can and must be defined as a pattern of thought and action that flows directly from Leninism,' asserted Alfred G. Meyer. 'Stalin's way of looking at the contemporary world, his professed aims, the decisions he made at variance with one another, his conceptions of the tasks facing the communist state – these and many specific traits are entirely Leninist.' Robert V. Daniels, contrasting 'the Trotskyists' with 'Stalin and more direct followers of Lenin,' elaborated: 'Leninism begat Stalinism in two decisive respects: it prepared a group of people ready to use force and authority to overcome any obstacles, and it trained them to accept any practical short-cut in the interest of immediate success and security of the movement.' Walt Whitman Rostow agreed: 'Lenin decided … to rule on the basis of a police-state dictatorship,' and 'Stalin, having cheerfully accepted the police-state dictatorship as the basis for rule, radically altered the tone of society' in a grimly totalitarian manner.[8]

A sharp contrast both to Stalinist and Cold War anti-Communist interpretations was represented by two outstanding scholars whose attitude toward the Russian Revolution approximated the sympathies of John Reed and his friends and whose understanding of events more or less corresponded to what Trotsky and Chamberlin had presented – E.H. Carr and Isaac Deutscher. A maverick member of the British elite, Carr shifted from a diplomatic career and editorial writing for the *London Times* to the writing of a remarkable number of biographical and historical studies largely focused on Russia. Deutscher, in contrast, was a Polish 'non-Jewish Jew' rising from humble beginnings. A militant in the early Communist movement who – opposing the Stalinist corruption – became a Trotskyist, by the end of the 1930s he was driven from his native land and left the revolutionary movement, morphing into a brilliant English-language journalist. Deutscher produced a massive biography of Stalin and a three-volume biography of Trotsky that – in multiple ways and with great erudition – set the historical record straight while advancing challenging interpretations. The first three instalments of Carr's monumental 14-volume *History of Soviet Russia* provided a meticulous account of the Bolshevik revolution from the standpoint of institutional history, at a high level of intellectual seriousness.[9]

The fact that Carr and Deutscher were each attacked and slandered by partisans of both Cold War power blocs highlights their importance in opening a vital space for scholars dealing with the Russian Revolution. Others – with somewhat divergent perspectives but displaying careful research and intellectual honesty – further opened that space with serious work in the 1970s. Robert C. Tucker ensured that English-language students and scholars would have easy access to reliable collections of writings by Lenin as well as Marx and Engels, but also a clearer comprehension of the actual role and meaning of Stalin.[10] One of his students, Stephen Cohen, played a decisive role in broadening the understanding of Bolshevism with his path-breaking biography of Nikolai Bukharin. In a similar fashion but with broader scope, Moshe Lewin made fundamental contributions in tracing the history involved in the making of the Soviet Union (in which he had lived for a number of years).[11] Strongly influenced by the Marxism associated with the émigré Menshevik current of Russian socialism, Leopold Haimson, Alexander Dallin, Israel Getzler, and Alexander Rabinowitch opened up additional new pathways in Soviet studies,[12] as did other scholars influenced by the rich traditions of Russian anarchism and populism, Paul Avrich and Teodor Shanin respectively.[13]

A radical ferment that developed and spread during the 1960s and 1970s among student-age youth in 'the capitalist West' (certainly in the United States, Canada, and Britain) would generate an explosion of exciting new work, highlighted in a seminal essay by Ronald G. Suny, 'Toward a Social History of the October Revolution' in the prestigious *American Historical Review*. Younger scholars, fluent in Russian and often accessing new material, giving centre stage to in-depth studies of the Russian working class, included Suny himself, Victoria Bonnell, Laura Engelstein, Rose Glickman, Tsuyoshi Hasegawa, Diane Koenker, David Mandel, Donald J. Raleigh, William Rosenberg, Steven A. Smith, Rex A. Wade, Reginald Zelnik, and others, including the Menshevik-influenced Leopold Haimson and Alexander Rabinowitch. Such work, judiciously integrated and popularized, found its way into a widely-read trilogy by W. Bruce Lincoln (*In War's Dark Shadow*, *Passage Through Armageddon*, and *Red Victory*) and in such outstanding collections as the 1997 *Critical Companion to the Russian Revolution 1914-1921*. Taken together, such impressive work seemed to corroborate the kinds of things that John Reed, Louise Bryant, Albert Rhys Williams, Bessie Beatty, Leon Trotsky, and William H. Chamberlin had conveyed in earlier years.[14]

Not surprisingly, there was a powerful conservative counter-attack, given special impetus by the 1989-91 'collapse of Communism' in Eastern Europe and the USSR, and by the right-wing triumphalism associated with the seemingly unstoppable and irreversible neo-liberal revolution associated with Ronald Reagan and Margaret Thatcher. Old-time Cold War anti-Communists such as Martin Malia and especially Richard Pipes wrote massive, hostile 'new' accounts of the Russian Revolution which simply ignored the work of all whose scholarship differed from their conservative interpretations, and such fat books were widely proclaimed to be the 'magisterial' and correct expositions of what really happened. They were joined, from the former USSR, by Communist careerists transitioning into anti-Communist careerists (such as Dmitri Volkogonov and Alexander Yakovlev), with supplements from disillusioned one-time radicals in the West who produced a *Black Book on Communism*. All of this was accompanied with an avalanche of well-funded promotion and super-charged 'now it can be told' hype designed to convey the impression that any other view is now simply unthinkable.[15]

An in-between terrain has been occupied by another layer of scholars who combine attitudes reminiscent of Cold War sensibilities (of one side or the other, or in some cases both) with a scholarly inclination to take more seriously the newer social history. For example, Sheila Fitzpatrick and J. Arch Getty have pushed hard for a 'more objective' appraisal of Stalin and Stalinism, in the process coming up with material and interpretations certainly worth considering. 'Stalin did not initiate or control everything that happened in the party and country,' Getty argues. 'The number of hours in the day divided by the number of things for which he was responsible, suggests that his role in many areas could have been little more than occasional intervention, prodding, threatening or correcting.' He could hardly have been the Evil Genius (or Benign Genius) behind all important things – he can only be understood adequately within the context of the complex political and social structures within which he functioned. Getty concludes: 'He was an executive, and reality forced him to delegate most authority to his subordinates, each of whom had his own opinions, client groups, and interests.'[16]

But one aspect of their approach involves positing an elemental consistency between Lenin and Stalin. According to Getty, Stalin and those associated with his repressive regime were partly animated by 'Bolshevik traditions of intolerance, fanatical unity against opponents, and easy recourse to violence'. For Fitzpatrick, Stalin's political characteristics (and Lenin's) were part of something by no means restricted to Bolshevism. 'All revolutionaries are enthusiasts, zealots,' she tells us. 'They are intolerant of disagreement, incapable of compromise; mesmerized by big, distant goals, violent, suspicious and destructive.'[17]

Variants of this approach can be found in the work of other influential scholars dealing with the Russian Revolution, such as Orlando Figes, who utilizes fragments of social history to deepen his point. Figes presents the struggle for a better world as an 'experiment' that went 'horribly wrong, not so much because of the malice of its leaders, most of whom had started out with the highest of ideals, but because their ideals were themselves impossible.' Bolshevik intellectuals, 'with their own idealized vision of what the workers were supposed to be,' were destined be foiled by 'the workers' actual tastes – vaudeville and vodka, for the most.' The struggle to mobilize the working class to take political power in order to usher in a glowing socialist democracy was, Figes concludes, doomed from the start: 'The state, however big, cannot make people equal or better human beings.'[18]

There are ample working-class biographies and autobiographies that collide with Figes's vodka and vaudeville stereotype: August Bebel from Germany, Louise Michel from France, J. Keir Hardie from Britain, 'Mother' Mary Jones from the United States, Alexander Shlyapnikov from Russia, and countless more from these and many other lands.[19] As was evident in the earlier social histories of the Russian Revolution (and also in the lived experience of many of us today), the working class is an immense human group reflecting a broad array of identities, ideologies, inclinations and tastes. Nor does the suggestion hold up that the Russian Revolution can be explained as impractical intellectuals taking control of the state for the purpose of somehow making everybody 'equal or better human beings' (although the revolutionaries certainly favoured *a society that would provide equal rights and a better life for all* – which is something else altogether, an eminently practical goal, and well worth fighting for).

The present volume provides a contrast and corrective to the neo-conservative and 'in-between' interpretations, as well as to the older anti-Communist and Stalinist distortions from the Cold War era, instead drawing from and highlighting the more valuable accounts of what happened, not least of which were the eyewitness reports from John Reed, Louise Bryant, and their friends. We see a story – the narrative highlighted by the materials in this volume – in which an oppressive political, economic and social order generates mass discontent within the population, exacerbated by converging crises, resulting in resistance and rebellion. These are advanced particularly by a small but growing working class – dynamic and strategically placed – which, in turn, is animated by its more conscious and activist elements that organize themselves into trade unions, political parties, soviets (councils), factory committees, workers militias, and more. A decisive role, within this complex mix, comes to be played by a specific revolutionary current steeped in Marxist theory and containing a number of strong personalities that have been shaped by considerable previous experience. The result is the world's first socialist revolution.

There has, of course, been additional work dealing with various facets of the revolutionary experience, and there are still many questions of fact and interpretation being wrestled with. For those concerned with what actually happened in history, and specifically with how revolutions actually happen (with an eye on the possible need for making revolutions of our own), such further 'wrestling' is important – and it is that to which we will now turn.

Multiple insurgencies

Rex Wade has summed up complexities of the Russian Revolution in a manner that deserves to be quoted at length.

> The Russian revolution of 1917 was a series of concurrent and overlapping revolutions: the popular revolt against the old regime; the workers' revolution against the hardships of the old industrial and social order; the revolt of the soldiers against the old system of military service and then against the war itself [i.e., against the First World War]; the peasants' revolution for land and for control of their own lives; the striving of middle class elements for civil rights and a constitutional parliamentary system; the revolution of the non-Russian nationalities for rights and self-determination; the revolt of most of the population against the war and its seemingly endless slaughter. People also struggled over differing cultural visions, over women's rights, between nationalities, for domination within ethnic or religious groups and among and within political parties, and for fulfillment of a multitude of aspirations large and small. These various revolutions and group struggles played out within the general context of political realignments and instability, growing social anarchy, economic collapse, and ongoing world war. They contributed to both the revolution's vitality and the sense of chaos that so often overwhelmed

people in 1917. The revolution of 1917 propelled Russia with blinding speed through liberal, moderate socialist and then radical socialist phases, at the end bringing to power the extreme left wing of Russian, even European, politics. An equally sweeping social revolution accompanied the rapid political movement. And all this occurred within a remarkably compressed time period – less than a year.[20]

This poses multiple questions that deserve attention. To narrow this to only a few issues:

(1) Given simply the occupational complexity of class, and the multiple facets of consciousness related to this, what were the consciousness and the underlying social reality involved in what Wade refers to as 'the workers' revolution against the hardships of the old industrial and social order'?

(2) What was the interplay of ethnic/national oppression, gender oppression, and class oppression (what some today might refer to as 'intersectionality')[21] in the social reality of 1917 Russia?

(3) What was the understanding (or what were the different, perhaps divergent, understandings) of such 'intersectionality' among the Bolsheviks, and how did this play out, or fail to play out, practically?

The key category for Russian Marxists was, of course, *working class* – for practical no less than theoretical reasons. In a classic study, Joseph Freeman observes: 'The growth of the working class continued so rapidly that between 1897 and 1913 the number of wage-earners in census industries increased 70 percent and in the domestic-craft industries 50 percent.' Rex Wade emphasizes that 'central to the history of the revolution, key players in all stages of its development, were the urban, especially industrial workers.... The revolution began as a demonstration of industrial workers and they never relinquished their leading role in both political and social revolution in 1917. They represented a potent force for further revolutionary upheaval if their aspirations were not met – as they almost certainly would not be, at least not in full.'[22]

The complex nature of the working class, and of working-class consciousness, has already been suggested. An aspect of this involves occupational differences – typographical workers were often seen as being more moderate, mine workers were often seen as being more militant, skilled workers (such a metal workers) were often seen as more politically advanced than unskilled workers (such a textile workers), the consciousness and mentality of many workers was permeated by earlier experiences in and continuing ties with the peasant village, workers fresh from the countryside were often scorned by seasoned city-dwellers, gaps sometimes tended to open between younger and older generations of workers, etc.[23]

Wade tells us that 'while their own economic, working and personal conditions were their most pressing concern, broader political issues also animated the workers.' A thick organizational network – involving trade unions, factory committees, local and district soviets, cultural and self-help groups of various kinds, workers' militia groups, etc. – all were means through which workers sought 'to use their newfound freedom and power to obtain a better life for themselves and their families.' He notes that these and other developments 'had the effect not only of solidifying working-class identity, but also of broadening the circle of those who identified themselves as workers.' Previously unorganized elements outside of the factories – cab drivers, laundry workers, bath house workers, restaurant waiters, bakers, barbers, retail clerks, lower-level white collar workers such as office clerks and elementary school teachers – all now identified themselves as part of the working class, organized unions, and sent representatives to the soviets.[24]

The question of who is or is not part of the working class, *and who self-identifies as a worker*, was complex in more than one way. The basic Marxist distinction – a proletarian is someone who sells labour-power to an employer in order to make a living – might, depending on context, be seen as subordinate to whether one has an education (and can be defined in some sense as part of the intelligentsia), and whether one works on a factory floor or someplace more 'refined'. Leopold Haimson discusses the example of pharmacy workers during the 1905 revolutionary upsurge, who formed a union – as employees in various workplaces were doing – but then were faced with the issue of whether they, as pharmacists' assistants, should self-identify as 'workers' (which would place them with predominantly working-class socialists of the Russian Social Democratic Labour Party) or as 'intelligentsia' (which would place them with professional groups in the 'bourgeois liberal' Union of Unions). Between 1905 and 1917, he notes, various working-class strata 'were alternatively drawn to (or indeed torn between) the representations of being class-conscious proletarians' or something other than that, which would have implications for political allegiances.[25]

There was also the matter of how class and class-consciousness intersected with ethnicity or nationality and with gender.

The vast empire of Tsarist Russia had been infamous as 'a prison-house of nations,' and what came to be known as Great Russian chauvinism combined with the ruling elite's ongoing efforts to squeeze wealth out of subject people's. Ethnic and national divisions in such a situation have the capacity to cut across class in multiple ways, with prejudices and 'blind-spots' and resentments (not to mention linguistic and other cultural differences) dividing workers and having complex impacts on class-consciousness and class struggle. Serious mistakes can be made, and were made, in such situations – but also new insights can develop and important corrections can lead to new opportunities. There is much to be learned (and more to be discovered, by scholars no less than activists) about what happened in the revolutionary struggle leading up to 1917, about the role of ethnic and national struggles within the overthrow of Russia's old order, and about the subsequent policies of the new revolutionary regime.[26]

No less complex, and sometimes similarly explosive, was 'the woman question'. One aspect of the complexity is 'intersectionality' – it is problematical to deal with gender abstracted from multiple other identities: is one in a rural or urban context, is one an aristocrat, a peasant, a bourgeois, an 'intellectual' white-collar worker, a factory worker, part of one ethnic community or another, etc.[27]

As with the 'national question,' there were Marxists – including among the Bolsheviks – who were inclined to take a reductionist and sectarian stand: the future socialist revolution carried out by the *working class* would bring an end to all bad things, including the oppression of women (or of subjugated nationalities and ethnic groups), and separate struggles against such oppression could divide workers and divert them from the class struggle and the primary task of overthrowing capitalism. This logic could also be convenient for not creating discomfort among male (or Russian-majority) workers and comrades, and keeping women (or other oppressed groups) 'in their place'.[28]

Despite such debilitating conservatism, even critical historians generally agree that the Bolsheviks were far more engaged in organizing for women's liberation than other groups on the left, and that Lenin was in advance of many of his comrades in supporting this work. A cautiousness and even prudishness prevented him from endorsing some of the more radical perspectives advanced by Alexandra Kollontai and Inessa Armand. The fact remains that the Russian Social Democratic Labour Party from the start, following the examples of Marx, Engels, and August Bebel, had, as Barbara Evans Clements puts it, 'a good record on women's issues' (the right to vote, equal civil, educational, and employment rights, special needs of women in the work place, including maternity leave and day-care for their children), and, 'publicly renouncing the sexism that was standard among European politicians in the early twentieth century, ... allowed its female members to achieve considerable prominence and personal freedom.'[29]

While Bolshevik women went out of their way to denounce 'bourgeois feminism,' they nonetheless needed to push their own comrades (many male, but some female) to support special efforts to agitate, educate and organize among working-class women. In the course of 1917, the political forces in the struggle for power, according to Richard Stites, 'were led by and overwhelmingly composed of men: government, parties, soviets, peasant associations, national organizations, cooperatives, industrial enterprises, and trade unions,' yet he also cites a pamphlet in which Alexandra Kollontai insists that 'in our revolution women workers and peasants played ... an active and important role'. Aspects of the truth can be found in both statements. The deep patriarchal patterns and male dominance of Russian (and European) culture naturally found reflection at all levels – but as Rex Wade observes, 'women entered public and political life in unprecedented numbers and ways,' reflecting the fact that during the First World War the number of women in the factories rose from 25 per cent to 43 per cent of the nationwide industrial labour force, and in the Moscow region, for example, they constituted 60 percent of all textile workers. 'Military defeats, economic breakdown, and soaring prices drew large numbers of women into sporadic strikes against deteriorating conditions,' according to Gail Warshofsky Lapidis, and – Wade points out – women 'voted in general elections and participated in selection of factory committees, soviets and trade union leadership. Some served as deputies in these and in city councils. Thousands became involved in the enormous variety of economic, social and cultural organizations that sprang up across Russia in the revolutionary year.' There is also the well-known point stressed by Lapidus: 'It was a massive strike touched off by women textile workers on International Women's Day that culminated in the February Revolution of 1917.'[30]

Revolutionary party

Essential for the making of the Russian Revolution was interplay between the broad masses of workers and peasants, in all their variety, with an organization of revolutionary intellectuals and activists having a predominantly working-class base and a Marxist ideology. This was the Bolshevik party whose central leader was Vladimir Ilyich Ulyanov – known to the world as Lenin. Both the Stalinist and Cold War anti-Communist versions of Lenin have him developing a tightly-organized, elitist, authoritarian 'party of a new type' with a personality to match (Stalinists presenting him as flawless, anti-Communists presenting him as deeply flawed) – an image, in its negative variant, captured after Communism's collapse in Robert Service's *Lenin, A Biography*. Inconsistent with portrayals provided by John Reed and his friends, by Trotsky and Chamberlin, and by a variety of later scholars (Carr,

Deutscher, Lewin, Cohen), it has been definitively demolished by the recent work of Lars Lih, in an exhaustive examination of the activity and thinking of Lenin and his comrades in Bolshevism's earliest incarnation – a massive volume entitled *Lenin Rediscovered* – as well as in his succinct and rich biography, *Lenin*.[31]

Lih's portrayal finds additional corroboration in Paul Le Blanc's *Lenin and the Revolutionary Party*, which presents Lenin's party as an essentially democratic collectivity rather than a one-man organizational dictatorship. Indeed, it is difficult to see anything but the kind of organization described by Lih and Le Blanc, given the complex multiple insurgencies we have noted, as capable of bringing about what happened in October 1917. This comes through, as well, in the eyewitness and partially eyewitness accounts of Bolshevik dissidents Eduard M. Dune, *Notes of a Red Guard*, and Victor Serge, *Year One of the Russian Revolution*. Lih has also emphasized the fact that Lenin did not see himself building a 'party of a new type,' that his model had been the massive German Social Democratic Party whose central theoretician, Karl Kautsky, saw socialism and democracy as inseparable. Lih has suggested that Lenin's outlook was basically indistinguishable from Kautsky's prior to 1914 (after which Lenin denounced him for betraying their common revolutionary perspective). While there was certainly much overlap between Lenin and Kautsky, however, recent work by Tamás Krausz, Alan Shandro and others compellingly present Lenin's perspectives as having their own quite distinctive quality.[32]

Lih's insistence of the Bolshevik party as a *collectivity* rather than a one-man show has been a particularly important corrective, and in the process he has advocated rehabilitation and respect for some of Lenin's comrades – such as Lev Kamenev and Gregory Zinoviev – who have been dismissed not only by Stalinists but also Trotskyists. Lih even suggests (quite controversially) that Kamenev was more right than wrong in the debate over Lenin's 'April Theses' of 1917, and that he essentially won the debate. While Nadezhda Krupskaya remembers the 'April Theses' debate differently (as do many others from the time, of various persuasions), she also conveys in her important reminiscences a vivid sense, with considerable detail, of the collective nature of the Bolshevik party – it was by no means simply Lenin calling the shots. This comes through as well in the attentive contemporary portraits one can find in Bolshevik Anatoly Lunacharsky's *Revolutionary Silhouettes* and the more substantial collection of contemporary biographies supplemented with the scholarship of Georges Haupt and Jean-Jacques Marie, in *Makers of the Russian Revolution*.[33]

There is need for more research – following along the lines of Ralph Carter

Ellwood's rich account of *Russian Social Democracy in the Underground* and August Nimtz's revealing exposition of the centrality of electoral work in Bolshevik strategy – to add new dimensions and detail to our understanding of the Bolshevik Party. But it also makes sense to reach for the kind of historical overview provided in Gregory Zinoviev's still valuable *History of the Bolshevik Party*, despite its brevity and other limitations. In this regard, the work of Vladimir Nevsky (1876-1937), a long-time Bolshevik activist, calls out to be made available. 'Like so many others in his generation, he was arrested in the mid-thirties and executed in 1937,' reports Lars Lih. 'After the revolution, Nevsky became a pioneering party historian whose magnum opus, published in 1925, was entitled *Istoriia RKP(b): Kratkii ocherk* [History of the Russian Communist Party (Bolsheviks): A Short Essay]. Despite the modest subtitle, this massive 500-page study constitutes the first history of the Bolshevik party to be fully documented and based on a full range of sources.'[34]

What went wrong?

John Reed, in *Ten Days That Shook the World*, recounts the conclusion of Lenin's speech after the Soviet seizure of power, that now 'the labor movement, in the name of peace and socialism, shall win and fulfill its destiny.' Reed added: 'There was something quiet and powerful in all of this, which stirred the souls of men. It was understandable why people believed when Lenin spoke.'[35] Yet within four years, Reed's friend Albert Rhys Williams, would write:

> Repressions, tyranny, violence,' cry the enemies. 'They have abolished free speech, free press, free assembly. They have imposed drastic military conscription and compulsory labour. They have been incompetent in government, inefficient in industry. They have subordinated the Soviets to the Communist Party. They have lowered their Communist ideals, changed and shifted their program and compromised with the capitalists.
>
> Some of these charges are exaggerated. Many can be explained. But they cannot all be explained away. Friends of the Soviet grieve over them. Their enemies have summoned the world to shudder and protest against them....

While abroad hatred against the Bolsheviks as the new 'enemies of civilization' mounted from day to day, these selfsame Bolsheviks were straining to rescue civilization in Russia from total collapse.[36]

Rosa Luxemburg saw problems as the Russian civil war unfolded in 1918.

'Whatever a party could offer of courage, revolutionary far-sightedness and consistency in a historic hour, Lenin, Trotsky and the other comrades have given in good measure,' but, Luxemburg warned, 'socialist democracy begins ... at the very moment of the seizure of power by the socialist party,' and 'with the repression of political life in the land as a whole, life in the soviets must also become more and more crippled,' leading not to socialist democracy but 'the dictatorship of a handful of politicians.'[37]

There were fluctuations in the people's fortunes after the brutalizing civil war. Important accounts – both contemporary and later – indicate improvements in material life and cultural freedom in the 1920s. 'There is no doubt that Lenin suffered his greatest defeat when, at the outbreak of the civil war, the supreme power that he originally planned to concentrate in the Soviets definitely passed into the hands of the party bureaucracy,' Hannah Arendt noted in *Origins of Totalitarianism*, but she insisted that 'even this development, tragic as it was for the course of the revolution, would not necessarily have led to totalitarianism.' Her elaboration, for which there is substantial and reliable corroboration, is worth pondering:

> At the moment of Lenin's death [in 1924] the roads were still open. The formation of workers, peasants, and [in the wake of the New Economic Policy] middle classes need not necessarily have led to the class struggle which had been characteristic of European capitalism. Agriculture could still be developed on a collective, cooperative, or private basis, and the national economy was still free to follow a socialist, state-capitalist, or free enterprise pattern. None of these alternatives would have automatically destroyed the new structure of the country.[38]

The fact remains that by the 1930s, claiming to be 'Lenin's faithful disciple and the prolonger of his work,' Joseph Stalin consolidated control over party and state.[39] This came after winning a set of factional conflicts, preceded in the mid-1920s by the crystallization around Stalin of a tight clique of top functionaries (thanks to his key position in the party apparatus as General Secretary), and decisively drawing on support within the lower levels of the party and state apparatus. Sincere Communists throughout the world, and many others as well, took Stalin's claims for good coin, seeing the consequent destruction of millions of lives – direct and indirect consequences of his modernizing 'revolution from above' – as representing instead the necessary defense of revolutionary goals and principles. An avalanche of material, against which no serious scholar can contend, has long since demolished this claim (although a U.S. Professor of Medieval

English Literature, Grover Furr, continues to lead a crusade in Stalin's defence).[40]

Overviews of Soviet and Russian history can be utilized to help sort through the meaning of matters dealt with in this book.[41] But those inclined to take seriously the approach animating the men and women who made the Russian Revolution will be especially concerned with how well Marxism can explain what happened – and Dutch historian Marcel van der Linden has provided a detailed survey of critical (but incredibly diverse) Marxist analyses. Both Ernest Mandel and David Mandel have identified with the particular analysis developed by Leon Trotsky in *The Revolution Betrayed.*[42]

Key elements in this analysis flow from an understanding that economic democracy (socialism), allowing the free development of each person as the condition for the free development of all people (as Marx and Engels had posited in the *Communist Manifesto*), depends on the immense economic surplus and productivity, plus the complex of socio-economic and global relationships among people and resources, built up by the modern world capitalist economy. An attempt to build socialism in a single country with a low level of economic development cannot be successful. As Marx stressed in *The German Ideology*, 'a development of the productive forces [generated by the Industrial Revolution] is the absolutely necessary practical premise [of Communism], because without it want is generalized, and with want the struggle for necessities begins again, and that means all the old crap will revive' – the exploitation and oppression of labouring majorities by powerful minorities that has characterized civilization for thousands of years.[43]

Stalin's commitment to building 'socialism in one country' was a recipe for bureaucratic tyranny. This is why Marx and Engels concluded with the appeal: 'Workers of all countries unite!' It is also why Lenin, Trotsky and the other leaders of the new Soviet regime utilized precious time and resources to build up a Communist International that might be able to facilitate victories of workers' revolutions in other countries. 'The contradictory social structure of the Soviet Union, and the ultra-bureaucratic character of its state,' Trotsky argued, are the direct consequence' of the unforeseen 'pause' in the process of world revolution.[44]

Despite remarkable progress in 'modernization,' and despite (but also because of) the fierce and murderous repressiveness of the Stalin regime, the socialist goals of the October Revolution could not be reached, and the bureaucratic tyranny that crystallized in the place of those goals proved incapable of being sustained beyond 1990, even with desperate but doomed attempts at bureaucratic self-reform.

What now?

The materials gathered in this volume are a continuation and a challenge. They are a continuation of a century-long process of trying to interpret and learn from the momentous things that large numbers of ordinary people did long ago in an effort to make the world a better place – a global society of the free and the equal.

And since our own world is still so very far from being that, with accumulating oppressions and potentially horrific crises continuing to afflict humanity, the consideration of such historical matters naturally poses the challenge of whether there are things that we can learn from the past, and apply fruitfully to our own time.

NOTES

1   See, for example, Paul Mason, *Why It's Still Kicking Off Everywhere: The New Global Revolutions*, London, Verso, 2013, and the on-line 'pages' of *International Viewpoint* (http://www.internationalviewpoint.org/) and *Links: Journal of Socialist Renewal* (http://links.org.au/).

2   Louise Bryant, *Six Months in Red Russia*, London, The Journeyman Press, 1982, pp. x, xi. Also see Virginia Gardner, *Friend and Lover: The Life of Louise Bryant*, New York, Horizon Press, 1982.

3   Bessie Beatty, *The Red Heart of Russia*, New York, The Century Co., 1918, pp. 479-80.

4   Albert Rhys Williams, *Through the Russian Revolution*, New York, Boni and Liveright, 1921, p. 275. Also see the later and partly autobiographical Albert Rhys Williams, *Journey into Revolution: Petrograd, 1917-1918,* Chicago, Quadrangle Books, 1969.

5   John Reed, *Ten Days That Shook the World*, New York, International Publishers, 1926, p. xii. Also see Robert A. Rosenstone, *Romantic Revolutionary: A Biography of John Reed*, Cambridge, MA, Harvard University Press, 1990.

6   Leon Trotsky, *History of the Russian Revolution*, Chicago Haymarket Books, 2007, and William Henry Chamberlin, *The Russian Revolution 1917-1921*, 2 vols, Princeton, NJ, Princeton University Press, 1987. The endorsements of Trotsky's work can be found in Carl Marzani, *The Education of a Reluctant Radical, Book 2: Growing Up American*, New York, Topical Books, 1993, p. 198, and Ian D. Thatcher, *Trotsky*, London, Routledge, 2003, p. 187. On Chamberlin, see David C. Engerman, 'Modernization from the Other Shore: American Observers and the Cost of Soviet Economic Development,' *American Historical Review*, Vol. 105, No. 2, April 2000, pp. 383-416, as well as Chamberlin's two outstanding books of reportage – *Soviet Russia, A Living Record and a History*, Boston, Little Brown and Co., 1930, and *Russia's Iron Age*, Boston, Little Brown and Co., 1934, – and his memoir, *The Confessions of an Individualist*, New York, Macmillan Co., 1940, pp. 63-159; Fitzpatrick's endorsement can be found on the back cover of the 1987 Princeton University Press reprint of his two-volume work on the Russian Revolution.

7   Commission of the Central Committee of the C.P.S.U. (B.), *History of the Communist Party of the Soviet Union (Bolsheviks) Short Course*, New York, International Publishers, 1939, pp. 196, 206, 224; Georgi Dimitroff, *The United Front*, New York, International Publishers, 1938, pp. 78, 280.

8   Bertram D. Wolfe, *An Ideology in Power: Reflections on the Russian Revolution*, New York, Stein and Day, 1970, pp. 187, 188; Alfred G. Meyer, *Leninism*, New York, Frederick A.

Praeger, 1962, pp. 282-3; Robert V. Daniels, 'The Evolution of the Communist Mind,' in *A Documentary History of Communism*, Vol. 1, New York, Vintage Books, 1962, p. xl, and Robert V. Daniels, *The Conscience of the Revolution: Communist Opposition in Soviet Russia*, New York, Simon and Schuster, 1969, p. 410; W. W. Rostow, *The Stages of Economic Growth: A Non-Communist Manifesto*, New York, Cambridge University Press, 1964, p. 160. For an informative general discussion, see David C. Engerman, *Know Your Enemy: The Rise and Fall of America's Soviet Experts*, New York, Oxford University Press, 2009.

9   E.H. Carr's *History of Soviet Russia*, 14 volumes, London, Macmillan, 1950-1978, is summarized in E.H. Carr, *The Russian Revolution from Lenin to Stalin 1917-1929*, New York, Macmillan Palgrave, 2004. Deutscher's foremost works are *Stalin, A Political Biography*, second edition, New York, Oxford University Press, 1967 and his three-volume biography of Trotsky, now gathered into one: *The Prophet: The Life of Leon Trotsky*, London, Verso, 2015. Also see Jonathan Haslam, *The Vices of Integrity, E.H. Carr 1892-1982*, London, Verso, 2000, Michael Cox, ed., *E.H. Carr, A Critical Appraisal*, New York, Palgrave Macmillan, 2000, David Horowitz, ed., *Isaac Deutscher, The Man and His Work*, London, Macdonald and Co., 1971, Isaac Deutscher, *The Non-Jewish Jew and Other Essays*, New York, Oxford University Press, 1968, and David Caute, *Isaac and Isaiah: The Covert Punishment of a Cold War Heretic*, New Haven, CT, Yale University Press, 2013.

10   Robert C. Tucker, *Stalin as Revolutionary: 1879-1929*, New York, W.W. Norton & Company, 1988, and *Stalin in Power: The Revolution from Above, 1928-1941*, New York, W. W. Norton & Company, 1990.

11   Stephen Cohen, *Bukharin and the Bolshevik Revolution: A Political Biography, 1888-1938*, New York, Oxford University Press, 1980; Moshe Lewin, *Lenin's Last Struggle*, Ann Arbor, MU, University of Michigan Press, 2005, *The Making of the Soviet System: Essays in the Social History of Interwar Russia*, New York, The New Press, 1994, and *The Soviet Century*, London, Verso, 2005.

12   Among the relevant texts here are: André Liebich, *From the Other Shore: Russian Social Democracy after 1921*, Cambridge, MA, Harvard University Press, 1997, especially pp. 271-326; Leopold Haimson, ed., *The Mensheviks from the Revolution of 1917 to the Second World War*, Chicago, Chicago University Press, 1974, and *The Making of Three Russian Revolutionaries: Voices from the Menshevik Past*, Cambridge, UK, Cambridge University Press, 1987; Alexander and Janet Rabinowitch with Ladis K.D. Kristof, eds., *Revolution and Politics in Russia: Essays in Memory of B.I. Nicolaevsky*, Bloomington, IN, Indiana University Press, 1972. Influential Menshevik contributions to the historiography (in some ways consistent with what Reed, Chamberlin and Trotsky present) include N. N. Sukhanov, *The Russian Revolution 1917, A Personal Record, Princeton*, NJ, Princeton University Press, 1984, Theodore Dan, *The Origins of Bolshevism*, New York, Schocken Books, 1970, and Raphael R. Abramovitch, *The Soviet Revolution 1917-1939*, New York, International Universities Press, 1962.

13   Paul Avrich, *The Russian Anarchists*, Oakland, CA, AK Press, 2005, and *Kronstadt 1921*, Princeton, NJ, Princeton University Press, 1991; Teodor Shanin, *The Roots of Otherness: Russia's Turn of the Century*, 2 vols, New Haven, CT, Yale University Press, 1985.

14   Ronald Grigor Suny, 'Toward a Social History of the October Revolution,' *American Historical Review*, Vol. 88, No. 1, February 1983; Daniel H. Kaiser, ed., *The Workers Revolution in Russia 1917*, Cambridge, UK, Cambridge University Press, 1987; W. Bruce Lincoln, *In War's Dark Shadow*, New York, Simon and Schuster, 1983, *Passage Through Armageddon, New York*, Simon and Schuster, 1986, and *Red Victory*, New

York, Simon and Schuster, 1989; Edward Acton, Vladimir Iu. Cherniaev, William G. Rosenberg, eds., *Critical Companion to the Russian Revolution 1914-1921*, Bloomington, IN, University of Indiana Press, 1997. Rabinowitch's *The Bolsheviks Come to Power: The Revolution of 1917 in Petrograd*, Chicago, Haymarket Books, 2009, appearing in 1976, was the earliest and one of the most influential of the new contributions.

15   Martin Malia *The Soviet Tragedy: A History of Socialism in Russia 1917-1991*, New York, Free Press, 1995; Richard Pipes, *The Russian Revolution*, New York, Alfred A. Knopf, 1990; Dmitri Volkogonov, *Lenin, A New Biography*, New York, Free Press, 1994; Alexander N. Yakovlev, *A Century of Violence in Soviet Russia*, New Haven, CT, Yale University Press, 2002; and Richard Pipes, *Alexander Yakovlev, The Many Whose Ideas Delivered Russia from Communism*, DeKalb, IL, Northern Illinois University Press, 2015; Stéphane Courtois, Nicolas Werth, Jean-Louis Panne, Andrej Paczkowski, Karel Bartošek, Jean-Louis Margolin, *The Black Book of Communism: Terror, Crimes, Repression*, Cambridge, MA, Harvard University Press, 1999.

16   J. Arch Getty, *Origins of the Great Purges: The Soviet Communist Party Reconsidered, 1933-1938*, Cambridge, UK, Cambridge University Press, 1985, p. 203. Even broader social and cultural scope is provided in Sheila Fitzpatrick, *Everyday Stalinism: Ordinary Life in Extraordinary Times in the 1930s*, New York, Oxford University Press, 2000.

17   J. Arch Getty and Oleg V. Naumov, *The Road to Terror: Stalin and the Self-Destruction of the Bolsheviks, 1932-1939*, New Haven, CT, Yale University Press, 1999, p. 14; Sheila Fitzpatrick, *The Russian Revolution*, Second Edition, New York, Oxford University Press, 1994, pp. 8-9.

18   Orlando Figes, *A People's Tragedy: A History of the Russian Revolution*, New York, Viking Press, 1996, pp. 736, 823-4.

19   See August Bebel, *My Life*, Chicago, University of Chicago Press, 1913; Louise Michel, *The Red Virgin, Memoirs of Louise Michel*, Tuscaloosa, AL, University of Alabama Press, 1981; Kenneth O. Morgan, *Keir Hardie, Radical and Socialist*, London, Weidenfeld & Nicholson, 1997; Philip S. Foner, ed., *Mother Jones Speaks: Speeches and Writings of a Working-Class Fighter*, New York, Pathfinder Press, 1983; Barbara Allen, *Alexander Shlyapnikov, 1885-1937: Life of an Old Bolshevik*, Chicago, Haymarket Books, 2016. Also relevant – among many other works – is Paul Mason, *Live Working or Die Fighting: How the Working Class Went Global*, Chicago, Haymarket Books, 2010.

20   Rex A. Wade, *The Russian Revolution, 1917*, New York, Cambridge University Press, 2000, p. 283.

21   Leslie McCall, 'The Complexity of Intersectionality,' *Signs*, Vol. 30, No. 3, Spring 2005.

22   Joseph Freeman, *The Soviet Worker: An Account of the Economic, Social and Cultural Status of Labor in the U.S.S.R.*, New York, Liveright, 1932, pp. 9-10; Wade, p. 89.

23   See Lewis H. Siegelbaum and Ronald Grigor Suny, eds., *Making Workers Soviet: Power, Class and Identity*, Ithaca, NY, Cornell University Press, 1994.

24   Wade, pp. 91-7.

25   Leopold H. Haimson, 'The Problem of Social Identities in Early Twentieth Century Russia,' *Slavic Review*, Vol. 47, No. 1, Spring 1988, pp. 5, 6. Also see Daniel Orlovsky, 'The Lower Middle Strata in 1917,' and Sergei V. Iarov, 'Workers,' in Acton, Cherniaev, Rosenberg, eds., *Critical Companion to the Russian Revolution*, pp. 529-33.

26   Marxist theoretical perspectives are examined in Horace B. Davis, *Socialism and Nationalism: Marxist and Labor Theories of Nationalism to 1917*, New York, Monthly Review Press, 1967, including an exposition of Lenin's important defense of the right of oppressed nations to self-determination – but the realities are messier. Important discussions of evolving perspectives of revolutionaries (Lenin first of all) and practices before 1917 are explored by Ronald Grigor Suny, 'Nationalism and Class in the Russian Revolution: A Comparative Discussion,' in Edith Rogovin Frankel, Jonathan Frankel,

Baruch Knei-Paz, eds., *Revolution in Russia: Reassessments of 1917*, Cambridge, UK, Cambridge University Press, 1992, Liliana Riga, *The Bolsheviks and the Russian Empire*, New York, Cambridge University Press, 2012, and Eric Blanc, 'Anti-Imperial Marxism: Borderland Socialists and the Evolution of Bolshevism on National Liberation,' *International Socialist Review* #100, Spring 2016.

27 Barbara Evans Clements, 'Women and the Gender Question,' in Acton, Cherniaev, Rosenberg, eds., *Critical Companion to the Russian Revolution*, pp. 592-603.

28 Gail Warshofsky Lapidus, *Women in Soviet Society: Equality, Development, and Social Change*, Berkeley, CA, University of California Press, 1978, p. 48, 51; Barbara Evans Clements, *Bolshevik Women*, Cambridge, UK, Cambridge University Press, 1997, pp. 18, 20,105-8; Wade, p. 118.

29 Lapidus, pp. 44, 51-52; Richard Stites, *The Women's Liberation Movement in Russia: Feminism, Nihilism, and Bolshevism, 1860-1930*, Princeton, NK, Princeton University Press, 1978, p. 301; Clements, *Bolshevik Women*, p. 12; Wade, p. 117.

30 Lapidus, pp. 37, 40, 48, 49; Stites, pp. 289, 317; Clements, *Bolshevik Women*, pp. 11, 12-13; Wade, pp. 118, 121, 124.

31 Robert Service, *Lenin, A Biography*, Cambridge, MA, Harvard University Press, 2000; Lars Lih, *Lenin Rediscovered*, Chicago, Haymarket Books, 2008, and *Lenin*, London, Reaktion Books, 2011.

32 Paul Le Blanc, *Lenin and the Revolutionary Party*, Chicago, Haymarket Books, 2015; Eduard M. Dune, *Notes of a Red Guard*, Urbana, IL, University of Illinois Press, 1993; Victor Serge, *Year One of the Russian Revolution*, Chicago, Haymarket Books, 2015; Lars Lih, 'Kautsky When He Was a Marxist' (http://www.historicalmaterialism.org/ journal/online-articles/kautsky-as-marxist-data-base, accessed 11 May 2016); Tamás Krausz, *Reconstructing Lenin, An Intellectual Biography*, New York, Monthly Review Press, 2015; Alan Shandro, *Lenin and the Logic of Hegemony: Political Practice and Theory in the Class Struggle*, Chicago, Haymarket Books, 2015.

33 Lars Lih, 'Zinoviev, Populist Leninist,' in Ben Lewis and Lars Lih, *Martov and Zinoviev: Head to Head in Halle*, London, November Publications, 2011, and 'The Ironic Triumph of Old Bolshevism: The Debates of 1917 in Context,' *Russian Review*, Vol. 38, No. 2, 2011; Nadezhda K. Krupskaya, *Reminiscences of Lenin*, New York, International Publishers, 1970; Anatoly Lunacharsky, *Revolutionary Silhouettes*, New York, Hill and Wang, 1968; Georges Haupt and Jean-Jacques Marie, *Makers of the Russian Revolution: Biographies of Bolshevik Leaders*, Ithaca, NY, Cornell University Press, 1974.

34 Ralph Carter Ellwood, *Russian Social Democracy in the Underground: A Study of the RSDRP in the Ukraine, 1907-1914*, Assen, The Netherlands, Van Gorum, 1974; August H. Nimtz, *Lenin's Electoral Strategy, From Marx and Engels Through the Revolution of 1905: The Ballot or the Streets – or Both*, New York, Palgrave Macmillan, 2014, and *Lenin's Electoral Strategy, From 1907 to the October Revolution of 1917: The Ballot or the Streets – or Both*, New York, Palgrave Macmillan, 2014; Gregory Zinoviev, *History of the Bolshevik Party, From the Beginnings to February 1917, A Popular Outline*, London, New Park, 1973; Lars Lih, 'The Fortunes of a Formula: From DEMOCRATIC centralism' to ' democratic CENTRALISM,' *Links: Journal of Socialist Renewal*, April 14, 2013 (http:// links.org.au/node/3300, accessed 11 June 2016).

35 Reed, *Ten Days That Shook the World*, 129.

36 Williams, *Through the Russian*, 276-277, 278. Outstanding contemporary critiques, holding up disturbingly well down to the present, are Bertrand Russell's crisp *The Practice and Theory of Bolshevism*, London, George Allen and Unwin, 1920, and Alexander Berman's passionate *The Bolshevik Myth, Diary 1920-1922*, New York, Boni and Liveright, 1925. George Leggett's devastating account, *The Cheka: Lenin's*

Political Police, Oxford, UK, Oxford University Press, 1987, adds important detail, as does Alexander Rabinowitch, *The Bolsheviks in Power: The First Year of Soviet Rule in Petrograd*, Bloomington, IN, Indiana University Press, 2007. A broader elaboration can be found in Samuel Farber, *Before Stalinism: The Rise and Fall of Soviet Democracy*, London, Verso, 1990, engaged with in John Rees et al, *In Defence of October, A Debate on the Russian Revolution*, London, Bookmarks, 1997. Diane P. Koenker, William G. Rosenberg, and Ronald Grigor Suny, eds., *Party, State, and Society in the Russian Civil War: Explorations in Social History*, Bloomington, IN, Indiana University Press, 1989, is invaluable, and aspects of the debate are deepened in Simon Pirani, *The Russian Revolution in Retreat, 1920-24: Soviet Workers and the New Communist Elite*, London, Routledge, 2008, and Kevin Murphy, *Revolution and Counter-Revolution: Class Struggle in a Moscow Metal Factory*, Chicago, Haymarket Books, 2007. Also relevant is Arno J. Mayer's *The Furies: Violence and Terror in the French and Russian Revolutions*, Princeton, NJ, Princeton University Press, 2000.

37   Rosa Luxemburg, 'The Russian Revolution,' in Mary-Alice Waters, ed., *Rosa Luxemburg Speaks*, New York, Pathfinder Press, 1970, pp. 375, 391, 393.

38   Hannah Arendt, *The Origins of Totalitarianism,* New York, Meridian Books, 1958, pp. 318-319. Corroboration regarding the relatively positive aspects of the 1920s, consistent with what Arendt says, can be found in Chamberlin, *Soviet Russia, A Living Record and a History*, Sheila Fitzpatrick, Alexander Rabinowitch, and Richard Stites, eds., *Russia in the Era of NEP: Explorations in Soviet Society and Culture*, Bloomington, IN: Indiana University Press, 1991, and Vladimir Brovkin, *Russia After Lenin: Politics, Culture and Society 1921-1929*, London, Routledge, 1998.

39   Walter Duranty, *I Write As I Please*, New York, Simon and Schuster, 1935, pp. 179, 181.

40   In addition to materials already presented – from scholars as diverse as Deutscher, Tucker, and Getty – see Tariq Ali, ed., *The Stalinist Legacy: Its Impact on Twentieth-Century World Politics*, Chicago, Haymarket Books, 2013, Roy Medvedev, *Let History Judge: The Origins and Consequences of Stalinism*, New York, Columbia University Press, 1989, Vadim Z. Rogovin, *1937: Stalin's Year of Terror*, Oak Park, MI, Mehring Books, 1998, and *Stalin's Terror of 1937-1938: Political Genocide in the USSR*, Oak Park, MI, Mehring Books, 2009, Matthew E. Lenoe, *The Kirov Murder and Soviet History*, New Haven, CT, Yale University Press, 2010, and Oleg V. Khlevniuk, *The History of the Gulag, From Collectivization to the Great Terror*, New Haven, CT, Yale University Press, 2004. For a sample of Furr's prodigious output, see *The Murder of Sergei Kirov: History, Scholarship and the Anti-Stalin Paradigm*, Kettering, OH, Erythros Press and Media, 2013.

41   An outstanding textbook is Ronald G. Suny, *The Soviet Experiment: Russia, the USSR, and the Successor States*, New York, Oxford University Press, 2010, but also useful is S.A. Smith, *The Russian Revolution, A Very Short Introduction*, Oxford, UK, Oxford University Press, 2002, combined with Stephen Lovell, *The Soviet Union, A Very Short Introduction*, Oxford, UK, Oxford University Press, 2009.

42   Marcel van der Linden, *Western Marxism and the Soviet Union: A Survey of Critical Theories and Debates Since 1917*, Chicago, Haymarket Books, 2009, Leon Trotsky, *The Revolution Betrayed*, Garden City, NY, Doubleday Doran, 1937. Trotsky's perspective is brilliantly contextualized and analyzed in Thomas M. Twiss, *Trotsky and the Problem of Soviet Bureaucracy*, Chicago, Haymarket Books, 2015.

43   Trotsky, *The Revolution Betrayed*, pp. 56, 59.

44   A useful account of the Communist International, related to issues discussed by Trotsky, can be found in C.L.R. James, *World Revolution 1917-1936: The Rise and Fall of the Communist International*, New York, Pioneer Publishers, 1937. John Riddell and his collaborators have produced multiple volumes documenting the

Communist International in Lenin's time, the vitally important first four congresses being covered in: *Founding the Communist International: Proceedings and Documents of the First Congress March 1919*, New York, Pathfinder Press, 1987; *Workers of the World and Oppressed Peoples, Unite! Proceedings and Documents of the Second Congress, 1920*, 2 volumes, New York, Pathfinder Press, 1991; *To the Masses: Proceedings of the Communist International, 1921*, Chicago, Haymarket Books, 2016; *Toward the United Front: Proceedings of the Fourth Congress of the Communist International, 1922*, Chicago, Haymarket Books, 2013. On consequences of Stalin's reorientation for the Comintern, see E. H. Carr, *Twilight of the Comintern, 1930-1935*, New York, Pantheon Press, 1982.

THE STAGES OF THE 1917 REVOLUTION

François Vercammen

During February 1917, in the midst of war, the autocratic Tsarist regime in Russia was overthrown by mass demonstrations. Eight months later, in October, the working class – supported by a popular uprising in the whole country – conquered political power and began to construct a new, socialist society. The twentieth century was transformed.

As predicted by some, and feared by others, the World War of 1914 gave birth to revolution.

The crisis of the regime

The 1917 revolution was the final climax to an endemic crisis that shook Russian society during the second half of the nineteenth century. A great military power in Europe (but also an imposing force in Asia), it was a society trapped in economic backwardness whereas further West the capitalist mode of production triumphed. The Tsarist state had tried to use its power to bring about certain changes: agrarian reform, democratization of the administrative apparatus, modernization of the educational system, social legislation, recognition of the right to form workers' industrial organizations 'from the top', cultural autonomy for the nationalities of the empire, etc. But each tentative reform was only partial and timid, and it was always followed by a counter reform – all the more brutal since it was necessary to regain control of temporarily 'liberated' social and political forces.

'Too little and too late': the crisis exploded in its totality for the first time in 1905. That revolution failed, but the reversal was only partial. In 1914, the declaration of war put a stop to a new wave of revolutionary strikes. Three years later history took its revenge: the world conflict became a powerful catalyst for all the suffering, the frustrations, and the hopes accumulated over the years.

Economic crisis: the regime was no longer able to feed its population. Political-institutional crisis: the autocratic state lost all legitimacy. Agrarian crisis: the hunger for land on the part of the peasantry was reinforced by the general difficulty of daily life. Crisis for the nationalities: they were increasingly suffocated by forced Russification.

The revolution of February 1917

Intolerable poverty during the winter of 1916-17 sparked off the revolution in February. Women – workers and housewives – lit the spark with their International Women's Day. Starting with textile workers, the strike extended rapidly and spontaneously to the entire proletariat of Petrograd – the capital of Russia at the time. In a few days the mass strike had been transformed into an insurrection, with the military garrison coming over to the revolution. The demand for 'bread' was quickly joined by demands for 'immediate peace' and 'down with the Tsar'. In the maelstrom of the insurrection workers found a way to organize themselves: through the formation of soviets (councils) – in the factories, in their neighbourhoods, and on a citywide level – as well as through a red guard (revolutionary militia). Even at the front, the soldiers elected their own committees and ... their officers! Later, during the summer of 1917, the peasantry, in its turn, joined in. Thus the entire social base of the regime was eliminated.

Dual power

Between the end of February and the end of October 1917, Russia lived through a very specific kind of revolutionary situation: dual power. Sufficiently resolute to turn out the Tsarist regime in February, the working class was not immediately ready to take 'full' power. But it covered the factories and cities with a dense network of councils, which quickly expanded to include the army and, finally, the countryside. In essence a counter-power, these soviets – more and more numerous, better and better coordinated – threatened at any moment to overthrow the bourgeoisie.

Two of these soviet structures played a decisive role: those which, elected on a territorial basis, exercised a political power 'in society' from the outset, and the factory councils, which embodied the dynamic power of the working class.

These councils, resulting from the urgent needs of the masses, also reflected their level of consciousness and their political prejudices. In order for the task of taking power to become clearly posed it was necessary for a revolutionary party to put it forward, to make it a priority. The organization capable of doing this was the Bolshevik Party. But that group remained a minority among the workers and in the soviets until September 1917. Thus, the history of dual power is also the history of a struggle between different political parties – representing the workers and popular movements – over this decisive question of the revolution: for or against the taking of power by the soviets.

The changing relationship of forces: February-June

At the outset, different reformist currents (Mensheviks, Social-Revolutionaries, Workerists) dominated these structures of self-organization. They led the soviets and, very quickly (by May 1917) were also taking part in the provisional (bourgeois) government. They attempted to contain the pressure of the masses through the politics of class collaboration.

The evolution of the situation within the workers councils during this period of dual power is, from that time forward, lightly linked to an intensifying class struggle.

At the beginning of April 1917, the first congress of the Soviets – declared to be 'pan-Russian' but in reality limited largely to St. Petersburg – had 480 delegates from the capital, 138 from local councils, and 46 from the army. It agreed to support the bourgeois-liberal government of Prince Lvov (demanding, however, to exercise control over that government!). It supported continuing the military effort; at the same time calling for an extension of the movement for workers' councils into all countries.

At the end of April, the government again tried to promote a pro-war policy, provoking large demonstrations and a strong strike movement for immediate economic demands. The pendulum was swinging to the left. At the (first) congress of factory committees in Petrograd, the Bolsheviks already had a majority because of their support for the call for 'an unconditional 8-hour work day', and 'workers' control' (by a vote of 421 to 335). Paradoxically, at the top echelons of the state and on the level of the national soviet structures, this leftward shift first translated itself – to the detriment of the liberals – by reinforcing the position of the reformists (Mensheviks, Social-Revolutionaries). Initially, they entered into a coalition government 'between the classes,' which they led from that point on.

At the beginning of June, the real first congress of workers' and soldiers' deputies met. With its 1,090 elected delegates (of which 822 were properly mandated and had the right to vote) it represented some 20 million people. Elected on the basis of universal suffrage, the congress constituted the most representative and democratic body that Russia had ever known. Based on a deep going political pluralism, it debated, over three weeks (3-30 June), all of the vital questions facing the population. The delegates included 283 SRs (Social-Revolutionaries), 248 Mensheviks, 105 Bolsheviks, and 73 unaffiliated individuals, with the rest divided between different small socialist groups. Its executive committee, which had the character of a virtual 'counter-government', was composed of 104 Mensheviks, 100 SRs, 35 Bolsheviks, and 18 socialists from other currents. After a short time it combined forces with the Executive Committee of the All-Russian Peasant Congress, which was held separately, and where the SRs held an absolute monopoly.

The coalition government, very popular at the outset, rapidly discredited itself. Similar causes bring similar results, but flavoured with an awakening class consciousness: the popular masses intervened directly one more time in the political arena, with their own methods of struggle. Aware of the pressures developing at the base, the Executive Committee of the workers' councils, under reformist leadership, tried to take over the movement by allowing a demonstration. On 18 June, in Petrograd, it was nevertheless the slogans of the Bolsheviks – especially 'All Power to the Soviets' (still under the leadership of the reformists) – which was by far the most popular.

Revolution and counter-revolution: July-August

The new relationship of forces was tested during the 'July days'.

The initiative had been taken with the demonstration of 18 June. The proletariat in the capital interpreted this first victory as a beginning of the final offensive. Going further than the Bolshevik party intended, the masses wanted to overthrow the government. However, this vanguard of the mass movement had failed to grasp the real situation. It was too far out in front. As a result, at the beginning of July, the pendulum swung sharply back again, quite far to the right. The bourgeoisie wanted to find a way to begin snuffing out the fire of the revolution. The man of the moment was named Kerensky.

Having become prime minister, Kerensky struck hard at the Bolshevik Party and the other revolutionary organizations. He tried to re-establish the cohesion of the army. He restored the death penalty, dissolved the insurgent regiments, and named General Kornilov to head the general staff. All of this was based on the 'legality' of the workers councils and on their higher bodies; Kerensky was attempting to transform their subversive reality! The (reformist) Executive Committee of the Workers Councils actively collaborated with this political approach, helping to empty the soviets of their revolutionary content. They became discredited in the eyes of the vanguard workers.

Kerensky thus organized a general offensive against the conquests which the masses had imposed after February, in addition, he postponed indefinitely the realization of popular demands – always acknowledging them but … always postponing them for future consideration. The dual power was eroded, without totally disappearing as such. The Bolshevik Party experienced grave difficulties, but maintained its majority position among the working class (as demonstrated by the municipal elections which the party won at the end of August).

Some in 'high places' believed that the hour for a radical counter-revolution had arrived: the military coup d'état. Kornilov turned his back on Kerensky and took his chances at the end of August 1917 (similar events spring to mind: Allende and Pinochet, September 1973 in Chile, or Ebert-Noske and Kapp, Germany, 1920). In three days, the 'army' with which Kerensky attacked the capital was routed. The soviets of Petrograd had taken the lead in the resistance. In this way they recaptured their place at the centre of the workers' counter power.

The revolution of October 1917

At the start of September the pendulum swung to the left just as sharply as it had swung right at the beginning of July.

Within the workers' councils, the Bolshevik Party became a majority – first in Petrograd and Moscow. Within the party, Lenin, still in exile in Finland, put the seizure of power and the organization of the insurrection on the order of the day. He posed the question: When? How?

Between April and September the party learned to struggle for a majority within the soviets using the methods of workers' democracy. From that point on it was through revolutionary initiative that these organs of workers' democracy would become the new state apparatus.

Faced with this turning point, the Bolshevik Party suffered a grave internal crisis before a clear line could emerge. A 'right' current, led by Zinoviev and Kamenev – constituting the majority at first in the central committee – hesitated, put off the moment for action and wanted to reject the idea of insurrection. Between Lenin and Trotsky, both partisans of immediate preparation for the uprising, there developed, at times, a debate over the precise tactic that should be followed in pursuit of it. The left wing of the party finally gained the upper hand in the central committee on 10 October 1917.

The national congress of workers', soldiers', and peasants' councils was called for the end of the month. At the same time, the Military Revolutionary Committee, an organ of the Petrograd Soviet, with Trotsky at its head, responded to a provocation by the district military commandant, Polkovnikov, who wanted to dissolve the city garrison which was completely behind the revolution. Thus the insurrection began as a measure of self-defence. In a few hours the bourgeois apparatus of repression was dismantled in Petrograd. Political power was within reach; it was up to the national congress of workers councils to make a final decision. Its political composition was now transformed from what it had been in June of 1917. Out of 650 delegates, the reformist bloc (the right wing Mensheviks and

SRs) controlled less than 100. The Bolsheviks, for their part, had an absolute majority of around 390 delegates. They were joined by the left wing Mensheviks and left SRs. The reformists, a minority, walked out of the congress, shifting to the side of the counter-revolution.

A new executive committee of the workers' councils – a real legislative body for the new soviet power – was elected on a pluralist basis: 67 Bolsheviks, 29 left SRs, with 20 seats given to different revolutionary groups. The executive committee, in turn, elected the first government of the new workers' state. 'We begin the construction of a new socialist order,' declared Lenin.

A joyous and painless revolution at the outset! But it would have to pass through terrible trials during the civil war years of 1918-1920, before consolidating itself.

The parties of the revolution

The democratic self-organization of the popular masses is a fundamental and examplary aspect of the Russian Revolution. But this did not determine, by itself, the question of what politics would actually be pursed by the 'counter-power'.

This self-organization encompassed a plurality of parties, with their specific programs, tactics, activities, etc. During the Russian revolution it was the interaction between these parties and the territorial councils which determined the outcome. The trade union movement was, for its part, extremely weak, and the activities of the factory committees remained subordinate, although important.

The political parties organized themselves very late and in a particular fashion, one which reflects the social reality of that epoch in Russia: a despotic state, paternalistic and totalitarian at the same time, overwhelming, suffocating or absorbing 'civil society'.

The Kadets: In 1917, aside from various monarchist groups which had become marginalized, the Kadets ('Constitutional Democrats'), constituted the main party of the dominant classes. This party formed the first provisional government, in the wake of the February 1917 revolution. Muliukov – professor, historian, and ideologue – was, along with Gutchkov, its principal leader.

The Workerists: Kerensky led, in 1917, the Popular Socialists, or Trudoviks (workerists). By then quite weak numerically, the party had known its hour of glory in the pseudo-parliaments of 1906-1914. There it represented the peasant masses who had been awakened to political life after 1905. This party grouped together political personalities, relying on the aspirations and dissatisfactions of the conservative petty-bourgeoisie in the provinces and in the countryside. Kerensky himself became a figure on whom the big bourgeoisie could rely.

The parties of the Second International: Three parties, all of which were members of the Second International, contested for the allegiance of the worker and peasant masses: The Mensheviks, the Bolsheviks, and the Social-Revolutionaries (SRs). All claimed to be socialist, that is to say Marxist, and revolutionary. Except for small minorities, each had in 1914 adopted a hostile attitude toward the imperialist war. Therefore, the process of political clarification was complicated. It was necessary for these parties to be tested in the fire of battle during the eight months of dual power. The events of the summer of 1917 were conclusive: splits between left and the right wings of SRs and Mensheviks; revolutionary unity within the Bolshevik party. This did not eliminate a certain continuing degree of political confusion among the rank and file and in the periphery of each of these parties, and also between them.

The SRs: Officially reconstituted in 1902, this party rested on a long revolutionary tradition which originated in the middle of the nineteenth century. It had been a strong political adversary to the RSDLP (Russian Social Democratic Labour Party). Completely hegemonic in the peasant movement, the SRs also had a strong influence in big urban enterprises. Poorly organized and confused politically, the SRs helped – between February and August 1917 – to guarantee an indispensable social base for the class collaborationist government, of which the Mensheviks constituted a political head. During the summer of 1917, the SRs split between a left, revolutionary wing (Spiridonova, Kamkov), very close to the positions of the Bolsheviks, and a reformist right-wing (Chernov, Gotz), collaborating closely with the Mensheviks. By the end of 1917, the left SRs largely surpassed the right in influence.

The Mensheviks: They formed after 1903 as the 'revolutionary right' wing of the RSDLP. The showdown of 1917 was not the only time that their majority (Dan, Lieber, Tseretelli) engaged in incurably class-collaborationist politics. They would pay the price in a left split, led by Martov and Martynov. These two, genuine 'centrists', opposed the war, had a base in the workers councils, and favoured a socialist revolution in 1917. But they hesitated and vacillated when confronted with the key problem of the revolution: the seizure and exercise of power.

The Bolsheviks: A faction within the RSDLP until 1912, the Bolsheviks became the key revolutionary party in 1913-1914, gaining the allegiance of worker cadres in the cities and the leadership of a general strike in Petrograd. The consolidation, implantation, and growth of the party came at the cost of internal struggles and debates: In 1914 there was a departure of the right-wing national chauvinists; in March and April 1917 the growth of a new opportunist wing (Stalin-Kamenev-Zinoviev), a majority – ready to support the liberal government, to accept the continuation of the war – which was opposed by the radical theses of Lenin. In July there was a struggle against an ultra left current in favour of immediately seizing power and a fight against sectarianism on the part of an older layer of cadre who were reluctant to fuse with other currents (including Trotsky's). In August there was a debate about revolutionary initiatives and shifting the foundation for workers democracy from the territorial councils to the factory committees. Finally, in October, there was the debate with the right wing of the party over insurrection, a discussion which was replayed again and again, in many different keys, during subsequent years. But in October, the Bolsheviks were a party of the masses which engaged in the struggle for power – a party recognized and supported by the popular movement.

The Mezhrayontsi: Trotsky, on the basis of his own revolutionary positions, had been a member of – or had been dragged along by – the Menshevik faction. He broke with them in August 1914. In July 1917, he rejoined the Bolsheviks, along with the Mezhrayontsi (the 'interdistrict' or 'intercraft' committees). Active and influential in Petrograd, this revolutionary Marxist group was a small minority: 60 to 80 members in 1915, 150 on the eve of February 1917, 300 in April (the Bolsheviks were 16,000 at that time in Petrograd), 4,000 in July – when the Bolshevik Party could count 180,000 members throughout the country.

The minority currents: The phenomenon of the 'intercraft' committees underlines the existence of many revolutionary currents and groups, marginal on the scale of the entire country but important at times in one city, one workplace, one sector. Among them were the anarchists, the revolutionary syndicalists, the 'maximalists' (an ultraleft split from the SRs), the Menshevik Internationalists (Martov, Martynov), and the United Social-Democratic Internationalists (small but influential because of the journal *Novy Zhizn* – New Life – of Maxim Gorky).

The international counter-revolution

The victory of October 1917 had powerful international repercussions. The call for an immediate end to the slaughter of the war and for the punishment of those responsible – the ruling classes of Europe – raised hopes in the trenches and combativity in the workplace.

The governments signed an armistice in November 1918. But many countries were already undergoing revolutionary crises – imperial Germany first of all. Along with Tsarist Russia, Prussian militarism was the principal barrier against subversion on the European continent after 1789 (the French revolution). The country was destabilized by a rapid succession of struggles. Between 1918 and 1923, the German proletariat tried to 'speak Russian'. But it lacked a revolutionary party at its head, with the same combativity and tradition of organization. The revolutionary wave was crushed for the first time in January 1919. It reappeared no less powerfully in 1920, then in 1921 and 1923.

A union was conceivable between the USSR – a vast country with rich agricultural lands, but backward and living under precarious circumstances – and a socialist Germany – powerful, industrial, situated in the heart of Europe with a large proletariat constituting a mortal enemy to European reaction. Confronted with this potential 'socialist bloc', a large imperialist coalition came together. It consisted of the German army (defeated but still imposing), a Russian army (out of power, but with which the White generals, that is the counter-revolutionaries, launched a civil war), and the military forces of France, England, and the United States – the 'victors' in the war. This coalition invaded the USSR.

In the political arena, the activity of social democracy, having passed to the side of the capitalist system, was decisive. Dominant within the world working class, it cut off solidarity, discredited the USSR, and blocked the development of a revolutionary movement in Western Europe. It had a single goal: to crush the socialist revolution and restabilize the bourgeois order. The USSR was devastated by the civil war. In Finland, Germany, Austria, Hungary, Italy, the proletariat was defeated – at times with the aide of private armies of a new type: the 'Freikorps' in Germany, the 'fascists' in Italy.

In the USSR, six years of uninterrupted war from 1914 to 1920, provoked an economic, social, and human disaster. The workers' state, completely isolated, stood fast. But the construction of socialism suffered badly under these frighteningly difficult conditions.

The end of a cycle

The first cycle of the international revolution, which ran from 1917 to 1923, now came to an end. Another cycle began, one of capitalist stabilization on a world scale. In the USSR the situation was favourable for the emergence of a privileged bureaucracy with Stalin at its head. Lenin, dying, undertook a 'last struggle' against the bureaucracy between 1921 and 1923. In Western Europe social democracy (the 'stinking corpse' as Rosa Luxemburg called it) renewed itself. It (re)gained the leadership of the workers' movement in most countries. Mass trade unions were consolidated during the 1920s, as a result of reforms imposed on the bourgeoisie – which feared revolution and mass struggle.

OCTOBER 1917:
COUP D'ÉTAT OR SOCIAL REVOLUTION?[1]

Ernest Mandel

There is currently a real campaign of denigration of the October 1917 Revolution underway, in both the West and in Eastern Europe. It is often very bitter. It is based on historical falsifications and myths that are just as great as Stalinist myths and falsifications. Fighting against it is not only indispensable from a scientific and political point of view. It is also a question of intellectual cleanliness. The fight for truth is also a fight for a minimum of decency in public life.

In the first chapter we will deal with three of the myths that are the most frequently encountered in current polemical writing.

The myth of a minority coup d'état

The first mystification deals with the nature of the October Revolution. It was only a diabolical coup d'état organized by that master of manoeuvres Lenin, and carried out by a small sect of professional revolutionaries. The comments, which followed the attempted coup d'état in Moscow on 26 August 1991, are very revealing from this point of view. Some went so far as to say that a second (failed) putsch made it possible to eliminate what a first (successful) putsch had created in 1917.

The truth is quite different. The October Revolution was the culminating point of one of the most deep-rooted mass movements ever known. In Europe of the period only the rising of the German workers in 1920 in reaction to the Kapp-von Luttwitz putsch, and the Catalan insurrection of 1936, in reaction to the military fascist taking of power by the Francoists, were of comparable scope, but nevertheless more limited and less long lasting.

Historical sources do not leave any doubt about the representativity of the Bolsheviks in October 1917. There is no need, to be convinced of this, to use the writing of those who were close to Lenin.[2]

The scope of the mass movement before, during and after the October

Revolution, is today well established.[3] Here we will simply cite some of the many testimonies from the Bolsheviks' opponents.

> ... the Bolsheviks were working stubbornly and without let up. They were among the masses, at factory-benches, every day without a pause. Tens of speakers, big and little, were speaking in Petrograd, at the factories and in the barracks, every blessed day. For the masses, they had become their own people, because they were always there, taking the lead in details as well as in the most important affairs of the factories or barracks. They had become the sole hope, if only because since they were one with the masses, they were lavish with promises and sweet though simple fairy tales. The mass lived and breathed together with the Bolsheviks. It was in the hands of the party of Lenin and Trotsky.
>
> To talk about military conspiracy instead of national insurrection, when the party was followed by the overwhelming majority of the people, when the party had already de facto conquered all real power and authority, was clearly an absurdity.[4]

The German historian Oskar Anweiler, who was a severe critic of the Bolsheviks, noted that:

> The Bolsheviks were in the majority in the councils of deputies in almost all the big industrial centres and also in most of the councils of soldiers' deputies in the garrison towns.[5]

Marc Ferro, another ferocious critic of the Bolsheviks, could not stop himself noting that:

> In the first place, Bolshevization was the effect of the radicalization of the masses and was thus the expression of the democratic will ...
>
> The radicalization of the masses is sufficiently explained by the ineffectiveness of governmental policy (with the participation of the socialists since May) which, under cover of necessity, instituted conciliation procedures between the ruling and popular classes. Negotiation, far from changing the established order, perpetuated it ...
>
> From that time on, in the towns and in the army, there was discontent. Also, those who from the beginning had contested the very principle of class collaboration were gratified, and among them the most intransigent, that is to say the Bolsheviks of the Lenin tendency. The workers demanded less inhuman working conditions. It was the brutal or cunning rejection

of this by the possessing classes which led to the factory occupations, the sequestration of the owners and then, after October, vengeance on the bourgeoisie ...

This movement had a popular basis whose forms of organization have been described. The fear of repression and anger against the treacherous leaders were enough to explain the elementary absolutist attitude [!] of the committees which structured during their participation in the movement which led to October, which was not the absolutism attitude of the Bolsheviks but in solidarity with the movement they led.[6]

For Dan, one of the main Menshevik leaders on the eve of the Revolution, the masses:

... began more and more frequently to express their discontent and their impatience with impetuous movements and ended ... by turning to communism ... Strikes followed one after the other. The workers sought to answer the rapid rise in the cost of living with wage rises. But all their efforts failed with the continuous drop in value of the paper money. The communists launched in their own ranks the slogan of 'workers' control' and advised them to take the running of the factories into their own hands, in order to stop the ''sabotage' of the capitalists. At the same time, the peasants started to take over the big properties, to chase out the land owners and to set fire to their manor houses for fear that the domains would escape from them between that point and the calling of the Constituent Assembly.[7]

The October Revolution took place under the slogan 'All power to the Soviets'. The historian Beryl Williams summed up the process, which led to October in the following fashion:

Soviet power, rather than party programmes or the Constituent Assembly, was seen by the masses as the solution to their problems and only the Bolsheviks were really identified with soviet power ... The party was now in a position to ride the popular wave into power.[8]

In the Second Congress of the Soviets, the supporters of the perspective 'All power to the soviets' won 69.6 per cent of the mandates. In the All Russian Congress of Peasant Deputies, which met 9-23 December 1917, there was a slight majority (Left SRs and Bolsheviks) in favour of soviet power. The historian Anweiler concluded, in examining the altitude of the masses in relation to the dissolution of the Constituent Assembly by the Soviet government in January 1918 that:

> In the ranks of the people it is rare that there were protests against the coercive measures of the Bolsheviks: and this was certainly not only because of intellectual and physical terrorism, which was still quite 'soft' at the time. The fact that the Bolsheviks had very largely anticipated the decisions of the Constituent Assembly on questions as important as peace and land weighed no less heavily in the balance ... The working and peasant masses were ... more inclined to the give their agreement to concrete measures by the new masters. Despite the deficiency of the soviets both in questions of organization and, often, representation, the masses considered them as 'theirs'.[9]

The myth of the bloody utopia: immediate socialism?

Second mystification and historical falsification: the Bolsheviks carried out their putsch in order to create in Russia, immediately or in the short term, an ideal society, a paradise on earth. They 'put utopia in power" in the world of the Soviet historian Alexander Nekritch, from whom we are used to a little more objectivity.[10]

In reality, the taking of power by the soviets had a very precise aim: to obtain a certain number of concrete goals. These were: immediate end to the war; distribute the land to the peasants; ensure the right of self-determination for the oppressed nationalities; avoid the crushing of Red Petrograd which Kerensky wanted to give over the German army; stop the sabotage of the economy by the bourgeoisie; establish workers' control over production: stop the victory of the counter-revolution.

We can summarize their goals in the classic Marxist formula: to carry out the historic tasks of the (national) bourgeois democratic revolution by establishing the dictatorship of the proletariat; that is to say the destruction of the state, particularly the apparatus of the bourgeois state. The revolution certainly rapidly grew over into the carrying out of socialist tasks. But this was not because the Bolsheviks were utopians. It was because the masses refused any self-limitation on their emancipation, as Trotsky had foreseen as early as 1906. Feeling themselves the masters in the state and in the street, they were not inclined to stay quietly in the factories, allowing themselves to be still and forever exploited.[11]

The initiatives to introduce workers' control multiplied spontaneously on the eve of and following the October revolution. They also led almost automatically to the expropriations of factories when industrialists tried to impose mass sackings or factory closures.[12]

Between November 1917 and March 1918, 836 enterprises were nationalized: three quarters of the orders of expropriation emanated from local organs such as factory committees, trade unions, local soviets, and local economic councils. Only 5 per cent were nationalized by the centre.[13]

The Bolsheviks did not hope to achieve 'utopia', that is immediate socialism in Russia alone. In fact, they unanimously rejected such an idea. Lenin never hid from the Russian masses that, for him, the historical role of winning power in Russia was to encourage the international revolution, particularly the German revolution, taking advantage of the fact that the relationship of forces was more favourable to the proletariat in Russia than in any other country in the world.

Julius Braunthal has emphasized the importance of this question for Lenin:

> The whole future of the international workers' revolution, of socialism, is at stake.' This argument recurred in practically all the articles and letters in which he pushed the Central Committee, in autumn 1917, to go into action. He repeated, 'the growing maturity and the inevitable character of the world socialist revolution can no longer be doubted … We are on the threshold of the world revolution. We would be real traitors to the International if in such a moment, in such favourable conditions, we did not respond to the appeal of the German revolution (for example [the sailors] of the German navy) by resolutions alone.[14]

Of course, it should not be assumed from what has been said that a socialist perspective was not an essential element in Bolshevik propaganda that it had not influenced, even in only a marginal way, the concrete measures taken.

For Lenin and the Bolsheviks at that point – contrary to their positions before April 1917 – 'soviet power', 'workers' power', or 'workers' and peasants' power' and socialist orientation were practically considered as synonyms.

But Lenin incessantly emphasized that this only meant that it was possible – and necessary – to begin following this path, nothing more. Lenin knew that a fully developed socialist society (in the traditional, Marxist, sense of the term: a classless society) could only exist after the victory of the international revolution. He repeated this in January 1918 before the Third Congress of the Soviets:

I have no illusions about our having only just entered the period of transition to socialism, about not yet having reached socialism … We are far from having even completed the transitional phase from capitalism to socialism. We never cherished the hope we would finish it without the aid of the international proletariat.[15]

The myth of a party-sect of fanatics

Third mystification and historical falsification: the October 1917 'putsch' was perpetrated by a small sect of power-hungry, fanatical highly centralized professional revolutionaries manipulated by Lenin.

In reality, from the months of February to October 1917, the Bolshevik Party became a mass party, bringing together the real vanguard of the Russian proletariat: the natural leader of the class, recognized as such. The number of professional revolutionaries (full-time organizers) in its ranks was extremely limited.[16] This party was the least bureaucratized mass party ever known. There were barely 700 full timers among 250-300,000 members. It functioned in a very democratic manner: there were numerous discussions and differences of opinion which were, in general, publicly expressed.[17]

This freedom of oppression did not only concern a few leaders who, when in minority, expressed their opinions publicly (like Bukharin or the 'Left Communists'), including in separate daily newspapers. It also concerned entire bodies of the party. Thus, for months during 1917, the party committee in Viborg sent its own agitators into the Baltic fleet, to oppose the arguments of the Petrograd committee, which it considered too tolerant of the Provisional Government.

Two Bolshevik currents publicly disagreed during the conference of factory committees before the October Revolution. The first was represented by Miliutin and Larin, supported by Ryazanov, Lozovsky and Shliapnikov. It wanted to combine workers' control with the demand for central planning. The second, represented by Skrypnik and Chubar, insisted above all on decentralized initiatives at the base.

This tradition remained alive. There was still a trace of it to be found in 1921, at the Tenth Congress of the Communist Party, while the battle on the banning of factions raged (we will come back to this later). During the discussion, Lenin had vigorously attacked Kiselyov, a delegate who had criticized certain extraordinary disciplinary powers that the draft resolution gave the Central Committee. Having obviously been carried away in his polemic, he immediately made a self-criticism:

Comrades. I am very sorry that I used the word 'machine-gun' and hereby give a solemn promise never to use such words again even figuratively, for they only scare people and afterwards you can't make out what they want. Nobody intends to shoot at anybody and we are sure that neither Comrade Kiselyov nor anybody else will have cause to do so.[18]

The Bolshevik Party was at that time a party fully integrated into Russian society and its living forces. This is the point tellingly made by the first platform of the Workers' Opposition, in its opposition to the rise of the Stalinist faction six years after the revolution:

The Party (was) ... that living independent collectivity which sensitively seizes living reality because it is bound to this reality with a thousand threads.[19]

While the October Revolution was not a putsch, nor was it simply the culmination of a spontaneous mass movement. It was also an insurrection methodically prepared and carried out by the Bolsheviks and their allies, supporters of soviet power: the anarchists and the Left Social Revolutionaries.

It was not a secret or minority insurrection. It was an insurrection organized in the full light of day, mainly within the institutions emanating from the soviets.

This was the result of a new legitimacy which had been accepted by the great majority of the workers and soldiers and, a little later, a good part of the peasants. The legitimacy of the soviets and the factory councils outstripped that of the Provisional Government, the military high command, the employers and the big landowners.

In the workplaces, the workers thus increasingly recognized the authority of the factory committees rather than that of the employers.[20]

In Petrograd, thanks to the agitation and organization masterfully led by Leon Trotsky, all the regiments of the garrison decided in public assemblies to no longer recognize the orders of the military hierarchy but those of the Soviet and the Military Revolutionary Committee.

It was in these conditions that the 'technical' overthrow of the Provisional Government should take place on 25 October with so little bloodshed. There were fewer deaths than are normally caused by road accidents during a normal weekend in the main countries of Europe. For those who counterpose the 'glorious February Revolution' to the Bolsheviks' 'bloody putsch', let us remind them that the first cost 1,315 victims in Petrograd, while the second hardly a dozen.[21]

In short, what was the revolution of October 1917? The culminating point of a formidable mass movement, guided towards the taking of power by a vanguard workers' party closely rooted in the masses. A party which sought above all to achieve the most burning immediate demands of the population, while aiming for broader national and international socialist goals.[22]

The international significance

The victory of the October revolution cannot be understood outside the context of the First World War of 1914-1918. Of all the Bolsheviks' slogans, that of an immediate end to the war, 'peace without annexations or indemnities' was the most popular. It became the main difference between the Bolsheviks and the other parties claiming to be socialist or revolutionary. It was above all the soldiers, of whom the great majority were peasants, who no longer wanted the war.

The falling apart of the army, which was mainly still Tsarist, disarmed the provisional government and then the first attempts at counter-revolution. This is what made possible the victory and then consolidation of the October revolution.

> Perhaps the most significant fact about the revolution of 1917 is that between spring and autumn this great [army], the largest ever put into the field by any country, was transformed into an 'enormous, exhausted, badly clothed, badly fed embittered mob of people, united by thirst for peace and general disillusionment'.[23]

The most clear-sighted Mensheviks later admitted this. Their leader Dan stated bluntly that 'the continuation of the war brought the Bolshevik victory in the Russian Revolution',[24]

In addition, the attitude of the Bolsheviks and the soviets after the taking of power in October 1917 made it possible to have a real evaluation of the policy of the new revolutionary state.

The right of the peoples to decide their own fate

Lenin's first speech to the Second Congress of Soviets to present the policy of the new regime brought into being in October was his report on the peace. In it we find a vigorous affirmation of the right to self-determination, whose democratic thrust is very relevant today:

If any country whatsoever is forcibly retained within the borders of a given state, if in spite of its expressed desires – no matter whether expressed in the press, at public meetings, in the decisions of parties, or in protests and uprisings against national oppression – it is not accorded the right to decide the forms of its state existence by a free vote, taken after the complete evacuation of the troops of the incorporating or, generally, of the stronger nation and without the least pressure being brought to bear, such incorporation is annexation, i.e. seizure and violence.

The government considers it the greatest of crimes against humanity to continue this war over the issue of how to divide among the strong and rich nations the weak nationalities they have conquered, and solemnly announces its determination immediately to sign terms of peace to stop this war on the terms indicated, which are equally just for all nationalities without exception.[25]

The Soviet government extended this principle of the peoples' right to decide their own fate to all the colonies and semi-colonies outside Europe. This was a revolutionary act which had incalculable historical repercussions. It gave a decisive impulse to the developing national liberation movements in countries like India, China and Indonesia, as well as significant support to already important anti-imperialist movements such as that in Turkey.[26]

In one of its very first statements during the peace negotiations with Germany at Brest-Litovsk, on 30 December 1917, the Soviet government proclaimed the extension of the right of nations to decide on their own fate, recognized by the American president Woodrow Wilson, to all colonial and semi-colonial countries. At the same time, this government abolished all unequal treaties with China, particularly those concerning the Chinese Eastern railway and the right to extra-territoriality of all Russian citizens in China, Mongolia and Iran. These principles were also incorporated into the first Soviet constitution, that of the Russian Soviet Federal Socialist Republic (RSFSR) of 1918.

The reaction of anti-imperialist forces in Asia was immediate. In China, the Bolsheviks were called the *huang-i-tang*, 'the party of the greatest humanism'. Sun Yat-sen, the Chinese nationalist leader, sent a message of solidarity to Lenin. In Iran, the national-democratic movement identified with the October Revolution, once Trotsky withdrew all the Russian troops and instructors from the country.

One of the effects of this policy was the famous conference of the Peoples of the East at Baku in 1920.

The Soviet regime for the first time in history even abolished secret diplomacy, deciding to publish all diplomatic documents and secret treaties. Most importantly, it decided to immediately start peace negotiations with all the belligerent governments who were prepared to do so.

October 1917: a revolution for peace

This appeal was accompanied by an appeal to the workers of the major imperialist countries to take the path of peace and socialism:

> While addressing this proposal for peace to the governments and peoples of all the belligerent countries, the Provisional Workers' and Peasants' Government of Russia appeals in particular also to the class-conscious workers of the three most advanced nations of mankind and the largest states participating in the present war, namely Great Britain, France and Germany. The workers of these countries have made the greatest contribution to the cause of progress and socialism: they have furnished the great examples of the Chartist movement in England, a number of revolution of historic importance effected by the French proletariat, and finally the heroic struggle against the Anti-Socialist Law in Germany and the prolonged, persistent and disciplined work of creating mass proletarian organizations in Germany, a work which serves as a model to the workers of the whole world. All these examples of proletarian heroism and historical creative work are a pledge that the workers of the countries mentioned will understand the duty that now faces them of saving mankind from the horrors of war and its consequences, that these workers, by comprehensive, determined, and supremely vigorous action, will help us to conclude peace successfully, and at the same time emancipate the labouring and exploited masses of our population from all forms of slavery and all forms of exploitation.[27]

And in conclusion, in a still more striking fashion:

> In the Manifesto of March 14 [1917], we [the soviets] called for the overthrow of the bankers, but, [before the October Revolution] far from overthrowing our own bankers, we entered into an alliance with them. Now we have overthrown the government of the bankers.
>
> The governments and the bourgeois will make every effort to unite their forces and drown the workers' and peasants' revolution in blood. But the three years of war have been a good lesson to the masses – [as is proved by] the soviet movement in other countries and the mutiny in the German navy, which was crushed by the officer cadets of Wilhelm the hangman ...

The workers' movement will triumph and will pave the way to peace and socialism.[28]

Trotsky, speaking to the peoples of Europe affected by the war, proclaimed:

The workers and soldiers must wrest from the criminal hands of the bourgeoisie the cause [the right to decide] of the war and take it into their own hands.

In other words, in the eyes of the Bolsheviks, the October revolution was a means to put an end to the war; in so doing it should encourage and speed up the development of the world socialist revolution.

Is this borne out by history? Incontestably.

The world war was a decisive turning point in the history of capitalism. It was the beginning of the epoch in which the destructive, barbaric, regressive features of the system were going to develop significantly in comparison to its capacity to maintain a periodic development of productive forces.

The First World War saw ten million human beings massacred, including the flower of Europe's young men, in the pursuit of goals to which no one today lends any legitimacy at all.[29] This was the first of a succession of disasters which led humanity 30 years later to the barbarity of Auschwitz and Hiroshima.

The most clear-sighted socialists – not only revolutionaries like Lenin, Trotsky and Rosa Luxemburg but also moderates like Jean Jaures – had foreseen this before 1914.

The Soviet government fought for immediate peace with Germany and Austro-Hungary during the Brest-Litovsk negotiations. A growing number of workers and soldiers from all countries already rejected the war, which explains the wide popularity throughout the world for the Soviet position, particularly when it was expressed in Trotsky's exemplary use of the negotiation table as an agitational method.

The representatives of Germany and Austro-Hungary complained of violation of all diplomatic norms.

What is this? Speaking directly to soldiers over the heads of their officers? Calling on them to disobey orders if not to mutiny? Calling on the colonies to rise? Calling on workers to strike. From a Foreign Affairs minister is this not trampling on the elementary rules of civilization and of 'friendship between nations'?

Very soon the French and British governments followed in the footsteps of their implacable enemies, the Central Powers, and denounced the Soviet revolutionaries in their turn.

On the other hand, for the peoples, the 'civilization' and 'norms of friendship between nations' that the belligerent nations claimed to stand for meant senseless massacre, destruction of entire towns, inhuman oppression and exploitation. It was the civilization of plague and death. Lenin and Trotsky incarnated the hope of a superior civilization, of life, liberty and equal rights for all women and men.

Imperialist propaganda – which right-wing social democracy also partly circulated – was much more virulent then than the anti-communist propaganda of the Cold War period or today. It had however a lot less effect among the toiling masses. They saw the sincerity of the Soviet regime.

The Soviet regime: internationalism in action

They saw that the first Soviet Constitution, that of 1918, eliminated the distinction between 'national citizens' and 'foreigners'. Anybody living in Soviet Russia and ready to work there would immediately enjoy all political rights, including the right to vote. John MacLean, the shop stewards leader from the munitions factory in Glasgow, Scotland, was imprisoned by the British government for having gone on strike. He was named Consul General for the RSFSR and thus achieved diplomatic immunity: which forced London to release him.

The Bolsheviks thus showed that they remained faithful to the best traditions of the socialist movement. The Second International had tragically failed in this domain on 4 August 1914 when its best leaders had accepted the logic of the war, in violation of their most solemn oaths and the resolutions adopted by their own organization during successive congresses.

After this historic capitulation, the practice of the new Soviet regime, which was in conformity with its principles, did more to stimulate a strong regrowth of internationalism within the masses than thousands of speeches, articles, pamphlets or books.

It was this, which made possible the creation of the Third International and unleashed a powerful movement of solidarity with the besieged Russian Revolution.

A socialist revolution: the revolution against the war

The new Soviet regime had in fact put into practice the resolutions adopted in 1907 and 1913 by the Second International itself. In fact, the policy of a socialist answer to the threat of war was not simply to denounce the dangers of unprecedented butchery on calling for a halt or an end to the massacre. Thanks to the consistent efforts of the left, then led by Lenin, Martov and Rosa Luxemburg at the 1907 Stuttgart Congress of the Socialist International, the unanimously voted resolution stated:

> In case war should break out anyway, it is their (the socialist parties) duty to intervene for its speedy termination and to strive with all their power to utilize the economic and political crisis created by the war to rouse the masses and thereby hasten the downfall of capitalist class rule.[30]

In 1912 in the Basle extraordinary congress, the Socialist International addressed a solemn warning to all governments:

> Let the governments remember that, given die present condition of Europe and the mood of the working class, they cannot unleash a war without danger to themselves. Let them remember that the Franco-German War was followed by the revolutionary outbreak of the Commune: that the Russo- Japanese War set into motion the revolutionary energies of the peoples of the Russian Empire: that the military and naval arms: race gave the class conflicts in England and on the continent an unheard-of sharpness and unleashed an enormous wave of strikes. It would be insanity for the governments not to realize that the very idea of a monstrous world war must inevitably call forth the indignation and the revolt of the working class. Proletarians consider it a crime to fire at each other for the profits of the capitalists, the ambitions of dynasties, or the greater glory of secret diplomatic treaties.
>
> If the governments cut off every possibility of normal progress, and thereby drive the proletariat to desperate steps, they themselves will have to bear the entire responsibility for the consequences of the crisis they bring about ...
>
> The proletariat is conscious that at this moment it is the bearer of the entire future of humanity. The proletariat will exert all its energy to prevent the annihilation of the flower of all peoples, threatened by all the horrors of mass murder, starvation and pestilence.[31]

Jean Jaurès, a great figure of French socialism, summed up this message in succinct terms in the final phrase of his speech to the Basle congress:

> In sharpening the danger of war, the governments should see that the peoples can easily make the count: their own revolution would cost fewer dead than the war of others.

Going even further, Victor Adler, the leader of Austrian social democracy stated that:

If the crime [of starting the war] is committed, a historic punishment will follow it: it will be the beginning of the end of the reign of these criminals.

With hindsight, these analyses and perspectives can seem rather unrealistic, in the light of the events of August 1914. Nevertheless, it should be noted that neither Lenin, Rosa Luxemburg and Martov, nor Jaures and Adler predicted that a revolution would immediately follow the outbreak of war – and revolutions did indeed break out three or four years later.

The period after the First World War

It is true that Adler himself capitulated in August 1914 to the 'criminals' that he denounced in 1913 and that he then did everything to prevent the revolution rather than prepare it. It is also true that the masses, including the social democrats, let themselves be swept up into the wave of chauvinism of the period.

These are unchallengeable facts. But it would be rather jumping the gun to conclude that they were necessarily the product of a reformist daily practice, combining economic strikes and the preparation of 'good' electoral results, or that this was the reflection of the growing integration of the proletariat into the bourgeois state and society.

Because in that case how could we explain the turn in the masses' attitude from 1917? That is to say from the moment that 'the political and economic crisis created by the war' in fact provoked poverty, famine, disease, massacres, the suppression of democratic freedoms, exactly as the Stuttgart and Basle resolutions had foreseen. How can the growing strike wave be explained, including of political strikes, against the 'paix de rapine' imposed by the German Ludendorff on the Russian Revolution at Brest-Litovsk in January 1918?

In May 1917, open mutiny erupted in the French army. Fifty-four divisions refused to obey orders. Over 100,000 *poilus* [rank-and-file soldiers] were court-martialled, 23,000 found guilty, 423 sentenced to death, and 55 actually shot according to official figures. Many others were shot without trial or pounded to death through artillery fire.[32] In August 1917, a mass strike in Barcelona was machine-gunned into submission, leaving 70 dead, hundreds of wounded and 200 prisoners. In February 1918, the Austro-Hungarian fleet mutinied at Catarro.

From October 1918 this turnaround led to an uninterrupted series of revolution. Rather later than the Bolsheviks had hoped. But nevertheless they were real revolutions: in Finland, in Austria, in Hungary, creation of soviet power in Bavaria, revolutionary crisis in Italy.[33] The world revolution was a tangible reality during these two years.

In December 1918, at a Herald rally in the Albert Hall, London, Robert Williams, general secretary of the Transport Workers' Federation, urged 'preparedness for revolution'. 'The sun of international socialism,' he said, 'is melting capitalism throughout Europe.'[34] In January 1919, a general strike broke out in Belfast, and in Seattle USA. In February 1919 a general strike in Barcelona lasted one month.

The world revolution was not only a tangible reality for the Bolsheviks, the revolutionary socialists, and for a good section of the 'centrist' socialist left throughout the world. It was also a tangible reality for the bourgeoisie.

The British Prime Minister Lloyd George wrote in relation to this:

The whole of Europe is fitted with the spirit of revolution. There is a deep sense not only of discontent but of anger and revolt amongst the workmen against the pre-war conditions. The whole existing order in its political, social and economic aspects is questioned by the masses of the population from one end of Europe to the other.

Lloyd George sent a confidential memorandum to the delegates to the Versailles Peace Congress on 23 March 1919:

If Germany ever goes over to the Spartakists, it is inevitable that she should throw in her lot with the Russian Bolsheviks. Once that happens, all Eastern Europe will be swept into the orbit of the Bolshevik Revolution and within a year we may witness a spectacle of nearly 300 million people organized into a vast Red Army under German instructors and German generals.[35]

Concerning the situation in Italy, during the wave of factory occupations in September 1920, the historian Gaetano Salvemini wrote:

The bankers, the big industrialists and the big landowners waited for the social revolution like sheep waiting to be led to the slaughterhouse.[36]

In his *History of the International*, the Austro-Marxist Julius Braunthal described the situation during the Socialist International's first post-war meeting, in August 1919 in the following terms:

Europe was in ferment. It seemed as if we were on the verge of decisive struggles between revolution and counter-revolution.[37]

And he added:

Immediately after the meeting of the founding congress of the IC there was a revolutionary upsurge in Europe which seemed to confirm Lenin's prognosis.[38]

In relation to Germany he noted that:

The imperialism of the Western powers imposed limits on the social revolution in Germany. But even within these limits, the conditions existed for a social revolution which would break the power of the big capitalist bourgeoisie; for heavy industry, mines and the chemical industry which was then owned by a few to become public property: to break [the power] of finance capital by imposing state control of the banks; the conditions for breaking the power of Junkers by the division [in a way favourable to the peasants] of big land properties, and above all by the development of an organ of the revolution's power – an armed force recruited among the workers and led by the socialists, as was the case of Volkswehr created by Austrian social democracy.[39]

In his report to the Third Congress of the Communist International, Trotsky cited two retrospective judgements of the European bourgeoisie which fully confirmed this analysis of the situation in 1919-20. The reactionary French newspaper *Le Temps* wrote on 28 April 1921:

Last year's May Day was set as the beginning of a general strike which was in its turn to usher in the first phase of the revolution. Today absolute confidence prevails in the nation's effort to surmount all the crises consequent upon the war.

And the daily newspaper most representative of the Swiss bourgeoisie *Neue Zurcher Zeitung* wrote at the same time about Germany:

Germany of 1921 bears no resemblance to Germany of 1918. Governmental consciousness has become so strong that communist methods meet with opposition among almost all the layers of the population, although the number of communists, who during the revolutionary days comprised a small and resolute handful, has since grown inorinately.[40]

It is true that outside Russia the revolutionary wave only had temporary victories: the creation of ephemeral soviet republics in Hungary and Bavaria. The first phase of the German revolution was defeated in January 1919. The Austrian revolution was stopped in a deliberate way by the (centrist) Austrian Socialist Party, which negotiated a compromise with the bourgeoisie.[41]

Defeats in Europe: the responsibility of the reformists

But this compromise was not a result of an objectively unfavourable relationship of forces. On this point we should note the terrible historic responsibility of the leaders of the Austrian SP. In fact, the taking of power by the Austrian socialists – which was perfectly possible at the time – would have fundamentally changed the situation in Europe in favour of the revolution. This would have assured a territorial junction with the soviet republics of Bavaria and Hungary, which had been recently established and were situated on either side of Austria. By their refusal to take power, the Austrian socialists interrupted the chain of the social revolution: if they had acted otherwise the three proletarian republics would have mutually strengthened each other, provoking a revolutionary momentum which could have spread throughout the whole of Europe.[42]

The German revolution started in 1918 and then suffered a heavy blow. But it then went through another upward phase which culminated in the impressive general strike of March 1920 against the Kapp-von Luttwitz putsch and was followed by a third wave in 1923 with the general strike against the Cuno government.[43]

And most importantly, if the Bolsheviks had 'illusions' in the world revolution, these illusions were shared by millions of wageworkers throughout the world.

There were only a handful of small revolutionary groups representing some tens of thousands of people outside Russia at the first Congress of the Communist International in March 1919. But in the months which followed, the sympathy 'for Moscow' would spread to such a point that the majority of organized workers in many countries (Spain, Italy, France, Norway, Bulgaria, Czechoslovakia) and a strong minority in others asked to join the Communist International. In Austria, Poland, Switzerland, the leaders of the Socialist Parties could only stop this tidal wave by themselves breaking with reformist social democracy and forming the so-called 'Two-

and-a-half International', which made oaths in favour of the dictatorship of the proletariat.[44]

It should be pointed out that the deep radicalization of the international proletariat after the October Revolution had its roots in the conditions in each country. It was not simply a product exported from Moscow.[45] It profoundly changed the international relationship of forces between the classes. To try to hold back this revolutionary wave with the aid of the reformists, the bourgeoisie had to grant the proletariat important reforms for which it had been fighting for more than 25 years, particularly the eight-hour day and simple universal suffrage. So deep was the radicalization that there was even a general strike in Switzerland and a call by the social-democrat leader Troelstra for a revolution in the Netherlands, two countries which had remained neutral during the war and which were a lot more stable than the rest of Europe.

This change in the international relationship of forces between the classes saved Soviet Russia from military suffocation in 1920 when the unanimous threat of a general strike by the British workers' movement prevented British imperialism from intervening alongside the counter revolutionary forces of Weygand and Foch during the Russo Polish war.[46] In this very precise sense as well the Bolsheviks' hopes in the world revolution were hardly illusory.

These hopes were undoubtedly excessive if we talk about decisive short-term victories. Lenin and Trotsky recognized this quite quickly. In a rather paradoxical fashion, they had sinned by an excess of spontaneism. The revolutionary wave seemed then so deep that they had rather under-estimated the role of the subjective factor – of the revolutionary leadership – in wresting a victory:

> What lies ahead of us is not chaotic, spontaneous assault, the first stage of which we observed in Europe in 1918-1919. It seemed to us (and there was some historical justification for it) that in the period when the bourgeoisie was disorganized, this assault could mount in ever rising waves, that in this process the consciousness of the leading layers of the working class would become clarified, and that in this way the proletariat would attain state power in the course of one or two years. There was this historical possibility. But it did not materialize. History has – with the assistance of the bourgeoisie's bad or good will, its cunning, its experience, its instinct for power – granted the bourgeoisie a fairly prolonged breathing space. No miracles have taken place.[47]

But it is undoubtedly the case that the masses wanted the revolution in a whole series of countries. There is much proof and many personal testimonies which underline this. If, despite this, the revolutionary struggle did not triumph outside Russia this is because there was not an adequate leadership or even that the hegemonic leaderships of the mass movement intervened actively to prevent this victory.

Despite the hesitations and the contradictions in his diagnostic, this is also the conclusion that Braunthal himself reached:

> Why is it that nothing like this [a social revolution] happened? In the last instance it is because the German social democracy did not intervene in the revolution as a revolutionary party, because the majority of the leaders as well as the masses (their own base) were far from thinking in revolutionary terms, and thus were not mentally prepared for the test of the revolution.[48]

The German people, the German and international proletariat, humanity as whole, have paid a terrible price for this bankruptcy, based on crimes. We will come back to this.

The national significance

The Tsarist regime was overthrown in February 1917, eight months before the October Revolution. It was then that the soviets – the workers', soldiers' and peasants' councils – were created. However, at the beginning of this crucial period, the Bolsheviks were not a majority in the soviets and were not in power. It was other political forces, the bourgeois liberals and Mensheviks, who formed the provisional government, and had the opportunity to prove themselves. But they turned out to be incapable of resolving all the burning problems that existed. It was this incapacity which explains the continuing growth of the Bolsheviks' influence and the creation of a new revolutionary situation in the autumn.

Immediate peace was not the only task which confronted the provisional government. The population felt the urgency of other problems and the soviets were committed to resolving them without delay (without that always meaning that the masses consciously supported the power of the soviets).

This is particularly true for the questions of land, workers' poverty, and political institutions.

In these three key fields of socio-political life, Russia carried a heritage of barbarism, of backwardness, of under development, to which were added the effects of a rapid and savage industrialization carried out by the autocracy.

The historic merit of the October Revolution is that it made it possible to rapidly clean out these Augean stables produced by Tsarism, for which the great majority of the Russian people – prisoner of these inhuman conditions – paid in human suffering.

It should be enough simply to describe these conditions to see once again the hypocrisy, if not the cynicism, of all those who hold the October Revolution responsible for the misery which existed in Russia until the early 1920s.

The agrarian question

The abolition of serfdom in 1861 was accompanied by heavy charges on the peasants. It is estimated that the capitalized yield of the land that the peasants were to receive at that time was around 648 million gold roubles, but the total price the peasants were obliged to pay was 867 million roubles. The peasants had in addition to pay an agricultural tax of 1.56 roubles per desiatin (a desiatin is equivalent to 2.7 acres). This makes in all 170 million roubles, while the bourgeois and the noble private owners only paid 0.23 roubles per desiatin.

According to a 1902 survey, the sums to be paid by the peasantry varied between 50 and 100 per cent of the net income per farm, according to size.

In addition, during the division of the land, the big landowners took the good land which had previously been available to the peasants, and too often only 'gave' them the right to buy less fertile land.

The peasants got practically nothing from the Tsarist state in exchange for this heavy contribution. In the heartlands of central Russia, living and working conditions remained as they had been for the last thousand years. The yield by hectare was a quarter of what it was in Britain, and less than a fifth for the average peasant farm (that is to say without including the land worked by the aristocracy and the bourgeoisie).[49]

In these conditions, the burden of the rent and taxes to be paid year after year made it impossible for the peasants to accumulate any reserves. This led on the one hand to a gradual exhaustion of the fertility of the land by over cultivation (we see that ecological problems do not only date from the Stalinist period!) and also led to periodic famines at every bad harvest. The worst was that of 1891.

More serious than this financial burden was the lack of land. It has been estimated that the size of a farm sufficient to feed a peasant family was 6.5 to

7 desiatin. The peasants working on formerly noble or public land received only 3.17 or 4.9 desiatin respectively. Given the growth of the population and the very limited rural exodus, the average amount of land available to each adult peasant was 4.83 desiatin in 1861 and 3.1 desiatin in 1905. Around 5 million adult men in the country could not really use their labour power, even at the low average level of productivity cited. The peasants needed 60 to 70 million desiatin of land in addition.

In 1905, in comparison with the 112 million desiatin in the hands of the peasants there were 101.7 million in the hands of the nobility, the clergy and the bourgeoisie, and 145 million desiatin in state and public lands. Agricultural enterprises of more than 50 desiatin each (15 times greater than the average peasant farm) occupied in themselves 80 million desiatin.

The conclusion is obvious; the peasants could only obtain the land they needed by radical elimination of the noble and bourgeois big property owners.

For as long as this agricultural revolution did not take place, the peasants could only continue to rent land belonging to the big landowners. At the end of the nineteenth century, in the so-called 'black earth' zone (the heart of Russia), the landowners leased 50 per cent of their property to the peasants; in the other parts of the country it was 35 to 40 per cent. The farm rents were extremely high, sometimes as much as half the harvest.

Adding up the cost of buying the land, the taxes and the rents, gives a total cost to the peasantry which implies inevitable pauperization of the majority of families in the countryside. Between 1888 and 1898, the number of horses owned by the peasants fell from 19.6 to 17 million. Their cattle livestock fell from 34.6 to 24.5 million. The number of farms without horses rose by 22 per cent) within the same period. (All these figures come from official surveys of the time.)

Teodor Shanin, correcting – no doubt advisedly – the figures that Lenin used in his 1908 text 'The Agrarian Programme of Russian Social Democracy during the First Russian Revolution', presents the following table for the stratification of the peasantry in European Russia towards 1905:

- 15.8 per cent of well-off peasant families had 15 desiatin or more;
- 51.4 per cent of peasant families had between 7 and 15 desiatin;
- 32.4 per cent of poor peasant families had less than 7 desiatin.

(In each case this is property per family and not by head of the population.)

He deduces that on average for the period 1897 1905 there were in Russia:

- Between 0.8 and 1.2 per cent of capitalist farmers (5.1 to 7.6 per cent of the peasant population);
- Between 6 and 8 per cent of landless workers (3 to 4 per cent of the peasant population);
- Between 2.6 and 3.9 per cent of rich peasants;
- Between 12.4 and 10.7 per cent of well-off peasants;
- 51.8 per cent of middle peasants;
- Between 24.2 and 26.4 per cent of poor peasants.[50]

The poor therefore represented a third of the village populations.

The barbaric conditions and poverty in which the peasantry lived under Tsarism was clearly expressed in their level of consumption. By head of the population, the average peasant farm, aside from expenses in food and housing, spent 5.5 roubles per year on clothing, 2.5 roubles for cultural-spiritual needs, 1.4 roubles for other material needs. Two peasant families each comprising 6 people, that is 12 inhabitants of the Tsarist countryside, consumed the same as one single American worker (without his family) in 1905. That is a difference of 1:12 (and at that time the consumption of an American worker was, obviously, very much less than it is today).

The massive exportation of wheat by Russia, the main source of its foreign currency before the export of oil, was only possible because the charges of rent and taxes forced the peasants to sell wheat even if they did not have enough to eat. If they had been able to really satisfy their needs, Russia would have been a country which imported not exported wheat.

In his once classic work on Russia, the very conservative Sir Donald Mackenzie Wallace, official representative of the British establishment, summed up the deterioration of the situation of the Russian peasants in the following figures: the annual tax arrears (that is the unpaid taxes) rose from 0.9 roubles per male inhabitant in 1882 to 6 roubles in 1893 and to 22 roubles in 1899 in the seven provinces of the black earth zone.[51]

Urban poverty

Urban and working class poverty was no less dramatic. Anatole Kopp, mainly using the figures of the Soviet author G. Pouzis, stated that in the 131 towns situated in the territories which constituted the Russian Soviet Federal Socialist Republic (RSFSR):

Only 9 per cent of houses were linked to this system (of drains). Of the 195,000 existing in 213 towns of the RSFSR, which before the Revolution had a water supply system, only 12.5 per cent were connected to it.[52]

In 1912, the number of people per apartment was 8.7 in Moscow, around 8 in Petrograd compared to 3.6 in Berlin, 4.2 in Vienna and 2.7 in Paris.[53]

The average working day was usually 10 hours, without counting the many hours of overtime. According to the historian Prokopovitch, in 1909 in Petrograd three times the average annual wage was necessary to keep a family decently. Working class poverty was thus enormous. In 1908, a working-class family spent 48 per cent of its income on food (which was extremely inadequate), 21 per cent on housing (usually miserable) and 15 per cent on clothing. For all other needs, particularly health care and even elementary education, there was only 15 per cent of a very meagre wage.

Pokrovski estimated that between 1892 and 1902, the real wage of a Russian worker had fallen by 20 per cent.[54] And in a later enlarged edition of his work, this communist historian, who was much praised by Lenin, described the miserable living conditions of the Russian workers at the end of the nineteenth century:

63.7 per cent of workers were illiterate … In the factories of Moscow the textile workers were almost always obliged to sleep on their looms. The whole family in fact slept on these looms two and a half metres long and two metres wide. They had to clean the dirty pieces with their clothes. The employers said to the doctor that the workers 'liked' to live like this.

The doctor who gave [this] information on textile workers became an inspector, which, let it be said in passing, immediately changed his attitude. Two years later, he describe] the workers' living conditions in most of the governmental enterprises of the Vladimir government: pollution, bail air, two families in a room with one or two windows.

The Russian workers then ate worse than the [German] after the imperialist war, during the civil war and the blockade. The usual food was salted meat, smoked fish. The only fresh mot was offal …

In these living and housing conditions, the workers were ill. In the Moscow textile factories, 134 women in 1,000 had tuberculosis. In addition there was an epidemic, which the doctors qualified as 'traumatic' and entirely 'proletarian': the injuries … In one [big] textile factory, in a three year period only one in three workers had not been injured.[55]

The rate of infantile mortality in the essentially working-class areas of Petrograd was at least double that of the 'mixed' areas. Almost a quarter of the babies born within the capital died before they were a year old.[56]

If we think that the descriptions from this Marxist source are excessive, this is the judgement of a very moderate bourgeois historian:

> It is frequently argued that the slums of Britain achieved an obscenity of inhumanity which no other society could conceivably equal. In the sense that the misery of the lower depths in English and Scottish slums equalled the misery of the lowest depths this is true. But by no means all British workers belonged to the lowest depths, while almost all Russian workers did so belong ... In Russia there were no gradation workers were wage-slaves in the strictest sense and their wages were insufficient to support a family.[57]

The academic of Russian origin, Nicholas V. Riasanovsky, whose works are frequently used in Western universities, wrote:

> ... despite the labour legislation and despite the fact that wages, undoubtedly rose in the years which preceded the First World War (which, let it be said in passing, Soviet historians continue to deny hotly), the Russian workers in general remained very poor. Badly paid, housed in overcrowded slums; almost illiterate and deprived of any other advantage, the proletariat of imperial Russia offered an excellent example of the' indigent and exploited workforce characteristic of the first phases of capitalism and which Marx described so powerfully in *Capital*.[58]

The English professors Kochan and Abraham cite an almost unbelievable fact:

> A circular [was] issued by Delyanov, the Minister of Education in 1887, banning lower class children from secondary schools: '... children of coachmen, cooks, washerwomen, small shopkeepers and persons of similar type, whose children, perhaps with the exception of those gifted with unusual abilities, should certainly not be brought out of the social environment to which they belong'.[59]

The super-exploitation of women workers was particularly serious. In 1914, women workers' wages were half those of men. In 1916 they had fallen to less than 4o per cent.[60]

Can the idea that the October revolution did a useful and healthy job in radically eliminating these abominations really be challenged?

The Tsarist state

The oppressive role of the Tsarist state had a precise financial dimension: 80 per cent of its budget was spent on the army and the repressive apparatus. This parasitic drain on the national income was essentially at the cost of the peasantry, but also at the cost of the workers, given the indirect taxes. Industry was financed above all thanks to foreign investment.

Russian industry was not competitive in the world market. Nor could the narrow base of the national market, given the poverty of the great majority of the population, give it sufficient outlets. In addition, imported products were cheaper and of better quality than the products of Russian industry. Thus there was an extreme protectionist policy and a constant tendency to military expansionism towards the East and South East. Countries like Turkey, Iran, Afghanistan, China, Korea as well as regions of the Caucasus were forced, by threats or bayonets, to buy Russian goods. The term 'Cossack capitalism (imperialism)' has been correctly used to describe this. It ended badly with the Russo-Japanese war at Tsushima when the Western armies were defeated.

But the most oppressive and repressive aspect of Tsarism was expressed in all the institutions (or their absence) formed by the autocracy and what they represented for the peoples of the empire: lack of democratic rights and freedoms; extreme bureaucratic arbitrariness; accentuated national oppression:

> With the emergence of national intelligentsia among nearly all the minority peoples, the government had either to concede the need for some local autonomy in the vulnerable borderlands or else to seek to convert these new forces to its own beliefs. The upshot was a vigorous policy of Russification. In the Ukraine, White Russia, Lithuania and Poland, the teaching of the vernacular was restricted or forbidden in schools and the use of Russian enforced. In the Baltic provinces, Livonia, Estonia and Courland, the government exercised similar discrimination against the German element ...
>
> It was probably the Russian Jews who now had to undergo the worst torments. [Dreadful pogroms took place.] 'One third of the Jews must die, one third emigrate and one-third assimilate.' said Pobedonostev [lay head of the Orthodox Church and one of the models for Dostoyevsky's Grand Inquisitor].

The apparent victory over Islamic nationalism in Transcaucasia merely encouraged the intelligentsia of Georgia and Armenia to feel secure enough to turn to revolutionary agitation. In Asia, the government's increasing support for a determined proselytizing movement was bound to offend the Islamic traditionalists among local population ... Central Asia and the Far East were the happy hunting grounds of Russian imperialist adventurers, dubious carpet baggers and pseudo viceroys ...[61]

In his 1,000-page book *The Russian Revolution,* Richard Pipes defends the preposterous thesis that the revolution was the result of the intelligentsia's devotion to utopian ideas and extreme thirst for power since the end of the nineteenth century.[62] But in order to support this conspiracy theory, he has to obliterate the powerful workers' strikes leading up to a general strike on 25 February, ('a startling event in wartime' as Moynahan adds) which occurred before the soldiers' mutiny of February-March 1917.[63] All this occurred because of the extreme deterioration of workers' living conditions, not because of the intelligentsia's incitement.[64]

In what is probably the most objective history of the Russian Revolution written by a non-socialist, William Henry Chamberlin wrote:

What were the outstanding characteristics of the first period of the deepening of the revolution? Loosening of discipline in the army, increasingly radical demands of the industrial workers, first for higher wages, then for control over production and distribution, arbitrary confiscation of housing in the towns, to a greater degree of land in the country districts, insistence in such non-Russian parts of the country as Finland and Ukraine on the grant of far reaching autonomy.[65]

Far from acting under the influence of radical utopia or of extreme thirst for power, the intelligentsia in 1917 was characterized by growing moderation, hesitation and absence of any will to exercise power, in the Iasi analysis determined by extreme class polarization in the country.

Is it surprising that at the time of the February 1917 revolution, the peasants, workers and oppressed nationalities emitted an almost unanimous cry: Enough is enough, Land, the right to self-determination, the 8-hour day and workers' control straightaway.

But the Provisional Government hesitated, dragged its feet, postponed the decision, put off decisions on these questions until after the Constituent Assembly, and the elections to the Constituent in turn were repeatedly postponed.

Is it surprising in these conditions that the masses increasingly took their fate into their own hands, that they sought to resolve their vital problems themselves that they identified with Bolshevik policies and the power of the soviets, when they resolved these problems from one day to the next?

The political significance

Both East and West, the condemnation of the October Revolution is generally based on the idea that the Bolshevik 'putsch' prevented the institutionalization and consolidation of democracy. Because of this it led to the establishment of a 'totalitarian regime'. Democracy or dictatorship, this was the alternative in October 1917 and in the months that followed.

Once again this is a flagrant mystification or falsification of history.

In reality, the polarization of social and political forces had reached a paroxysm in Russia. This polarization was such that it did not leave any space for an experiment in institutionalized or indeed prolonged bourgeois democracy. From July 1917, days which were marked by a radicalization of popular demands, the bourgeois parties – and the military cliques to which they were linked – had adopted a much more repressive course.

Kornilov's military *coup d'état* in August 1917 did not fall from the sky. It reflected the sharpening of the socio-political struggle. Its failure simply reinforced the thirst for revenge on the part of the possessing classes and their henchmen. This was seen on the eve and immediately after the October insurrection.

This hate of the Russian property-owning classes took on a rarely seen force. It can for example be compared to that of the French bourgeoisie at the time of the Paris Commune in 1871 and the Spanish reaction in the summer of 1936.

Jacques Sadoul noted pertinently that they:

> ... wanted to establish an absolutist regime which would drown the revolution in blood, and massacre and deport the Jews, Bolsheviks, socialists and Kadets.[66]

Russian reaction and German imperialism

This class hatred was so deep that in the space of a few months, the nobility and the 'patriotic' monarchists who were indignant about the soldiers' lack of enthusiasm for Kerensky's offensive on the Polish-Galician front in June 1917, called for the arrival of German troops in Petrograd in order to crush the revolutionary hotbed and became strongly Germanophile.[67] Again it is Sadoul who points out:

... since the arrival of [German ambassador] Mirbach in Moscow, the monarchists feel at ease. The first visit of the German ambassador was to the Grand Duchess, sister-in-law of Nicholas II. He then saw other notorious royalists. It is obviously a question of preparing a restoration of the Tsar. The absolutist monarchists are ready to accept everything without shame, and particularly a military alliance with Germany and Ukrainian independence.[68]

A member of the German embassy, the Freiherr Karl von Bothmer, completely confirmed this:

For some lime, monarchist circles have been being very active and are talking freely to us ... During these discussions, I have met a series of important personalities who are sympathetic to us. They all said the same sort of thing: We can do nothing without you. You have to intervene directly, then we can act.[69]

Counter-revolutionary repression

This class hatred was not directed in the first place against the Bolsheviks and their allies. It was directed above all at the popular masses, starting with the 'wild' peasants in their villages, demanding that the 'plunderers' should be brought into line.

It was the bourgeoisie and the nobles, with the hesitant support of the reformist parties, particularly the right Social Revolutionaries, who started the Civil War after the Russian Revolution. They showed proof of an unlimited cruelty in tire period of 1918-21.

This line of cruelty based upon deep contempt for the masses was expressed most clearly by the Tsarina Alexandra herself. She wrote to her husband: 'Be Peter the Great, Ivan the Terrible, be Tsar Paul – crush them all under your feet.'[70]

And on the very eve of the revolution she still wrote to the Tsar: 'Dearest, show the power of your fist – that is what Russians need ... They themselves ask for this – so many have said to me recently: 'We need the knout'.'[71]

The American journalists A.R. Williams, who lived in Russia during the revolution, cited the following passage by N. Chiffrin in the anti-Bolshevik daily *Le Jour* of 7 September 1919:

As you know, the Bolsheviks have changed the names of the old regiments. The Moscow troops have on their backs K.L. – Karl Liebknecht. We (the northern White Army) took one of these regiments prisoner. We took it before the war tribunal. The trials on the White front are very short. Each soldier is interrogated and if he admits to being communist then he is immediately condemned to death by hanging or bullet. The Reds know this perfectly well.

Lieutenant K. stood before the prisoner regiment and declared: 'Those among you who are real communists, show their courage and step forward.' There was a long and oppressive pause after these words. Then more than half the regiment stepped forward in line. They were condemned to death by firing squad. But before the execution, each soldier had to dig his own grave ...

The condemned men were ordered to undress ... so that their uniforms would not be stained by their blood nor cut to pieces by the bullets. The communists slowly look off their shirts and tied them up in a bundle ... Then, naked, they dug their graves ... A command, a flash in the night, the shots rang out ... The communists were still upright, very straight. A second salvo. The bullets went straight to their hearts, the blood gushed out ...[72]

To the smallest detail this description prefigures the methods used by the Nazi Special Forces, the SS, during the Second World War: massacre of political commissars and Jews forced to dig their own graves. They were, what is more, prisoners of war. This was the action of 'defenders of democracy' against the 'Bolshevik dictatorship'.

The Freiherr von Bothmer reported in his above-mentioned book:

The Czechoslovaks [prisoners of war whom imperialism armed against the Soviet power during the summer of 1918] and the Siberians acted with an extreme lack of scruples in relation to the members of soviets who fell into their hands. The large number of executions made a deep impression on all Bolsheviks.[73]

The German writer Alfons Paquet, the correspondent in Russia of the *Frankfurter Zeitung*, also noted that, after the temporary occupation of Jaroslav in July 1918, the Bolshevik members of the soviet were executed by the counter-revolution with, on this occasion, the active participation of the SRs.

Does it need to be recalled that at the same time the terrorists of the left SRs killed some of the most important Bolshevik leaders, including Volodarski and Uritsky. One left SR, Fanny Kaplan, made an attempt on Lenin which was nearly successful.

Bolshevik writers asserted quite correctly:

It was under the salvos of the Czechoslovak rifles, behind the mountain of dead bodies of the finest flower of the proletariat of Siberia and the Urals, ... that the so-called 'people's army' (the Whites) was formed.[74]

The attempts by conciliatory parties to create a regime called the 'Constituent Assembly' failed rapidly. A series of coups d'état gave power back into the hands of military dictators like the admiral Kolchak or the general Wrangel.[75]

White dictatorship or soviet power

The concrete choice was not between bourgeois democracy and Bolshevik dictatorship. It was between counter-revolutionary dictatorship or soviet power.

There is no doubt about the dictatorial character of the counter-revolution. John Rees gave a good description of the terror used by the reactionary forces:

'The greater the terror, the greater our victories,' declared Kornilov. We must save Russia he argued 'even if we have to set fire to half of it and shed the blood of three-fourths of all the Russians!'

Ataman Semyonov was placed under the authority of the White general Kolchak.[76] The spectacle of the zones under his control left no ambiguity as to the nature of his rule:

Innocent men and women dangled by the scores from telegraph poles in the vicinity of his capital, and his men machine-gunned freight cars full of victims at execution fields along the railway ...

By the orders of another White leader, Baron Urgan-Stemberg, 'men and women suffered death by beating, hanging, beheading, disembowelling and countless other tortures which transformed living human beings into what one witness called a formless bloody mass'. Even his own staff physician described one of the Baron's written orders as 'the product of the diseased brain of a pervert and a megalomaniac affected with a thirst for human blood'.[77]

The pogroms

In 1918-1921, the Ukraine was the theatre of the worst pogroms, massacres of the Jewish communities that Europe was to know before the 'final solution' of the Nazis. According to Zvi Gitelman, there were 2,000 pogroms, 1,200 of which were in the Ukraine. The author estimated the total number of victims at 150,000. These massacres were accompanied by unbelievable cruelty:

> Men were buried up to their necks and then killed by the hooves of horses driven over them, or were literally pulled apart by horses driven in opposite directions. Children were smashed against walls in view of their parents: pregnant women were a favourite target, their unborn children killed in their mothers' sight. Thousands of women were raped and hundreds were left insane by their experiences.[78]

These pogroms were coldly and consciously organized by the counter-revolutionary leaders. As the American author and scholar Bruce Lincoln notes:

> No longer spontaneous outpourings of racial and religious hatred, pogroms now became coldly calculated incidents of wholesale rape, extreme brutality and unprecedented destruction. In a single day at the end of August, in the Jewish settlement of Kremenchuk, the Whites raped 350 women, including pregnant women, women who had just given birth and even women who were dying.[79]

According to Salo W. Baron, after the pogroms organized under the 'socialist' Petljura, the massacres left in their wake some 100,000 new widows, and 200,000 new orphans. No less than 28 per cent of all Ukrainian Jewish houses were said to have been burned, and in addition 10 per cent abandoned by their owners.[80]

The counter-revolution also drew on the support of the German occupying army. When it conquered the town of Odessa and its surroundings, it published a statement dated 16 November 1918, also reproduced in its newspaper *Neue Nachrichten,* and which in particular asserted that:

> We have penetrated into Russian territory with the intention of re-establishing order and freeing the country from the Bolshevik usurpers … All the elements harmful to Russia, that is the Bolsheviks and those who support them, are now declared outlaws. Whoever shelters them will be taken before a military tribunal.[81]

The list of atrocities committed by the Whites can be prolonged indefinitely:

The assassinations by Yudenich (650 people shot or hung in the town of Iamburg alone in August 1919) by the Baltic gangs and the Germans of von der Galtz (approximately 4,000 victims) ... by Kolchak (a thousand Red soldiers burnt alive at Perm during his withdrawal) ...[82]

The social counter-revolution

The 'political alternative' to the power of the soviets had, obviously, a precise socio-economic content as is the case during any social revolution. Where the Whites established their dictatorship, the gains of October were rapidly if not immediately eliminated. The landowners took back their estates. The rights of the national minorities were suppressed. The soviets were ferociously persecuted. The democratic rights of the workers were totally denied.

This is what caused the defeat of the Whites.

A major factor in Kolchak's defeat was the low morale of his forces; there were frequent desertions to the communist side in the course of the battle. Another was his failure to win over the population, which, although far from pro-communist, preferred Soviet rule in the last resort.

There were many reasons for the victory of the Red Army in the civil war, but most of them add up to one simple fact: the people as a whole, in spite of the unpopularity of the communists, preferred the Soviet regime to the available alternatives. The peasants disliked both sides, and wished above all to be left alone; but when it came to the choice, they preferred the Communists, who gave them land, to the Whites, who took, or threatened to take, it away.[83]

Chamberlin states likewise:

On July 16 [1918], the Siberian government ordered the suppression of all existing Soviets and forbade the election of new ones. Throughout July and August the policy of the Siberian government was directed to the restoration of private property in every form ...

When the Whites began to bring back the landlords, the peasants organized guerrilla bands and fell upon them.[84]

This is why the Whites lost. They could not win or reconstitute a popular base. Their armies were, in general, officer armies, without the ability or even the desire to recruit conscripts. We see to what extent these officers feared the peasants.

A third way?

Confronted with this diagnosis, which it is difficult to contest, opponents of October often react in two diametrically opposed directions. Some consider that there was no basis for a (bourgeois) democratic regime in Russia whether this was for social reasons (extreme instability; absence of middle classes, the traditional support of democracy) or for ethno-cultural reasons (lack of democratic traditions in the Russian empire, tendency of the masses to vacillate wildly between resigned passivity and chaotic and uncontrollable explosions).

In these conditions, for these people the 'totalitarian deviation' of the Bolsheviks was inevitable but was nevertheless worse than an authoritarian right-wing regime.

For others, there was nevertheless the possibility of a third way. In their opinion, if the Kerensky regime had not been overthrown by the 'Bolshevik putsch' it could have gradually stabilized, carrying out moderate repression against both the far right and the far left.[85] Once the Constituent Assembly was convoked and the distribution of the land to the peasants carried out in an orderly and legal fashion, a bourgeois democracy comparable to that in Poland, although certainly with limitations that Western Europe did not experience, could have stabilized.

This is not a realistic view. It underestimates the explosive character of social contradictions. To think that the capitalists would have accepted social legislation which undermined the competitiveness of their factories, to think that the landowners would have accepted a division of their property, because these reforms had been carried out by a Constituent Assembly elected by universal suffrage, is to misunderstand the lessons of European history of the 1920s and 1930s.

During this period, bourgeois democracy was not only severely restricted or indeed suppressed – except to a very limited extent – in Poland and the Baltic countries, and strongly restricted in Finland. It was also eliminated in Italy, in Germany and in Spain, three countries that were a lot more developed that Russia in 1917.

The Menshevik leaders themselves recognized this. Dan wrote:

> Having assessed the effective relationship of forces, it [the Menshevik CC] reached the conclusion that – independently of their subjective intentions – the victory of the elements marching on Petrograd would have necessarily meant the victory of the worst of counter-revolutions.[86]

The price of October 1917

The choice was thus truly either victory of the socialist revolution or victory of a counter-revolution that would have been among the most bloody ever known, which would have brought to power a Russian Hitler still worse than the German Hitler we know.

It is in the light of this diagnosis and of everything that it implies that we can reply to the question whether, in the final analysis, the price paid by the October Revolution was too high or not. Our answer is a definite no. A defeat of the revolution in 1917 would have cost the Russian people and Europe much too dear.

In order to distort the calculation, the opponents of the October revolution use the sort of magical disappearing trick that they use for the French Revolution. They add up pell-mell the victims of the revolution and of the counter-revolution, the economic effects of the first and of the second and then say that all that is the cost of the October Revolution.

How can the French Revolution be held responsible for the victims of the Napoleonic Wars? How can the October Revolution be held responsible for the victims of the White terror and pogroms?

Sophists argue that the Civil War and the White Terror are only products of the revolution. The answer is in the question: was not the Revolution itself the product of the Ancien Regime? Here we come up against a conception of history as a continuous flow without being attached anywhere in time or in space. This conception does not make it possible to ever draw out any conclusions. While saying that it is an attempt to understand the movement of history as a whole, this method in facts hides the precise responsibility of given social and political forces, in relation to specific actions.

Revolutions are at present not very popular, to say the least. This "spirit of the time" is reflected in what R.V. Daniels, author of *The Conscience of the Revolution* and *Red October*, writes in the *New York Times Review of Books* of 26 April 1992: 'Mr Moynahan shows what a revolution really means. The normal bonds of society give way to mindless murder and mayhem.'

This is nothing but anti-working-class and anti-peasant prejudice. Why is the revolutionary masses upsurge 'mindless' and 'mayhem' while the ruling state's and private violence is supposed to be 'normal'? The Tsarist-capitalist participation in the First World War cost between 5 and 6 million deaths. Was that not 'mindless' murder? Why was the pre-war rule based on the knout, countless executions and deportations, barbaric oppression (pogroms!) and mass starvation 'normal' and the masses' revolt against these evils a dissolution of the 'normal bonds of society'? Was slavery also 'normal' and revolts against slavery 'mindless murder and mayhem'?

Moral judgement and class prejudice

There is, moreover, an aspect of this question which we should not try to hide. In time of revolution, the toiling population is first of all carried towards generous reactions. But, faced with civil war, when it sees itself repeatedly provoked and subject to aggression from its class enemies, it also tends to use direct, indeed sometimes 'savage' violence. Babeuf already pointed out in his letter to his wife, commenting on the execution of the Princesse de Lamballe after the taking of Bastille, that these excesses were the largely inevitable product of years of confrontation by the people with the violence and cruelty of their oppressors.[87] To hope, in these conditions, that the masses in all circumstances would show themselves to be scrupulously respectful of all the rights of women and men is really to demand a miracle.

In the final analysis, what is hidden by all these abstract, pseudo-moral condemnations of revolutionary violence – without any consideration of the precise historic context – is open class prejudice. The traditional violence of those in power is 'normal'. It represents a 'lesser evil' whatever its extent. The rebellious response of the risen people is by definition 'worse', even if its scope is much less than that of the property-owners. The hypocrisy hits us in the face.

This class prejudice often hides a fear of the masses whose social support is once again quite obvious. As a rather moderate French historian says:

> After 1861, the intelligentsia and the state had the constant preoccupation of controlling the people through fear of their anarchic and destructive potential. The common fear (due to ignorance) prevents them from having an objective idea of the people, based on a concrete knowledge of the reality of the country. Thus both have succumbed to the popular stikhiinost (elementary force) of the beginning of the twentieth century.[88]

It is just as mistaken to want to add together the cost of the October 1917 revolution and that of the later Stalinist regime. Stalinism is in fact the product of a real bureaucratic counter-revolution. To confuse the two, is an under-estimation, or indeed a negation of the scope of this later, or the radical break that the 'Soviet Thermidor' – the bureaucratic counterrevolution - constituted in relation to October and the period which immediately followed.[89]

The cost of Stalinism was dramatic for the Soviet and international proletariat.

The scope of this Stalinist counter-revolution expresses the historic tragedy which occurred a lot better than any subtle analyses of the so-called responsibility of Lenin's ideas (or indeed those of Marx) for Stalin's crimes. During the 1920s and 1930s. Stalin assassinated a million communists. Can we seriously say that this is 'a detail of history'? Is it not odious to throw butcher and victims into the same bag?[90]

The Bolshevik orientation: a critical analysis

In general, the October Revolution was the product of objective social contradictions, which acquire an irrepressible explosive dynamic, as well as the evolution of the relationship of forces between the classes and the social layers operating in this framework. It also resulted from the activity of the Bolshevik Party in untangling these knots of contradictions in the interests of the toiling masses and the international proletariat.

This said, in the light of the later evolution of the Russia of soviets and of the USSR, we should ask whether some of the policies put into operation by the Bolshevik party, after the taking of power, did not encourage the process of bureaucratic degeneration of the first workers' state.

This bureaucratic degeneration, in the 1920s and 1930s, was certainly not initiated nor fundamentally caused by the orientation of this party. It also had its roots in the objective contradictions of Soviet society and the international situation which then prevailed. However, decisions like the concrete attitude to the Bolshevik party – or different components of its leadership – at precise moments also had an effect on the process of bureaucratization of the regime. We should try to understand some of the mistakes which were made.

The banning of the soviet parties

The most serious of these mistakes was the banning of the soviet parties at the very moment that the revolutionary government had definitively won the civil war of 1918-20. Trotsky, although not very inclined to self-criticism of the decisions of the leadership and government of which he was the most influential member after Lenin, made two explicit judgements on this. In 1936 he wrote:

> The prohibition of factions ended in a prohibition to think otherwise than the infallible leaders. The police-manufactured monolithism of the party resulted in a bureaucratic impunity which has become the source of all kinds of wantonness and corruption.[91]

Two years later, in the Transitional Programme that he wrote in 1938 for the founding conference of the Fourth International, he came out explicitly in favour of multi-partyism:

Democratization of the soviets is impossible without legalization of soviet parties. The workers and peasants themselves by their own free vote will indicate what parties they recognize as soviet parties.[92]

It is undeniable that the workers considered the Mensheviks in 1920 as a soviet party, because they had quite a number of elected representatives, particularly in Charkov and Moscow.

The same remark also applies to the anarchists.

The banning of the soviet parties, as well as the banning of factions within the government party which was its logical follow-on (each faction is in fact another party in formation), were undoubtedly seen as temporary measures, related to particular circumstances, which would therefore be repealed when the objective situation improved. Obviously we should ask what were the precise consequences of these specific decisions, put into effect at a particular moment.

But we should also ask another question: what were the consequences of the theories which were put forward to justify such bannings, even if they were conjunctural? I think that the theoretical justifications caused a lot more harm in the more long term, than the measures themselves – and continue to do so today.

The danger of substitutionism

The banning of soviet parties was based on a substitutionist conception of building socialism – and of socialist/communist policies in general. That is a conception which Trotsky had always vigorously denounced (except in the 'black years' of 1920-21) and that Lenin also fought against during a good part of his life.

In this conception, the proletariat in its majority is not conscious enough to rule a country. The social democrats are of the same opinion and even add: to lead a trade union. Another argument was introduced later: that of losing its class character and its corruption (including through colonial super profits).

This starting point very quickly leads to the conclusion that the party must rule instead of the actually existing working class. The party apparatus, or even its leadership, or even its 'infallible leader', are then the decisive instruments for changing society. Stalin expressed the real content of substitutionism in a formula which leaves no room for misunderstanding: 'the cadres decide everything'.

The substitutionist doctrine of the party feeds a verticalist, statist, paternalist and authoritarian conception of the regime, even when the worst excesses and crimes of Stalinism are avoided. It can certainly be hedged around with all sorts of restrictive clauses: the party (the party leadership) rules in place of the working class but is based on it, mobilizes it, notes its reactions, corrects its own mistakes in the light of experience, etc.

But this does not in the least change the fundamental attitude. It is not the working class which rules and which democratically takes decisions. A small minority rules in its stead.

In these conditions the soviets are emptied of at least one vital component of their content. They can at the limit be an effective fighting instrument against the class enemy. But they no longer assure the direct exercise of power by the proletariat and (or) the toiling masses as a whole.

Without real multi-partyism, in practice, the soviets cannot experience real democracy. They cannot really choose between different alternatives in economic, social, cultural policies.

To the extent that the suppression of soviet democracy takes on a repressive aspect, this repression no longer targets simply the big, medium and petty bourgeoisie. It also hits the working class. We can even say that the more numerous the proletariat is, the more hegemonic it is from a social point of view, the more it is the target.

Self-emancipation

Such a conception and such political orientation are contrary to Marx's main contribution to socialist theory (including the theory of revolutionary organization): the idea of the self-liberation and the increasing self-organization of the proletariat. The emancipation of the workers will be the doing of the workers themselves, not that of the trade unions, the parties, the governments or the state. These are indispensable instruments in the historical process. But they can never replace the activity of the wage-workers themselves and other layers of the exploited and oppressed. The fundamental emancipating role of their self-activity cannot be ignored.

It would be to misunderstand the driving role of material and social interests in history to think that the substitutionist ideology created the hydra of bureaucratization. It was rather the existence of the workers' bureaucracy which produced the ideology of substitutionism. But once it existed, this ideology in its turn encouraged the objective process of bureaucratization.

The position of Rosa Luxemburg

This is what Rosa Luxemburg understood when she warned the Bolshevik leaders of the danger in her first comments on the Russian Revolution:

But with the repression of political life in the land as a whole, life in the soviets must also become more crippled. Without general elections, without unrestricted freedom of press and assembly, without a free struggle of opinion, life dies out in every public institution, becomes a mere semblance of life, in which only the bureaucracy remains as the active element.[93]

This quotation from Luxemburg does not correctly describe the state of public life in Russia in 1918. There was then a strong diversity and discussion of political ideas, and legal or quasi-legal activity of many organizations. Rosa wrote her pamphlet in prison and did not have sufficient information available.

But she offered a remarkable and prophetic critical diagnosis of the more long-terms trends, particularly from 1920-21. To have formulated them already in the summer of 1918 – 'only the bureaucracy will remain an active element' – shows an exceptional lucidity and capacity for theoretical analysis.

We consider that Rosa was also right when she wrote that:

The basic error of the Lenin-Trotsky theory is that they too, just like Kautsky, oppose dictatorship to democracy ... The latter naturally decides in favour of 'democracy', that is, of bourgeois democracy ... Lenin and Trotsky, on the other hand, decide in favour of dictatorship [of the proletariat) ...

... to spur the working class ... to create a socialist democracy to replace bourgeois democracy – not to eliminate democracy altogether.

But socialist democracy is not something which begins only in the promised land after the foundations of socialist democracy are created: it does not come as some sort of Christmas present for the worthy people who, in the interim, have loyally supported a handful of socialist dictators. Socialist democracy begins simultaneously with the beginnings of destruction of class rule and of the construction of socialism. It begins at the very moment of the seizure of power by the socialist party. It is the same thing as the dictatorship of the proletariat.

Yes, dictatorship! But this dictatorship consists in the manner of applying democracy, not in its elimination, in energetic, resolute attacks upon the well-entrenched rights and economic relationships of bourgeois society, without which a socialist transformation cannot be accomplished. But this dictatorship must be the work of the class and not of a little leading minority in the name of the class – that is it must proceed step by step out of the direct participation of the masses; it must be under their direct influence, subjected to the control of complete public activity; it must arise out of the growing political training of the mass of the people.[94]

Rosa Luxemburg is much less lucid when, in the same pamphlet, she criticized the orientations of the Bolshevik Party and the Soviet regime on the nationality question and the peasant question. On these questions she adopted dogmatic positions which did not take into account the immediate or historic political and economic necessities (concerning the period of transition). She criticized the central slogans of the right to self-determination and the distribution of the land to those who worked it in the agrarian reform as 'petty-bourgeois' and opportunist.

However, if the Bolsheviks had opposed the desire for self-determination of the peoples integrated by force into the Tsarist Empire; if they had opposed the great desire for land from the majority of the peasants, they would have lost power. What happened in the USSR after 1928, and what is happening today is a tragic confirmation of this.

In fact, if the leadership were wrong in this question – Lenin and Trotsky much less than the others – it was through leftist sectarianism and not by an excess of opportunism. We can moreover use the argument of 'parallelism' with Kautsky's reasoning against Rosa. Kautsky also used the argument of opportunism to the peasants against Rosa.

The workers' and peasants' alliance and war communism

It is difficult to judge at what point the policy of requisition of wheat by the Soviet regime under siege, called 'war communism' was unavoidable, to a certain extent at least, in 1918-1920. But it is certain that it threatened more and more to break the workers-peasants' alliance, that is the very basis of the Soviet regime.[95]

It is no less certain that it led to a greater and greater decline of productive forces, particularly the production of foodstuffs, which threatened to bring about the collapse of the whole Russian economy.

Agricultural, essentially cereal production, fell by almost 30 per cent, horse livestock by 25 per cent, cattle livestock by 20 per cent, pig livestock by 28 per cent, and industrial production by almost 60 per cent. In exchange for the same quantity of wheat, the peasants only received 5 per cent of the same industrial products that they had received in 1917-18. Thus they refused to sell wheat for money that had practically no value. And thus it was necessary to requisition the wheat.

But this also led to an absolute fall in wheat production and not simply a retreat by the peasants to a subsistence economy. And as wheat production fell, there was in time less and less to requisition.

Then followed a general trend to speculation and the black market, which was particularly hard on the poorest layers of the population.

Trotsky, head of the Red Army during the Civil War, found himself at the head of an army that was essentially composed of millions of peasants. He travelled constantly throughout this enormous country. Because of this he saw better than Lenin and the other leaders of the party the immediate concerns of the peasantry. He thus proposed, one year before Lenin, abandoning 'war communism' in favour of the early adoption of a more flexible policy, the 'NEP' (New Economic Policy). At this point he ran into the resistance of Lenin and the majority of the leadership.[96]

On this question we agree with the assessment of the Soviet historian Roy Medvedev who considers that the attempt to continue the policy of requisitioning wheat after the end of the Civil War provoked the social crisis of 1921, including the Kronstadt rising. This was a serious error which cost them dearly.[97]

Moreover, during 'war communism' the proletariat was weakened, not only numerically hut also physically and morally. In 1921, an industrial producer during production only consumed 30 per cent of the energy that used in 1913-14, and less than half of that used in 1916-17. This led to a severe fall in work productivity, which Chamberlin estimated as having declined in 1920 to 20 per cent of the 1913 level.[98]

Some people have idealized the policy of 'war communism', emphasizing the passage to 'directly communist' forms of production and distribution. Kritsmann, whose statistics we have used in what has just been said, talks about the 'heroic years of the great Russian Revolution'.[99] Many Bolshevik leaders have followed suit.

Making a law out of necessity, these latter theorized the constraints of lack and rationing. They idealized the return to a 'natural' economy (more exactly to an economy of three sectors: a subsistence economy, an exchange economy and a monetary economy).

All Marxist tradition and the good sense of the proletariat argue against this 'communism of poverty', however sympathetic and stimulating – for the future! – were the very egalitarian 'models' developed and applied at this time.[100] This 'model' did not unleash any dynamic able to bring the country out of growing famine. And it caused a confusion that Stalin was cynically able to call on in 1928-34.

The question of peace negotiations

The Civil War and the intervention by the imperialist powers, particularly German imperialism, against Soviet Russia partly explains the origins and deviations of 'war communism'.

But here we touch on another important mistake that was made during the Brest-Litovsk negotiations by most of the Bolshevik leaders and cadres with the notable exception of Lenin, who at that point reached the summit of his political lucidity. This is the delay in reaching separate peace with each of the Central Powers

There was an important difference between the peace conditions proposed by these empires during the first phase of the negotiations of Brest-Litovsk, opened in December 1917, and the conditions obtained from them after the interruption of the negotiations by the Soviets and the continuation of the advance by the German army.

The first were still acceptable to a large section of public opinion in the working class and the urban petty-bourgeoisie. The second were widely felt as a national humiliation and a betrayal of the interests of the proletariat of the Soviet Union and of the international proletariat. In addition, they meant the control of the Ukraine by imperial Germany and the repression of the Ukrainian peasant movement. They provoked the break in the coalition between the Bolsheviks and the left SRs. They gave a strong stimulus to the Civil War.

The majority of the Central Committee and the Bolsheviks refused to sign the peace conditions resulting from the first phase of the Brest-Litovsk negotiations. They used as an argument for their position – as did Trotsky for his intermediary position 'neither war nor peace' – the fact that this position corresponded to the sentiments of the majority of the urban population. But it did not correspond to the sentiments of the majority of the peasant population, without mentioning those of the soldiers in the army which was in full flight of decomposition.

And above all it did not lead to any concrete alternative: immediate overthrow of the rule of the Hohenzollern and Habsburgs. What could guarantee this? Immediate organization of the 'revolutionary war'? With a non-existent army?[101]

The only result of the refusal to sign the peace conditions immediately was to allow the German army to occupy new and very important territories, and in particular to take the immensely rich Ukraine away from the Soviet Republic. Lenin predicted this every day. We have seen once against that the price that the Revolution had to pay for this mistake was very high.

The Red Terror

The question of the Terror – and the creation of the Cheka (the secret political police) – are directly linked to the consequences of the Brest-Litovsk peace. Both can only be explained in the light of these events.

The question of the terror – independent of the question of its unacceptable excesses – is less clear than some claim. The experience of the Spanish Civil War in 1936 is a clear illustration of this fact. At that time not only the Stalinist but also the anarchists and the social democrats of the right, centre and left without distinction, as well as many autonomous and unorganized groups of workers, applied wide ranging measures of 'red terror'. They had no choice.

Confronted with an implacable, murderous and torturing enemy, who takes the women and children of militants as hostages, who shoots prisoners of war and political opponents en masse, something has to be done to limit the losses. This is a question of common sense: to force the murderers to stop if they do not want to pay too high a price for their crimes.

We should note moreover that Lenin tried to avoid being forced to use terror after the October revolution. In particular he said:

> We are accused of making arrests. Indeed, we have made arrests; today we arrested the director of the State Bank. We are accused of resorting to terrorism, but we have not resorted, and I hope will not resort, to the terrorism of the French revolutionaries who guillotined unarmed men. I hope we shall not resort to it, because we have strength on our side. When we arrested anyone we told him we would let him go if he gave us a written promise not to engage in sabotage. Such written promises have been given.[102]

But the counter-revolutionaries acted with total cynicism and lack of scruples, despite the initial generosity of the Bolsheviks. The generals Krasnov, Kaledin and others, the pupil-officers arrested during the October insurrection, were released on the promise that they would refrain from any anti-governmental action. They immediately broke their word, took arms and caused the death of thousands of workers.

The people make these mistakes once, twice, and then reply harshly. Is this surprising?

Among the particularly cynical action of the future 'victims of the Terror', A.R. Williams points out the Whites' use of Red Cross lorries to cross the front lines and bring munitions to the White armies.[103]

Williams even reports on a moving expression of the generous spirit of the revolution during the taking of the Winter Palace. The pupil-officers gave themselves up. The crowd was mad with rage, having discovered among other things the torture chambers in the depths of the palace. Antonov-Ovseenko, who led the Red Army detachment, cried: 'I'll shoot the first one to touch a prisoner'. He ended by convincing the crowd:

> Do you know where this madness leads? When you kill a White Guard prisoner it is the revolution you kill and not the counterrevolution. I have given twenty years of my life in exile and in prison for this revolution... [It] means something better, it means life and liberty for all. You give your blood and your life for die revolution, but you should also give it something else ... your intelligence. You should put commitment to the revolution above satisfying your passions. You have the courage to bring victory to the revolution. Now, in the name of your honour, you should give proof of magnanimity. You love the revolution. The only thing I ask you is not to kill the thing you love.[104]

But having suffered from the savage violence of the counter revolutionaries the climate changed. Again, should we be surprised?

Moreover, we should be clear on the limits of the Terror. Up to March 1920, the total number of victims of the Red Terror was officially estimated at 8,620 people. Morizet estimates the number at a little more than 10,000. After the defeat of the White Armies of Denikine and Kolchak, the death penalty was abolished for several months by the Soviet government. It was only reintroduced from the time of the Polish offensive against the Ukraine in May 1920.

The atmosphere in Soviet Russia was far from the universal fear described by so many historians. We can see this from reading what Morizet, any eyewitness, said about the trial of a high-ranking White officer, Galkin, by the Revolutionary Tribunal at Moscow on 14 July 1921:

> I do not think I have ever seen a public or magistrates more sympathetic to the accused that on that day. The four hundred workers or soldiers who crowded into the chamber, the three judges and the prosecutor, all four of them young, all looked with a sort of friendship on this little man of thirty-five, in his worn clothes, that a debonair under-officer guarded, revolver in hand to obey the rules. There was no barrier between them and him. Four armed soldiers, interested in the discussions above all vaguely covered the free space around the garden bench reserved for the accused, the table of defence and ours.

Rather than a terrible audience of the Revolutionary Tribunal, one would have thought oneself watching an impassioned discussion between men who disagreed on the answer to a question of conscience.[105]

Galkin was given a light sentence, and then rapidly pardoned, although he had taken arms against the soviet regime. But he stated that he detested still more the counter-revolutionary White dictators after the experience he had of them. The Tribunal believed him.

The Cheka

The question of the Cheka is very different from what we have just been talking about: temporary measures during a cruel civil war. The Cheka was the creation of an institution, an apparatus, with the inevitable tendency of any institution and any apparatus to become permanent, and to escape any control.

A fascist torturer can be shot after a public trial, even a summary one. But a secret political police cannot be submitted to public control.

The archives of the Cheka, which have begun to be published thanks to *glasnost* (the policy of 'transparency' under Gorbachev), showed that the worm was in the fruit from the very beginning, despite the personal honesty of Felix Dzerzhinsky, the first leader of the Cheka, who nobody suspects of improper intentions. The mention of just one fact is enough: the members and informers of the Cheka gave themselves a bonus (a part of the 'spoils') for any goods seized from 'speculators' or those who committed 'economic crimes'. There is no doubt of the dynamic to corruption this represents. Chamberlin fully confirms this judgement.[106]

The same goes for the tendency of the Cheka to escape from all control. This dangerous dynamic was affirmed very early. One anecdote illustrates this. Lenin had the greatest admiration and friendship for the left Menshevik leader Martov. One day Lenin called him into the Kremlin, gave him a false passport and said: 'Leave the country immediately. If not the Cheka will arrest you in a few days and I would not be able to stop them.'

G. Leggett, a reactionary who was extremely hostile to the Bolshevik regime, admits however that this independence was only conjunctural at first:

In the inevitable clash between the arbitrary violence of the Cheka and the system of Soviet law evolved by the People's Commissariat for Justice, the Cheka gained the upper hand whenever the regime came under threat: when the crises receded the [People's Commissariat] won the advantage.[107]

Lenin himself was resolutely favourable to the constitution of a state based on law and the need to make decisive steps in this direction. In a conflict which set Dzerzhinsky against Kamenev in 1921, concerning the reforms of the political police after the end of the Civil War, Lenin supported Kamenev who had proposed to limit the competence of the Cheka to questions of espionage, political crimes, the protection of the railways and food stores. All other repressive activity should be the responsibility of the People's Commissariat of Justice.

It should also be noted that the Cheka was hardly a creature of the Bolshevik Party or of Lenin. It was above all the left SRs who played a key role in its creation. But all that being said, it is none the less true that the tendency to become independent, less and less controllable was present from the beginning of the Cheka. Victor Serge used the term 'professional degeneration'. This is why we think that the creation of the Cheka was undoubtedly a mistake.

Lenin's organizational conceptions

Did the organizational conceptions of Lenin open the road to the excesses of the October Revolution and the Stalinist dictatorship?

One of the theses frequently put forward by the critics of Bolshevism is that the excesses which occurred after 1918 – the dissolution of the Constituent Assembly, the Terror, the prolongation of war communism – were in the last analysis the result of Lenin's organizational conceptions. We can sum up the conceptions attributed to Lenin, the ultimate source of all evil, by these authors in the following way: revolutions are 'made' by the revolutionary party and not by the masses; this party should be a highly-centralized, limited troop of professional revolutionaries; it – because of this – largely escapes the control of the working class; this class is unable to raise itself to the level of revolutionary political action, let alone reach a revolutionary political consciousness.[108]

Other authors, such as Louis Fischer, go a step further and say that Lenin's organizational conceptions, as they were classically expressed in the pamphlet *What Is To Be Done?*, were inspired by not very pleasant psychological traits of the person in question: blind hatred of Tsarism and the property-owning classes; a thirst for vengeance for the execution of his brother by the autocracy; the conviction that violence, terror, 'the extermination of the enemy' play an essential role in all revolutions.

All these affirmations, in whatever variant, are in the best of cases a unilateral view of historical reality, of the writings of Lenin and the actions which he inspired or led.

Lenin and power

Above all, the portrait of Lenin as a monomaniac for absolute personal power does not tally with the image of him that emerges from the many accounts of those who knew him. Nikolai Valentinov, who was very critical of the Bolshevik leader, said:

> It is a huge mistake, and many, almost all, make it to consider Lenin a heartless man of iron, a producer only of political resolutions, completely indifferent and insensitive to the beauties of nature. He loved the fields, the meadows, the rivers, the mountains, the sea, the ocean.[109]

The rather limited importance that Lenin gave to his personal role is revealed by his reaction when the Central Committee proposed to start publishing his Collected Works: 'Why? It's quite useless. Thirty years ago we wrote anything. It's not worth reproducing all that.'[110]

Lenin's simplicity and honesty in rejecting all kinds of material privileges appears clearly from the following facts:

> Lenin gave away the gifts of food and fuel which peasant admirers brought to the Kremlin ... Commissars' salaries were fixed at two thirds of the rate for the highest category for industrial technicians ...
>
> War communism had not killed the theatres of Moscow or stifled the exuberance of the avant garde. The demand for theatre seats was so enormous that both Lenin and Balabanova [then secretary of the Communist International - EM] – united at least in determination not to accept preferential treatment – were turned away one evening from the Arts Theatre where a Stanislavsky production of Chekov's Three Sisters was playing.[111]

The myth of Lenin as cynical and unscrupulous in the 'struggle for power' is based above all on a rather disgusting calumny, that he accepted 'German gold' in 1917 to finance Bolshevik propaganda. This calumny was the basis of persecutions of the Bolsheviks after the revolutionary days of July 1917.

In what is one of the best biographies of Lenin, Ronald W. Clark demonstrates a certain agnosticism on this question, going almost so far as to say there is no smoke without fire. He then recounts, without totally dismissing it, the assertion by an employee of the German Foreign Affairs Ministry, that 50 million gold marks were 'invested' in the Bolshevik movement.[112]

But the same Ronald Clark cites in passing the most striking proof of the unfounded nature of this calumny: *Pravda,* the main journal of the

Bolsheviks, was always short of money.

Urgent and constant appeals were launched for a few tens of thousands of roubles.[113] How could a movement, which had received millions of gold marks, be so short of money?

Brian Moynahan takes up this slander in a completely uncritical way, without mentioning the unreliable nature of the so-called 'witnesses'.[114] Moynahan's treatment of Lenin in the period February-September 1917 is characterized by extreme bad faith, if not clear falsifications. He alleges for example that in the famous 'sealed train' organized by the Swiss social democrats Grimm and Platten, Lenin failed to involve other socialists than Bolsheviks in the trip.[115]

Wrong. Among the 32 Russian emigrants in the separate train carriage which, on the basis of an agreement with the German government, went through German territory to return to Russia, because the British and French authorities blocked their return by sea, there were nineteen Bolsheviks, six members of the Bund, three members of the group Nashe Slovo close to Trotsky, and four members of other organizations. Furthermore, the agreement made with the German government stated clearly that there would be no discrimination between 'defeatist' and 'defensist' emigrants; all Russian emigrants had the right to board this carriage. In fact, at least some of the Bundists were defensists.[116]

In fact, this trip, and all the conditions with which it took place, was approved by a declaration of a series of international socialist militants, among them Stroem, the general secretary of the Swedish Socialist Party, and Lindhagen, the socialist mayor of Stockholm, as well as Fritz Platten.

Moynahan presents the trip as having been identified by public opinion both internationally and in Russia as a pro-German manoeuvre.[117] But how can one reconcile this version with the fact that upon arrival in Petrograd, Lenin was welcomed officially by the Menshevik leader of the soviet, Nikola Chkheidze? And what about Radek's agitation against German militarism. What about the fiercely defeatist Trotsky's behaviour on his way back to Russia, reported by Moynahan himself:

> The British released him [from the prison camp in Amherst Canada], to the relief of the camp commandant. Trotsky had been converting the [interned German] submariners with enough success for German officers to plead with the commandant to muzzle him. 'Camp life had become a perpetual meeting.' The British colonel agreed to ban him from speaking.[118]

Who acted there in the interests of German militarism?

What is to be done? and the years 1905-1907

Finally, it is impossible to use only the pamphlet *What Is To Be Done?* – written in 1902 – to judge Lenin's organizational conceptions. The theses put forward in this work, undoubtedly with a certain exaggeration that Lenin himself was to admit later, cannot be detached from the precise historical context: a small party working in the strictest clandestinity.

Lenin never raised these theses to the level of a general theory of organization valid for all countries (including Russia) in all periods, independently of the period and the concrete conditions in which the class struggle was developing.

The alternative conceptions then proposed by the Mensheviks underestimated the constraints of illegality, the threat that they represented for the continuity of class activity, the – necessary but difficult – role of political centralization of fragmented struggles and above all the key nature of the struggle for political independence and later for the hegemony of the working class in the revolution. The split during the Second Congress of the party, in 1903, already contained in a latent fashion the germs of the central political differentiation between Bolsheviks and Mensheviks concerning the role of the Russian bourgeoisie in the revolution (the division between these two currents of the RSDLP was formalized in 1912).[119]

Even in the 1902 pamphlet *What Is To Be Done?*, we find passages that sound very much 'Luxemburgist-Trotskyist':

> The organization of professional revolutionaries has no meaning apart from its connection with the 'genuine revolutionary class that is spontaneously rising to struggle'.[120]
>
> Everyone will probably agree that 'the broad democratic principle' presupposes the two following conditions: first, full publicity, and secondly, election to all offices … We call the German Socialist Party a democratic organization because all its functions are carried out publicly; even its party congresses are held in public.[121]

These quotes are already sufficient to reject the thesis defended by Ingerflom.[122] That author believes that Lenin's organizational concepts were derived from a broad understanding – which he is supposed to have shared with Axelrod of all people – of the historical consequences of the absence of 'civil society' in traditional Russia. Hence even the proletariat, contrary to what Trotsky and Rosa Luxemburg thought, was unable to gain class-consciousness. Lenin is supposed to have thought that the party is prior to the class and the class struggle: it has to constitute the class, so to speak.

All these affirmations do not hold in the light of the sum total of Lenin's writings even prior to the 1905 revolution.

After the very important experience of the 1905 revolution, Lenin broadened this clarification still further, in a partially self-critical fashion, by using the image of having 'bent the stick too far in one direction'. His opponents having 'bent the stick' – that is the argument – 'in one direction' he had to bend it in the other to re-establish the balance:

> From 1903 to 1907 … the Social-Democratic party, despite the split in its ranks, gave the public the fullest information on the inner-party situation (minutes of the Second General Congress, the Third Bolshevik and the Fourth General, or Stockholm, congress). Despite the split, the Social-Democratic Party earlier than any of the other parties was able to take advantage of the temporary spell of freedom to build a legal organization with an ideal democratic structure, an electoral system, and representation at congresses according to the number of organized members …
>
> Basically, of course, their success was due to the fact that the working class, whose best representatives built the Social-Democratic party, for objective economic reasons possesses a greater capacity for organization than any other class in capitalist society. Without this condition an organization of professional revolutionaries would be nothing more than a plaything, an adventure, a mere signboard.[123]

Lenin expressed himself in a still clearer way when he asserted that:

> It seems to me that comrade Radin is wrong in raising the question … the Soviet of Workers' Deputies or the Party? I think that … the decision must certainly be: both the Soviet of Workers' Deputies and the Party (…). It seems to me that the Soviet of Workers' Deputies, as an organization representing all occupations, should strive to include deputies from all industrial and professional and office workers, domestic servants, farm labourers, etc. from all who want and are able to fight in common for a better life for the whole working people, from all who would have at least an elementary degree of political honesty, from all but the Black Hundreds.[124]
>
> [At the 1906 Unity Congress] we were all agreed on the principle of democratic centralism, on guarantees for the rights of all minorities and for all loyal opposition, on the autonomy of every Party organization, on recognition that all Party functionaries must be elected, accountable to the Party and subject to recall.[125]

The principle of democratic centralism and autonomy (sic) for local Party organizations implies universal and full freedom to criticize, so long as this does not disturb the unity of a definite action ...[126]

The Central Committee has absolutely no right to call upon the party organizations to accept its resolution in favour of supporting the demand for a Cadet Ministry. It is the duty of every party member to take an absolutely independent and critical stand on this question and to declare for the resolution that in his opinion more correctly solves the problem within the framework of the decisions of the Unity Congress. The St Petersburg worker Social Democrats know that the whole Party organization is now built on a democratic basis. This means that all the Party members take part in the election of officials, committee members and so forth ... that all the party members determine the line of tactics of the party organizations.[127]

An author like Louis Fischer knew his sources perfectly. However, he deliberately does not comment on the passages in Lenin's writing, which go in this direction.[128] This is manifest intellectual dishonestly, something that he is well acquainted with.

Fischer lived in the USSR between 1923 and 1936 as a foreign correspondent, particularly for the American periodical The Nation. As such he made an apology for the Moscow that was extremely useful to Stalin and international Stalinism.[129] However, in the biography of Lenin, which he wrote thirty years later, he said:

Stalin's vendetta against Trotsky plunged Soviet Russia into a bloodbath. In reality directed against Trotsky, the Moscow Trials of the 1930s cost the country its top leaders ... In 1937 it was the turn of the military leaders of Russia and, in their thousands, its best industrial managers, writers, planners, administrators ... It will always be impossible to measure what disasters this mad policy brought for Russia.[130]

The person who in 1936-38 was an advocate of this 'mad policy' did not find it necessary to formulate a single word of regret, of excuse or of self-criticism. He preferred to cross to the other side of the barricade.

Yesterday the wonderful Stalin was the successor of the wonderful Lenin. Today the despot Stalin is a by-product of the Leninist inclination for personal power and violence. We see what these two symmetrical positions have in common: in the last analysis Stalin derives from Lenin, yesterday for good and today for evil.

A non-monolithic party

We touch here on a much more general historical falsehood that is found in many authors who deal with the history of Soviet Russia in 1918-20.[131] Where was this so-called monolithic Bolshevik Party that was a result of the claimed Leninist obsession for hyper-centralization?

In reality, we have never seen a workers' party with so many differences of opinion and so much freedom of expression, including in public, as the Bolshevik Party of this period – and certainly not the German or Austrian social-democratic parties even in their best moments. We could cite many different illustrations of this. But we will simply mention the following:

- During the discussion on the opportuneness of the October insurrection, Zinoviev and Kamenev, the main members of the Central Committee, publicly disagreed with the position of the majority in an article published in the journal of Maxim Gorky.

- During the discussion on the formation of a coalition government of all the workers' parties, after the Second Congress of the Soviets, six members of the Central Committee and a number of members of the Council of Peoples' Commissars, publicly took a position against the decision of the majority. They also resigned from their posts to give more weight to their opposition.[132]

- Ryazanov and Lozovsky, two Bolshevik leaders voted against the dissolution of the Constituent Assembly in January 1918 at a meeting of the Central Executive Committee of the Soviets.

- During the negotiations on the Brest-Litovsk agreement, the 'left communists' around Bukharin published a daily newspaper to defend in public their minority position.

- The current known as the 'democratic centralist' tendency led by the 'left communists' like Ossinsky, put forward in the review *Kommunist* from 1918 a plan for workers' management of industry which was very different from that of the majority of the Central Committee. It started, very timidly, to put it into practice.[13]

- The Workers' Opposition led by Shliapnikov, Miasnikov and Kollontai, established in 1920, defended its minority positions publicly.

- Again in 1921, I. Vardin (Megaldze), the director of the Cheka, against Lenin's opposition, proposed to legalize all the opposition parties and groupings which accepted the Soviet system of government. They were to be authorized to present separate lists of candidates in the elections to the soviets and a free press in line with their size.[134]

An episode recounted by llyin-Zhenevsky, deputy People's Commissar for Defence, is a good illustration of this liberal atmosphere. At the end of March 1918 there was the First conference of soldiers and sailors of the Red Army. At the opening of the conference, there was a proposal to elect an honorary presiding committee of Lenin, Trotsky and Zinoviev. The anarchists were opposed. The proposal was adopted but only with a small majority, a lot of the Bolsheviks voting with the anarchists.

Against the opposition of the leaders of the Bolshevik delegation and of Ilyin-Zhanovsky representing the government, a bloc of anarchists and 'left' Bolsheviks forced through that the conference should have legislative and decision-making powers. The same bloc also imposed a substantial increase in soldiers' and sailors' pay that the government said it could not fulfil.[135]

It could be objected that Lenin violently – a violence that remained essentially verbal and did not lead to any disciplinary measures – opposed these ruptures of discipline.

This is true but this is not the essential point.

Because what these episodes show is that the party formed by the organizational conceptions of Lenin was non-monolithic; that very many leaders and cadres, as much workers as intellectuals, maintained a great independence of thought, an ultra-sharp critical spirit and that the daily practice of this party reflected much more this critical independence than any sort of monolithic or hyper-centralist education.

In addition it should be noted that Lenin's inspiration was not really different. At the Tenth Party Congress, in March 1921, when factions were banned, he opposed the proposal to ban tendencies as well. He stated clearly that when the party is divided on important questions it is impossible to prevent the election of the leadership on the basis of different tendency platforms.

He himself, on more than one occasion when he was in a minority in the leadership, decided to look elsewhere and sought to organize a minority tendency or defend minority positions in public.

These facts cannot be hidden without distorting the history of the Soviet Russia of Lenin's time.

An internal tension in Leninism

It is true that in the writings and practice of Lenin there are also different features of paternalism, authoritarianism and substitutionism. In fact, the total organizational theory and practice of Lenin seems to be dominated by a balancing act, as explained in the works of Marcel Liebman, Paul Le Blanc and above all the excellent essay by Stephen Cohen already mentioned.[136]

In a first approximation this balancing act can be summed up as follows: in the phases of a revolutionary upsurge, the tumultuous rise of the mass movements, the democratic and even libertarian emphases predominate in Lenin's practice. In the periods of revolutionary slump, the decline of activity of the mass movement, the themes of centralism and replacement of the class by the party take predominance.

To explain this duality by Machiavellism is misplaced and unjust. The starting point for such an attitude is a psychological interpretation, which can hardly be proved.[137]

At the limit, this psychological interpretation could be replaced by a sociological one. The democratic and libertarian Lenin acted under the pressure of the workers' vanguard and masses. The hyper-centralist and substitutionist Lenin sought a pragmatic solution in a situation where, in practice the masses were not active.

But this sociological explanation is not fair to Lenin either. It does not take into account the whole of Russian history from 1918 to 1923. In particular it does not make it possible to understand the almost desperate violence with which Lenin reacted from 1922, if not the end of 1921, faced with the growing bureaucratization of the state and of the party (a bureaucratization of which he then became aware). It does not explain 'Lenin's last fight' against the tentacular bureaucracy, nor the violence of his final confrontation with Stalin, nor the truly pathetic tone he used on this occasion: 'I suppose I have been very remiss with respect to the workers of Russia for not having intervened energetically and decisively enough ...'[138]

Any 'sociological' explanation can only ignore a historical fact, that is nevertheless difficult, and that Paul Le Blanc correctly counterposed to the too mechanical view of the 'balancing act', as Liebman formulated it. It was in the years of reaction, in 1908-11, in the struggle against the 'liquidating' tendency that Lenin to a large extent grouped together and trained the Bolshevik cadres, which made it possible for his party to become hegemonic in the Russian workers' movement from 1912.

An independent mind

The Russian example illustrates a more general historical rule: it is in non-revolutionary periods that the programmatic, political and organizational bases are created for the 'breakthrough' of the revolutionary party during the later years of struggle.

The thesis whereby the party conceived by Lenin was a party essentially composed if not dominated by bourgeois intellectuals and not workers has no factual basis.[139] This opinion is put forward by Alfred Meyer, which even asserts that democratic centralism was a system that 'functioned pretty well, while the party was commanded by a strong leader who ruled it with an iron grip'.[140]

This second assertion fits the facts no more than does the first.

To demonstrate the contrary we can cite Beryl Williams, who is nevertheless very hostile to the Bolsheviks and to Lenin:

> As the Bolsheviks popularity rose, so did party membership. In the process the party was to change out of all recognition. By October, it was a mass party, not the elite intellectual grouping of 1903 or of popular imagination. Figures for membership are difficult to establish, but it would seem that the party grew tenfold in the course of the year to rather more than a quarter of a million. The vast majority of members by October were workers ... Again in contrast to popular belief, they were not highly organized or united, although they probably had more cohesion and certainly stronger leadership than their rivals. But there were great differences in approach between the Central Committee, local 'sub-elites' in district committees and soviets, and 'sub-sub-elites' in the factories. Local activists, like their supporters, tended to act with remarkable independence.[141]

This honest description gives a much more faithful picture of the real functioning of the party than the different legends about 'democratic centralism' under Lenin. It makes it possible to understand why Lenin had serious clashes with these 'committee men' at least four times; in 1905-16; at the beginning of the revolution in February 1917; on the eve of October; and from 1921-22. The first three times the clash ended to his advantage, thanks to the support he won from the broad workers' vanguard, including outside the party. The fourth time he lacked this support, with the tragic consequences that we know.

Towards a coherent conception

Lenin never really presented a total, completely coherent conception of the party and its organizational principles. But it does seem, that in the light of historical events he moved in this direction. An element of this process of clarification was the gradual assertion of the dialectical unity between the self-activity of the class and the role of the vanguard party, except in the 'black years' of 1920-21 (some would say 1919-21).

Authors like Leopold Haimson assert that the Russian intellectuals and Marxists have never been able to resolve the problem of the contradiction between spontaneity and consciousness, between the action of the masses and the action inspired and organized by the vanguard. However, the October Revolution gave this answer, illustrated by die striking and classic formula given by Trotsky in his *History of the Russian Revolution:*

> Without a guiding organization the energy of the masses would dissipate like steam not enclosed in a piston box. But nevertheless what moves things is not the piston or the box, but the steam.[142]

It remains the case that the organizational model of *What Is To Be Done?*, even applied in a limited period, has produced problems: a certain type of leaders, 'committee men' unable to adapt to tumultuous mass movements, Lenin's companion Krupskaya wrote on this subject:

> The 'committeeman' was usually a rather self-assured person. He saw what a tremendous influence the work of the committee had on the masses, and as a rule he recognized no inner-party democracy. 'Inner-party democracy only leads to trouble with the police. We are connected with the movement as it is,' the committeeman would say. Inwardly, they rather despised the Party workers abroad, who, in their opinion, had nothing better to do than squabble among themselves – 'they ought to be made to work under Russian conditions'. The committeeman objected to the over-ruling influence of the Centre abroad [that is of Lenin! EM]. At the same time, they did not want innovations. They were neither desirous nor capable of adjusting themselves to quickly changing conditions.[143]

In any case, the real history of Soviet Russia between 1918 and 1923 can only be understood in by taking into account all these contradictory elements and not as some original sin of Lenin.

Those who want to find the origins of Stalinism should first of all look at the social forces and their mutual relations, which is more in line with the principles of historical materialism than to simply look at ideas. But, as for the intellectual sources, Stalinist organizational conceptions do not continue those of Lenin: they represent their brutal and terrorist negation.

Re-establish soviet democracy immediately?

How was it possible to effectively oppose the bureaucratization process in the Russia of 1920? That is, in a country which was drained bloodless, hit by famine, whose transport system was totally disorganized, with a working class reduced to less than half if not a third of what it was in 1917. A working class on a rapid road to demobilization, not because of the end of the Civil War, but because of the absolute necessity of finding an individual supply of food. In such social and material conditions, the immediate re-establishment of soviet democracy, indeed decisive steps to workers' management were a total utopia.

The leadership of the party and of the state were supposed to give the priority to an upturn in production, particularly agricultural production, a rise in work productivity and the re-establishment of employment.

Lenin and Trotsky's mistake was to generalize the exceptional conditions of the time. From the beginning of the NEP in 1921-22, the numerical weakening and the tendency to decomposition and social degeneration of the working class were halted.

It was at this point that a gradual broadening of soviet democracy could have speeded up the socio-political re-establishment of the working class, making easier its slow re-politicization. But by limiting what remained of democracy in a draconian fashion at this very moment, the Soviet leaders on the contrary made worse the de-politicization of the proletariat and of the party.[144]

It is impossible to judge to what point a 'new course' would have met with success. But the tragic results of the policy followed in 1921 are too obvious not to conclude: what was utopian in 1920 was no longer so from 1922.

The strategic dimension

The October revolution raises the key strategic question which confronts the whole of the socialist workers' movement: how should a party, which identifies with the working class and socialism (or communism), behave in a revolutionary situation. This question refers back to another, broader, question, that of long-term socialist (or communist) strategy: a question that we will not go into here.

Revolutions do not fall from the sky. They cannot be mechanically detached from the periods which precede them, the periods in which the conditions which lead to their explosion slowly mature. In the same way, what the parties identifying with the working class do and are depends to a large extent on their composition and their activity in pre-revolutionary or non-revolutionary phases (although we cannot deny that the revolution itself can noticeably modify some of these factors).

It is schematic but useful to sum up the two fundamentally counterposed strategic philosophies during a revolution by the formula: fatalism or voluntarism.

Fatalism or reasonable voluntarism

The fatalist approach is based on the idea that the 'objective conditions' and the 'balance of power' determine practically everything, that the course of events is largely independent of decisions of parties and their leaders, that the task of these latter is essentially to draw the boundaries between what is 'objectively possible' and the rest (which would be adventurism and illusions).

We should therefore have the courage to say to the masses that a series of their aspirations are impossible.

The Mensheviks embodied this orientation during 1917. Their main contacts abroad were the Austro-Marxists whose leader and theorist Otto Bauer has gone down in history as the very prototype of the fatalist Marxist.

The voluntarist approach to strategy in a revolutionary period is on the other hand based on the idea that, whatever the weight of objective factors (economic, social, historical and cultural tradition), which partially determine the course of events, this is not totally predetermined. The concrete actions of social classes (and the main sections of them), the activity and precise orientation of parties and their leaders can also have a decisive effect on the course of events.

'Parametric' determinism

It is not a question of counterposing a determinist approach (identified with 'fatalism') to an agnostic or teleological philosophy of history (which would then be identified with 'voluntarism').[145] We are discussing here voluntarism which respects the major historical-materialist constraints.

We must avoid mechanistic and linear determinism, which has done a lot of harm, replacing it with a richer determinism, based on the dialectic of objective and subjective factors.[146] We express this understanding of what is 'possible' by the concept 'parametric determinism', an understanding of history which makes it possible to take into account what is 'latent' and 'virtual'. Such a concept was already used by Marx in Volume I of *Capital.*

The course of events is neither totally predetermined nor totally undetermined. The possible outcome of the revolution oscillates within predetermined limits.

In Russia in 1917, neither a return to a semi-feudal regime nor the rise of capitalism based on parliamentary democracy, nor the totally finished building of a classless socialist society were possible. But in the predetermined framework, the action of the masses, of the parties and their leaders could lead to several possible variants: victory of an ultra-reactionary bourgeois counter-revolution (which could only be bloody, repressive, and destructive of the workers' movement and all independent activity of the working and peasants masses); victory of the revolution through the soviets taking power, making it possible to start building a new society (in fusion with or at least with the support of the international revolution).

The fatalist approach was, in great measure, the product of the 'Marxism' of the Second International, inspired by Kautsky. It was a conception strongly marked by a mechanistic determinism of semi-Darwinian inspiration.[147] It implied that, even when confronted with a revolutionary explosion, the socialists could not in the final analysis do otherwise than submit to the inexorable march of events. The voluntarist approach implied on the contrary that socialists were conscious of the possibility of influencing in a decisive fashion the historic outcome through their own action. This is the principal merit of the Bolsheviks, who tried to do just that. And this is the main lesson that Rosa Luxemburg learnt from the October events, a lesson which led her to moderate her criticisms of Lenin and Trotsky and to support the Russian Revolution in an enthusiastic fashion:

> Whatever a party could offer of courage revolutionary farsightedness and consistency in a historic hour, Lenin, Trotsky and the other comrades have given in good measure. All the revolutionary honour and capacity which Western social democracy lacked were represented by the Bolsheviks. Their October uprising was not only the actual salvation of the Russian Revolution; it was also the salvation of the honour of international socialism.

and again:

> What is in order is to distinguish the essential from the non-essential the kernel from the additional excrescences in the policies of the Bolsheviks. In the present period when we face decisive final struggles in the entire world, the most important problem of socialism was and is the burning question of our time. It is not a matter of this or that secondary question of tactics, but of the capacity for action of the proletariat the strength to act the will to power of socialism as such. In this, Lenin and Trotsky and their friends were the first, those who went ahead as an example to the proletariat of the world: they are still the only ones up to now who can cry with Hutten: 'I have dared!'

This is the essential and the enduring in Bolshevik policy. In this sense theirs is the immortal historical service of having marched at the head of the international proletariat with the conquest of political power and the practical placing of the problem of the realization of socialism, and of having advanced mightily the settlement of the score between capital and labour in the entire world. In Russia the problem could only be posed. It could not he solved in Russia. And in this sense, the future everywhere belongs to 'Bolshevism'.[148]

Was it right to take power?

Of course the counterposition between these two options, fatalism and opportunism, should not be exaggerated, even though they do remain two fundamentally different options. Too great a simplification of the problem can confuse things and make the choice more difficult.

There is, in this sense, the possibility of adventurist, putschist, 'Blanquist' excesses in the 'voluntarist' course: attempts to seize power by minorities who do not enjoy the support of the majority of wage-workers.[149]

But the existence and the danger of such deviations can only be an excuse to avoid the real strategic choice which existed in Russia just before the October Revolution.

The Bolsheviks obviously enjoyed the support of the majority of the proletariat. The people obviously wanted a radical, revolutionary change. Was it right, in these precise circumstances, to take power?

The revolutionary Marxists of today, like those of 1917 and the following years, remain convinced that the answer is an unreserved 'yes'.

Determinism, political choices, experience

Recently, the critical study of Bolshevik tactics in the years which followed the October Revolution, has given rise to a confrontation on the nature of historical determinism between John Rees and Samuel Farber. The first accuses the second of having abandoned all materialist determinism, because he presents a range of alternatives, analyses, and other choices which could have been possible for revolutionary socialist policy in Russia in 1918-23:

> Marxism does not suggest that in every circumstance, political will or ideology can play a key role. The degree to which workers can 'make their own history' depends on the weight of objective factors bearing down on them. ... In Russia (after October 1927) the limits of action were reduced to withstanding under ever narrowing constrictions, a siege. Every ounce of willpower and political consciousness was necessary to keep the workers' state from being overcome. The 'subjective factor' was reduced

to withstanding, under ever narrowing constrictions, to a choice between capitulation to the Whites or defending the revolution with whatever means were at hand.[150]

But this way of posing the problem has two fundamental weaknesses.

First of all it does not respond to the essential objection, that is that soviet democracy was definitively suffocated at the moment when the soviet parties were banned, after the Civil War, and not when the alternative was either to capitulate to the Whites or to defend the revolution with all the means available. It was thus suffocated after the victory, when there was no White army still present on Soviet territory.

The measures then taken were inspired by the idea that, precisely because of the victory in the Civil War, the revolutionary mobilization of the Civil War was going to decline. This demobilization, in the eyes of the Bolsheviks, could threaten soviet power still more than the White armies. John Rees does not mention this explanation. Thus he does not unmask its illogical and mistaken character.

Rees then dissolves these concrete problems in an abstract and general formula. The question was not to know whether if, in general, 'all means necessary', should be used to defend soviet power and prevent a White victory. The question is to know whether this or that concrete measure made easier or more difficult the victorious pursuit of the Civil War.

Was this the case in the creation of the Cheka? Was this the case in the continuation and stepping up of wheat requisitions in 1919-20 and in general the excesses of 'war communism'? Was this the case with the banning of the soviet parties?

The Soviet power, the leaders of the Bolshevik Party, had a real choice: to take or not take these measures. Were they right? Were they wrong?

John Rees argues as if the question was not even posed. And curiously, he does not mention the central argument which could, if not totally justify, at least largely explain the behaviour of the Bolsheviks in this regard. It was formulated by Rosa Luxemburg in her pamphlet on the Russian Revolution.

The socialist revolution, as well as the beginning of building a classless society, constituted a totally new experience. There was absolutely no handbook of pre-established rules that could be referred to. The Russian Revolution was an immense historical laboratory, both exalting and dramatic. Advances could only be made by experimentation, in feeling the way.

Only practice can show if this or that concrete measure – we are not talking here about general orientation – is correct or false. Any dogmatic approach, starting from pre-established schemas, is counter-productive (as is any purely pragmatic orientation). Both avoid the big strategic choices.

Many things are clear after the event, but were not at the time. They could not be so. As Napoleon Bonaparte said: 'We'll start fighting then we'll see.' Lenin liked to repeat these words of a master tactician.

Mistakes and socialist democracy

It is just because this is the case that the revolution has a vital need of pluralist soviet democracy, of an active political life, of the masses' right in practice to criticize and to intervene. Because if the revolution as the beginning of building a classless society is an immense laboratory, then mistakes are inevitable: it is thus vital to have mechanisms which make it possible not so much to avoid mistakes – which is impossible – but to correct them as quickly as possible, and then to avoid them being repeated in the future. Lenin himself noted that the fashion in which a party behaved in relation to its own mistakes determined its future.

And it is in this context that soviet democracy acquires all its value.

Democracy and social equality

Samuel Farber is thus, in my opinion, correct as opposed to John Rees for the general method of approach. But, once again, he is only right in a general and abstract fashion and not in a large number of the concrete judgements he makes. In fact he uses purely formal criteria of democracy excessively, criteria, which turn out to be, in practice, much less democratic than they seem at first sight.

Farber insists strongly on the importance of a 'state based on law', the need for written laws, the principle according to which the accused is presumed innocent until proven guilty, etc.[151] Our movement incorporated most of these principles into the theses which it adopted during its 1979 and 1985 congresses, entitled 'Socialist Democracy and the Dictatorship of the Proletariat'. We did not wait for the upheavals in Eastern Europe nor the publication of Farber's book to assert and defend these rights.[152]

But Farber does not deal with a series of other problems which although not 'formal' are nevertheless very real. Problems which could be an obstacle to the guarantee of human rights for women and men as long as market and monetary phenomena exist, that is to say during the whole transitional period. These include the corruptibility of judges and the need to limit the number of lawyers that an individual can use because if not those who have with more money have greater possibilities of defending themselves or – under civil law – of accusing others. To overcome these problems, changes required include: free legal defence; the need for strict public control and thus elimination of the principle that a 'closed case' cannot be reopened; substantial modifications of the procedural codes to make them more transparent to the mass of citizens; the generalization of the principle of the revocability of judges, thus eliminating of the principle that they are appointed for life; and the maximum extension of the principle of trial by jury.

There is no reason why these juridical changes would undermine or limit the rights of individuals or the 'state based on law'. They are in fact necessary conditions if we want all women and men, and not only privileged minorities (including bureaucrats and intellectuals) to enjoy their formal rights to the full! However, the severe criticism of 'revolutionary justice' rejects them dogmatically, as if on principle.

Social inequality in the legal system is a well-known scandal in our 'states based on law'. Three recent events provide a rather spectacular confirmation of this, if one is needed. Prince Victor-Emmanuel, claimant to the throne of Italy, has been acquitted of the murder of a young German after the legal process dragged on for eleven years. Would a citizen of average means be able to drag things out for so long?

In Japan, after 24 years, the Hitachi Corporation has won a case against one of its employees, sacked for having refused to work overtime. A lawyer who has established a workers' advice centre, Mr Kawahito, said about this case:

> Like many of Japan's laws, this one is deliberately unclear. Today's decision was wrong because Japanese workers will now be unable to refuse overtime and the incidence of *karoshi* (death from overwork) will rise further ... One in four white-collar workers now fear death from overwork, according to a recent Tokyo survey by Nippon Kayaku, a medicine manufacturer ...
>
> Clearly, the Supreme Court has favoured big business and believes economic power comes from overtime. It has given priority to economy over human life.[153]

The Kennedy family spent one million dollars in less than six months to defend a member of the family accused of rape.[154] Could an ordinary person do that?

The United States, Italy and Japan are of course capitalist countries and not post-capitalist societies. But this does not change anything in the fact that these three cases illustrate the ambiguity of the concept of the 'state based on law'. They show that the independence of the judicial power can enter into open conflict with equal opportunities, when there is an inequality of wealth, of income, of social status: phenomena which will survive during the period of transition to which Farber refers.

A coalition government?

The problem of the choice of possible actions obviously has a much broader dimension than that of the undoubtedly very limited possible variants of Bolshevik tactics. This choice is posed for all those who from 1917 until today, from Plekhanov to Eric Hobsbawm, say decidedly: they should not have taken power, the October Revolution was 'premature'.

What should have been done? Wait passively for events to occur? Deliver the country to the rabble army of Wilhelm II? Russian and international reformists do not put forward anything coherent, except absurd illusions in an impossible bourgeois democracy.

Centrists like Martov and Otto Bauer/Hilferding defended an alternative solution in a hesitant and timid way. Martov called it 'a unified revolutionary democratic government': a coalition of all the parties identifying with socialism.

A whole wing of the Bolsheviks also looked to such project (as we saw in the previous chapter). It was however fundamentally impossible, not because of the supposed 'sectarianism' of the Bolsheviks but for much deeper reasons.

In fact, the right SRs and the right Mensheviks did not want to give up at any price the policy of 'national defence', that is to say the continuation of the war which had unavoidable implications. The centre-left Menshevik Dan, who was a (more and more hesitant) supporter of 'revolutionary national defence', wrote on this:

> The continuing defence of the country, while waiting to sign a democratic peace, required that an army of several million people be maintained, and that everything should be done to prevent it becoming disorganized. As a consequence the application of the agrarian reform had to be put off until after the meeting of the Constituent Assembly. In fact, a revolutionary expropriation of the big landowners and the distribution of land would have inevitably provoked the desertion of millions of peasant soldiers who would not have stayed at the front at such a time.[155]

In other words, neither the majority of the Mensheviks nor the right SRs were ready to accept immediate peace, the immediate division of the big properties and workers' control over production. The Menshevik minister of labour, Skobelev, agreed to re-establish the authority of the manufacturers and managers in the enterprises, a demand of the employers' association. On what programme could a governmental coalition then be established?

The 'conciliators' made the exclusion of Lenin and Trotsky a condition for the constitution of such a 'workers' united front' government. It was obviously an unacceptable condition for the Bolsheviks who nevertheless held the absolute majority of mandates in the congress of soviets!

A coalition government of the Bolsheviks, left SRs, left Mensheviks (the 'internationalists' around Martov) would at the limit have been possible. It was moreover partially constituted because a coalition government of the Bolsheviks and left SRs was formed. But it was Martov's group which from the outset refused to follow this path.

Do nothing? The German example

It could be argued that, after all, it was better not to follow a revolutionary path which could only lead to failure. This is only in appearance a Pontius Pilate position.

In reality, by refusing to act, one influences events as much as one does in acting – because one opts for the status quo and leaves the field open to the class opponent who can take the initiative freely.

Scholastics say, not incorrectly, that there are sins of omission as well as of commission.

This fundamental question of strategic choice can be most clearly illustrated by comparing the behaviour of the German social democrats who had the majority during 1918 with the behaviour of the Bolsheviks in 1917 (the right wing of the USPD occupying a middle position quite similar to that of Martov in Russia).

Let us leave aside the question of the social composition of the leadership of the German social democratic party and the material interests represented. Let us even leave aside the question of the real motivation of this majority current. The disastrous historical balance sheet of reformism is clear.[156]

The SPD refused to take power. It refused to envisage the possibility of an advance, however moderate, to socialism. It refused to purge seriously the state apparatus inherited from the Empire – particularly its military, legal and diplomatic branches. It went over to the side of the established order one hundred per cent, and was at most prepared to undertake some timid reforms.

This policy was concretized in a number of ways: finalization of the agreement on institutionalized negotiations (class collaboration) between the trade-union bureaucracy and the employers; formation of a coalition government with the bourgeoisie; liquidation of the workers' councils not only as bodies of political power but even as bodies of workers' control and dual power within the enterprises; above all, a secret agreement with the command of the imperial armed forces, on the joint proposal of Ebert, social-democratic leader, and General Groener:

> There can no longer be any discussion today on the question of the alliance made in November between Chancellor Ebert and the army chiefs, even in the version of a telephone agreement between Groener and Ebert in the night of November 9 to 10 cannot be formally substantiated. From November 10, Marshal Hindenburg telegraphed to the military commanders that the central command had decided to collaborate with the Chancellery in order to 'prevent the spread of terrorist Bolshevism in Germany'.

General Groener [wrote] some years later: 'We made an alliance against Bolshevism'.[157]

But what Ebert, Noske and Groener called 'Bolshevism' was, in Germany, a very broad popular movement challenging bourgeois society, independently of the existence of adventurist and minority ultra-left groups. For example, the general strike for the defence of the workers' councils in February-March 1919, or the formidable mass mobilization against the Kapp-von Luttwitz putsch in March-April 1920.

Reformism and counter-revolution

In a revolutionary period, the refusal to get involved in the revolution and the taking of power almost inevitably means being part of the counter-revolution. The choice is then no longer between action and inaction. It is between revolutionary action and counter-revolutionary action. The reformists are in fact led to repress the spontaneous, semi-spontaneous or organized movement of the toiling masses; opposing it first by manoeuvres and lies and then by violent action.[158]

The role of Gustav Noske, the social-democratic minister, is notorious on this. He did not hesitate to write:

> Nobody made the slightest objection when I expressed the opinion that order should be re-established by the force of arms. The war minister, colonel Reinhardt, wrote an order naming general Hoffman as the commander in-chief ... The objection was made that the general would be too unpopular with the workers ... I insisted that a decision must be

made? Someone said: 'Couldn't you do it yourself?' I replied briefly and firmly: 'I don't see any objection. Someone has to play the role of the mad dog. I'm not afraid of this responsibility'.[159]

Nor did the same Noske hesitate to post the following warning on the walls of Berlin a few' months later:

The brutality and the bestiality [sic] of the Spartakists who fight against us force me to give the following order: any one taken arms in hand in the struggle against the government will be summarily shot.[160]

These massacres were justified in the name of hostility to 'Bolshevism'. It can be noted, not without a certain irony, that these same people were indignant about the Red Terror against 'people taken arms in hand against the government' (however, Trotsky never considered or practised execution of members of the White Army).

But the fundamental fact is elsewhere. Leaders of parties that call themselves socialist take on themselves the right to forbid the broad masses to organize strike or even to organize unarmed demonstrations, in the name of priorities, of 'principles', of political judgements which are very far from being shared by everyone, and which turned out to be far from a papal infallibility.[161]

The Mensheviks, even the left wing, opposed initiatives for workers' control that emanated directly from the workplaces in Russia. They even look on themselves the right to repress the workers when they ignored their judgements. This pretentious and paternalist arrogance has the same substitutionist arrogance as underlies Stalinist behaviour. This parallel between reformist and Stalinist behaviour should be highlighted.

Let us repeat: all this is the absolute opposite of the doctrine and orientation of Marx, centred on the concept of the self-emancipation of the working class.

Marx and Engels had a premonition of this substitutionism and its implications when, in their famous letter of September 1879, they condemned the position of the reformist Manifesto of the 'Zurich Three' (Hochberg, Bernstein and Schramm) in very ironic terms:

If we want to win to [our] cause the upper layers of society (as the Zurich Three hope), we must not frighten them at any cost. The Zurich Three think that they have made a tranquillizing discovery: the party must show that it is not ready to take the road of a bloody and violent revolution but that it has decided ... to take the road of legality, that is of reforms. The logical conclusion of this argument is thus that if Berlin shows itself again to be so badly brought up as to have another March 18 [that is a revolutionary explosion], the social democrats, rather than participating in this struggle as 'rabble burning to climb onto the barricades' [terms used by the 'Zurichois'] they should rather 'take the road of legality', dismantle the barricades and, if necessary, march in step with the glorious troops against the exclusive, brutal and unlettered masses.[162]

This is a forecast and condemnation of the behaviour of the reformists Ebert and Noske forty years before the facts!

The main justification that the German social-democrats put forward for their policy of opposition to the socialist taking of power during a revolutionary crisis, is that democracy had to be defended, indeed defended at all costs, including against millions of workers – it does not matter here if they form a (slight) majority or a strong minority of the proletariat and the electorate.

To do this they had first to ignore or deny the reality of the counter-revolutionary threat.[163] But by taking the path of repression, by using the old state apparatus of the property-owning classes for this purpose, they opened the road to a process of consolidation of 'elites' – thus also paving the way which led to the bloodthirsty regime of the Nazi dictatorship. The Weimar Republic gave birth to the Third Reich. It was in 1918-19, in 1920 and 1923 that all was decided, in the repression of the revolution and the German masses – the reformists not only playing a passive role but getting actively involved in the counter-revolutionary camp.[164]

The Nazi dictatorship and the Second World War cost humanity 50 million deaths. That was the concrete alternative to the October Revolution. That is the most striking historical justification for this revolution.

By way of conclusion

International and Russian reaction attacked the October Revolution with extreme violence during the years which followed the Bolshevik revolution, stating that it only had purely destructive effects.

Great cultural wealth

The French newspapers, particularly *Le Temps*, had whole columns denouncing the 'Asiatic barbarism' which had allegedly stamped out all artistic, scientific and literary life in Soviet Russia. In July 1920, the French Academy of Sciences suppressed a report by Monsieur Victor Henri, posted in Russia, on the scientific activity in the country. In 1925, *The Times* of London published a Note of the Admiralty stating that the Soviet government had brought nothing to Russia except blood, poverty and famine.[165]

The Prussian country squire Karl von Bothmer, summed up the central argument of this campaign of denigration when he wrote:

> No constructive force has shown itself. Nowhere are any creative forces appearing. [The government] only maintains itself through criminal means, without being able to show it has achieved anything.[166]

At the same lime as von Bothmer was writing this, Beryl Williams more honestly noted that:

> The combination of artistic experimentation and intense intellectual debate over cultural matters was to give rise to a period or artistic vigour and utopian dreams in the period of the revolution and the civil war.[167]

She noted that in fact at the end of 1918, there were already three times more museums in Russia than before the Revolution.[168]

In fact, the rise of the theatre and cinema in the USSR, and of painting, posters and avant-garde sculpture, of urbanism and architecture, or psychology and psychiatry, of analysis of the economic situation, of historiography, not to mention literature, impressed the whole world. This cultural flowering was greater than the famous 'golden years' of the Weimar Republic, whose base and material wealth was nevertheless much broader.

The rise of education

The Revolution also undertook an immense effort of literacy and extension of education. The budget for public education which had been 195 million roubles in 1916 and that the February revolution increased to 940 million roubles, was increased again to 2.9 billion roubles in 1918 by the Bolsheviks and then to 10 billion in 1919. The number of primary schools was increased from 38,387 in 1917 to 52,274 in 1918 and to 62,238 in 1919. Pre-school teaching, which was practically non-existent under Tsarism, already covered 200,000 children in 1921 and 561,000 in 1921.[169]

Unafraid of making himself ridiculous, professor Norman Stone does not hesitate to assert that before 1917 Tsarism was already on the road to successful modernization of Russia. He cites its 'rapid scientific and cultural development'.[170]

But in Tsarist Russia there were at most a few thousand scientists. The great majority of the population was illiterate. Thanks to the work started by the October Revolution, there were, at the beginning of the 1980s, more than two million scientists; 125 million graduates of secondary education; 14.8 million citizens with post-secondary diplomas; and more than 80 per cent of the workforce who had secondary education certificates.[171]

As for the industrial leap forward, whatever its price the balance sheet is at least clear.

A humanist revolution

So much for the 'non-achievements' of the Russian Revolution.

But let us leave the material domain for the moral and spiritual, which the opponents of the revolution have talked so much about, not without a certain hypocrisy.

Even von Bothmer has to recognize that the Russian Revolution, in forbidding any sale of alcohol, made alcoholism practically disappear from the big towns. There were no drunks in Moscow and Petrograd.[172]

When we know the extent to which the plague of alcoholism affected Russia before October, – and after the re-establishment of the state monopoly on selling alcohol under Stalin – and when we know its ravages in the Soviet Union of today, then we understand quite easily the importance of this question.

In the same way the publicist Alfons Goldschmidt felt himself in total security in Petrograd and Moscow. The streets were clear. In the midst of the famine lorry loads of flour passed. They were not attacked. There was no pillage of food shops.[173]

The humanism of the revolution was also expressed in a generous cultural-moral pluralism that was touching and also naive. The German writer Alfons Paquet was a slandering critic of the revolution who could not, despite himself, help sympathizing with it.[174]

He describes how on the first anniversary of October, a long list of 'freedom fighters' was inscribed on the white walls of the former military academy. The list included the names of Victor Hugo, Emile Zola, Ibsen, Emile Verhaeren, Nekrassov, Saltykov, Michalovski, Byron, Chopin, Koltzov, Constantin Meunier, Mussorgski, Pushkin, Rirnsky-Korsakov, Scriabin, Beethoven, Marx, Engels, Auguste Blanqui, Bebel, Lassalle, Jean Jaurès, Plekhanov, Spartacus, Gracchus Babeuf, Garibaldi, Robespierre, Danton, Jean-Jacques Rousseau, Robert Owen, Herzen, Bakunin, Voltaire, Pertel, and many others.[175]

In 1918-19 the works of Pushkin, Lermontov, Gogol, Tolstoy, Turgenev, Dostoyevsky, Goncharov, Grigorovich, Ostrovsky, Ryleiev, Zola, Anatole

France, Merimée, Walter Scott, Romain Rolland, Aulard, Louis Blanc, Jean Jaures, Bebel, Plekhanov and Kautsky (these two firm opponents of the October Revolution), were published in print runs of between 25,000 and 100,000.[176]

At the same time, the revolution stimulated a formidable participation by the masses in cultural life: 'Theatre audiences were solidly proletarian, dressed in shabby clothes, topped by threadbare overcoats in teeth shattering cold.'[177]

On May Day 1920, 20,000 people in Petrograd saw a spectacle entitled *The Liberation of Work,* which told the story of the historical fight for emancipation, from the slave revolts of Antiquity to the Russian Revolution. The celebrated film of Serge Eisenstein, *The Battleship Potemkin,* was filmed with the participation of thousands of citizens of Odessa.[178]

Class spirit

Between this popular-proletarian spirit and the very nature of the revolution in the institutional domain there is an undeniable inter-connection. Let us cite once again Alfons Paquet who nevertheless recognizes what was the essential in this spirit:

> The first incomparable contribution of the Russian Revolution is to have taken up in full radicalism and with an iron hand, the fight against the egoism of capitalism, whether in a private or state form. The merit of Bolshevism is to have made that possible …
>
> The collapse of Europe is happening before our eyes, but the basis of its reconstruction has already been established. Let us try to understand fully the ideas of the revolution and draw hope from them for the future.

And he made this conclusion of striking topicality:

> One day, for example, the workers [of the towns bordering the Rhine which are] Basle, Strasbourg, Mannheim, Mayence, Ruhrort [a mining agglomeration], Emmerich and Rotterdam could form a joint council of the Rhine basin and thus could make their influence felt in the transformation of this axis in a great European river route, going beyond country borders and the law established by those on top … The idea of such councils could also, in many ways, serve the European goal, that is the building of a joint peace economy.[179]

There is here undeniably a class spirit. It is undoubtedly on that basis that supporters of the power of private property, the power of wealth to, put it in the dock. It remains for us in line with the requirements of social justice and historical facts, totally defendable from all points of view, starting with the moral point of view.

Alfons Goldschmidt, in Petrograd, saw this class spirit: 'The first impression: a proletarian city. The worker rules. The worker dominates the streets.'[180]

Alfons Paquet noted: 'Councils exclusively composed of proletarians rule the enterprises, the urban neighbourhoods, the villages, the districts and the provinces.'[181]

The Bolshevik government distributed arms to the workers in almost all towns in the country during the civil war. Is this not proof that this was not the government of a clan or a sect but a class government, convinced that it enjoyed the confidence of the majority of this class?

Many historians have asserted that the Bolsheviks lost members and indeed the support of the working class after the Brest-Litovsk peace and the start of the Red Terror in 1918. Even a well-disposed critic, William G. Rosenberg, said so.[182] But this statement is contradicted by the systematic call for the mobilization of factory workers in the Red Army, in order to defend Soviet power. In fact, the vast majority of workers replied positively to this appeal.[183] There were of course undoubted fluctuations in the attitude if the working class in relation to the Bolsheviks in 1918, 1919, 1920. But whatever its critical aspect, the support of the majority of the workers remained.

The Red Army was moreover impregnated with this proletarian class spirit. *The Soldier's Handbook* contained passages such as:

You must be among your comrades. Your leaders are brothers who are more experienced than you. In battle, in exercise, in the barracks, at work, you must obey them. As soon as you are out of the barracks you are absolutely free ... If someone asks you: how do you fight? Answer: I fight with the rifle, the bayonet, the machine gun and also with the truth which I address to those enemy soldiers who are workers and peasants so that they know that in reality I am not their enemy but their brother.[184]

Chamberlin also notes:

Intensive education propaganda was a feature of the organization of the Red Army. Amateur plays and communist lectures were given in the soldiers' clubs which were established wherever circumstances permitted. Vivid posters endeavoured to bring home to the workers and the peasants what would happen to them if the factory owner recovered his factory, the landlord took back his land and the old Tsarist officials and the Cossacks returned to rule.[185]

Among many other testimonies which attest to this class spirit, there is a fact cited by S.A. Smith. When at the end of December 1917, it was necessary to reduce employment in the munitions factories and the Putilov factories in Petrograd, the workers drew up lists of priorities. No party membership, even that of the Bolshevik Party, was taken into account.[186]

Hope

The historical meaning of the October Revolution was admirably expressed by Maxim Gorky, who was however a severe critic:

> Whoever honestly thinks that the irrepressible aspiration of humanity to freedom, to beauty and to an existence guided by reason is not a useless dream but a real force which, by itself, could create new ways of living – that it is in itself a lever which could change the world – every honest person must recognize the general significance of the activity of these consistent revolutionaries. The revolution should be conceived as a vast attempt to give shape to the guiding ideas and response envisaged by the chief thinkers of humanity ...
>
> Come with us, towards the new life for which we are working. Forward to liberty and beauty of existence.[187]

There is a further justification for the revolution, supplied by the stubbornly anti-Bolshevik author Leonard Shapiro, on the basis of his own memories as a young boy in Petrograd at the end of 1920:

> Life was extremely hard. There was near starvation level ... Yet my recollection, no doubt influenced by the adults around me, is one of enthusiasm and excitement. Life was new, hopeful, it was moving forward to some great future. In spite of the hardships and the brutality of the regime, the spirit of euphoria evoked by the fall of the monarchy in March 1917, was not yet dead.[188]

And David Mitchell notes:

Libertarians who like [Victor] Serge, meant business, could feel that Trotsky was right, that a bold, sometimes bloody, but always spirited attempt was being made to usher in the springtime of a new world.[189]

We cannot say more. History is a severe but fair judge; it simply has to be given the time to do its work. In 1810, indeed in 1815, there was no longer very much sympathy for the French Revolution of 1789, except in very limited revolutionary circles. But in 1848, not to mention 1889, the judgement had profoundly changed. We are convinced that it will be the same for the verdict made on the October Revolution.

Translated by Penny Duggan and Steve Bloom

NOTES

1   Ernest Mandel wrote 'October 1917: coup d'état or social revolution' after the collapse of the USSR, a process which commenced in 1989. It was first published in 1992 as Notebook for Study and Research no. 17/18, IIRE, Amsterdam.

2   See in particular David Mandel, *The Petrograd Workers and the Soviet Seizure of Power*, London, Palgrave Macmillan, 1984; R. Lorenz, *Die russiche Revolution 1917: Der Aufstand der Arbeiter, Auern and Soldaren*, Nymphenburger Verlagsangestalt, 1981; John Reed, *Ten Days which Shook the World*, New York, Dover, 2006; Steven Smith, *Red Petrograd, Revolution in the Factories, 1917-18*, Cambridge, Cambridge University Press, 1985; and obviously Leon Trotsky, *History of the Russian Revolution*, Chicago, Haymarket, 2007.

3   See as well as the books mentioned in the previous note: E.H. Carr, *The Russian Revolution from Lenin to Stalin 1917-1929*, London, Macmillan, 1979; G. Comte, *La revolution russe par les témoins*, Paris, La Table Ronde, 1963; Marc Ferro, *October 1917 - A Social History of the Russian Revolution*, London, Routledge, 1980; R. Kohn, *Die russiche Revolution in Augenzeubenberichten*, Munchen, 1977; Marcel Liebman, *Leninism under Lenin*, London, Merlin Press, 2010; Roy Medvedev, *The October Revolution*, New York, Columbia University Press, 1979. Among the analyses of the post-Stalinist Soviet Union, particularly in relation to the role of the working class: A.G. Egorova, *Rabacij Klas v Oktjabr' skoj revoljutcii*, Moscow, 1967; G.A. Trukan, *Rubacij kas v bobe za pobedu Improcenie sovetskoj v losil*, Moscow, 1975. For a pre-Stalinist Soviet work, see P.N. Amosov et al., *Oktjabrs koja Revolujutcija I Fabzavkomy*, Moscow, 1927.

4   Nicholas Sukhanov, *The Russian Revolution 1917*, Volume II, Oxford, OUP, 1955, pp. 528 et 579.

5   Oskar Anweller, *Les Soviets en Russie* 1905-1921, Paris, 1917, p. 231.

6   Marc Ferro, *Des Soviets au communisme bureaucratique*, Paris, Gallimard/Juliard, 1980, pp. 139-140, 164.

7   Dan, in Martov-Dan, *Geschichte der russischen Sozialdemokratie*, Berlin, 1926, pp. 300-301.

8   Beryl Williams, *The Russian Revolution 1917-1921*, London, Blackwell, 1987, pp. 38, 39.

9   Oskar Anweiler, op. cit. p. 274.

10   Alexandre Nektritch, *L'armée rouge assassinée*, Paris, Grasset, 1965.

11   On this see what remains the most impressive eyewitness account: Victor Serge, *Year one of the Russian Revolution,* Chicago, Haymarket, 2015. Many striking testimonies are reproduced in S.A. Smith op. cit.

12   S.A. Smith, op. cit., p. 233.

13   Thomas F. Remington, *Building Socialism in Soviet Russia,* University of Pittsburgh Press, 1984, p. 39.

14   Julius Braunthal, *Geschichte der internationale,* Vol. II, Berlin-Bonn, 1978, p. 113.

15   Lenin, *Collected Works,* Volume 26, Moscow/London, p. 489.

16   In trying to show that from the beginning there was a tendency to bureaucratization of the mass movement, Ferro in fact proves the contrary. At the second conference of factory committees, the main base of the Bolsheviks, the members elected directly by the workers were 93 per cent, the members designated by the trade unions, the parties and the soviets 7 per cent. At the third conference, that of October 1917, these percentages were respectively 88 per cent and 12 per cent (op. cit. p. 118). It is difficult to consider as 'bureaucratized' or 'becoming bureaucratized' a body of which 88 per cent of its members are factory workers, directly elected by their workmates.

17   Trotsky points out in his *History of the Russian Revolution* that the Bolshevik party named 14 people as its representatives in the presiding committee of the Second Congress of the Soviets, six of whom were opposed to the insurrection.

18   Lenin, *Collected Works,* Vol. 42, p. 289.

19   Quotation from the platform known as that of 'the 46'. See *Documents of the 1923 Opposition,* London, New Park, 1975, p. 7.

20   See in S.A. Smith (op. cit. pp. 58-60, 63-64, 85-86, 139 f.) the many initiatives of workers' control in the enterprises. The Red Guards themselves came from the militias established by these committees.

21   E.H. Carr, *The Bolshevik Revolution, Vol. I,* Penguin, London, 1950, p. 160:
The almost effortless success of the Petrograd coup of 25 October 1917 seemed to show that it indeed had behind it the vast majority of the population. The boast of the Bolsheviks that the revolution itself cost remarkably few lives and that most of these were lost in attempts of their opponents to wrest the victory from them when it had already been won was justified.
For the figures, W.H. Chamberlain, *The Russian Revolution, Volume I, 1917-18,* Princeton, Princeton University Press, 1952 (second edition), p. 85.

22   S.A. Smith (op. cit. pp. 150-156) correctly opposes the thesis of many Western historians that the Bolsheviks were congenitally opposed to institutionalized workers' control. But it is to be regretted that he himself makes concessions to this thesis on the basis of the 'black years' of 1920-1921. On this question he hardly mentions the later position of Lenin and Trotsky at the Third and Fourth Congresses of the Communist International and those of Trotsky, the Left Opposition and the Fourth International in favour of workers' control from 1923.

23   William H. Chamberlain, op. cit. p. 223.

24   Martov-Dan, op. cit. p. 304.

25   Lenin, *Collected works,* Vol. 26, p. 250.

26   David Mitchell, *1919 Red Mirage,* London, Jonathan Cape, 1970, p. 160.

27   Lenin, 'Report on Peace, 26 October', *Collected Works,* Vol. 26, pp. 251-252.

28   Ibid., pp. 253.

29   Obviously this does not mean that there were not deep going reasons for the war, particularly the rivalry between Britain and Germany in the division of the spoils arising from the dismantling of the Ottoman Empire and the domination of the Middle East, whose oil wealth began to be suspected. There was also the rivalry between Tsarist Russia and the German-Austro-Hungarian Coalition for domination over the Balkans.

30   John Riddell (ed.), *Lenin's Struggle for a Revolutionary International Documents: 1907-1916, The Preparatory Years*, New York, Monad Press, 1984, pp. 35.

31   Ibid., pp. 89-90.

32   David Mitchell, op. cit., p. 18.

33   Bavaria is German border region which meets Austria. This geographical position is important, as we will see later, because there was a simultaneous revolutionary upsurge in Bavaria, to the west of Austria, in Hungary on the east border of Austria and in Austria itself.

34   Mitchell, op. cit., p. 32.

35   Mitchell, op. cit., p. 171.

36   Gaetano Salvemini, *The Fascist Dictatorship in Italy*, New York, 1927, pp. 30-31.

37   Julius Braunthal, op. cit., p. 175.

38   Ibid., p. 186.

39   Ibid., p. 232.

40   Leon Trotsky, *The First Five Years of the Communist International, Vol. I*, New York, New Park Publications, 1945, p. 177.

41   R. Rosdolsky (*Die revolutionare Situation on Œsterreich im Jahre 1918 und die Politik der Sozialdemokraten – Der Œsterreische Januarstreik 1918*, Berlin, 1973) has shown on the basis of archive material how the Austrian social-democratic leaders maneuvered, in close association with the imperial government to first channel and then suffocate this strong general strike in Vienna, Otto Bauer, leader of the left wing of the Austrian SP, recognizes that the end of the general strike before it became a revolution was massively resisted within the proletariat.

42   For a presentation of this question, see the Introduction by Yvon Bourdet to a selection of texts by Max Adler, *Démocratie et conseils ouvriers*, Paris, Maspero, 1967. Yvon Bourdet essentially justifies the refusal of the Austro-Marxists to conquer power, under-estimating both the international revolutionary potential of the period and the seriousness of the short-term consequences of the political choice, while emphasizing that the failure of the Austro-Marxist project of a 'slow revolution' allowed the later rise of fascism.

43   During the general strike against the far-right putsch of Kapp/von Luttwitz, for the first and only time, even the reformist trade unions called for the constitution of a 'pure' workers' government composed of the SPD, the USPD and the trade unions.

44   The revolutionary wave even affected the faraway town of Seattle in the United States where a general strike broke out which took semi-soviet forms of organization.

45   The left Menshevik leader, Martov, tried after the event to give a 'sociological' interpretation of the international workers' radicalization which followed 1917. He stated (J. Martov, *Bolscevismo modiale*, Einaudi, Toronto, 1960; the Russian original dates from 1919) that is radicalization was essentially among the soldiers and unorganized workers, who took the standpoint of 'consumers' opposed to the standpoint of the 'producers', traditional social-democratic skilled and semi-skilled workers. This cannot be sustained in the light of the facts. Not only in Russia and Italy but also in Germany, the wage-workers opting for the Communist International were above all skilled and semi-skilled workers in the big factories, while the reformist received their main support from more or less unskilled workers from small and medium enterprises and the less developed sectors of the economy. The division in Germany between the USPD and SPD first, and then between left and right in the USPD (up to March 1921), and then in 1923 between the CP and social democracy, has exactly the same sociological basis. As for Russia, S.A. Smith and D.P. Koenker have shown that the Bolsheviks received all the support from the skilled workers of the big enterprises. See Kaiser (ed.), *The Workers' Revolution in Russia in 1917 - The view from*

Below, Cambridge, Cambridge University Press, 1987.

46   On 9 August 1920, a Council of Action was organized by the Parliamentary Committee of the British trade unions, the Executive Committee of the Labour Party and the Parliamentary group of this party with the goal of warning the government: that a war is being prepared by the Allies against Soviet Russia on the Polish question. It states that such a war would be an intolerable crime against humanity. It thus warns the government that all the industrial strength of the workers will be used to prevent the war... and that a Council of Action will be immediately formed to take all the measures necessary to implement this resolution.

47   Leon Trotsky, Ibid., p. 219.

48   Braunthal, op. cit., p. 232.

49   All these figures can be found in L. Trotsky, *1905,* Paris, 1969, pp. 34 et seq.

50   Teodor Shanin, *Russia as a 'Developing Society',* Vol. 1, London, 1985, pp. 98, 101.

51   Donald Mackenzie Wallace, *Russia on the Eve of War and Revolution,* (ed. Cyril E. Black), New York, Random House, 1961, p. 346.

52   Anatole Kopp, *Changer la vie, changer la ville,* Paris, UGE/10-18, 1975, p. 261.

53   James H. Baker, 'St. Petersburg and Moscow on the eve of the revolution', p. 50 in Daniel H. Kaiser, *The Workers' Revolution in Russia, 1917 - The View from Below,* Cambridge, Cambridge University Press, 1987.

54   M. Pokrovski, *Geschichte Russlands,* Leipzig, Hirschfeld, 1929, p. 275.

55   M. Pokrovski, *Russische Geschichte,* Berlin, Buchergilde Gutenberg, 1930, pp. 249-252.

56   S.A. Smith, op. cit., p. 13.

57   Edward Crankshaw, *The Shadow of the Winter Palace,* London, Penguin, 1978, p. 344.

58   Nicholas Riasanovsky, *Histoire de la Russie,* Paris, Robert Lafont, 1987, pp. 463-4.

59   Lionel Kochan and Richard Abraham, *The Making of Modern Russia,* London, Penguin, 1983, p. 223.

60   S.A. Smith, op. cit p. pp. 47-48.

61   Kochan-Abraham, op. cit., pp. 223-224, 196-197.

62   Richard Pipes, *The Russian Revolution,* New York, Vintage Books, 1990.

63   See in this respect, among other sources, Moynahan's fiercely anti-communist book *Comrades* (pp. 49-56).

64   Ibid., pp. 4, 7.

65   Chamberlain, op. cit., p. 143.

66   Jacques Sadoul, *Notes sur la révolution bolschevique,* Paris, La Sirène, 1920, p. 288.

67   Kerensky, a reformist, was the head of the Provisional Government. The political situation within the armed forces and the soldiers' desire for peace were such that they did not manage to organize effective military offensives against the German forces, for which he was strongly reproached by the right. We should remember that a large part of Poland had been incorporated into the Russian empire.

68   Jacques Sadoul, op. cit., p. 322.

69   Karl von Bothmer, *Mir Graf Mirbach in Moskan,* Tubingen, Osiander'sche Buchhandlung, 1922, p. 56.

70   Moynahan, op. cit., p. 34.

71   Moynahan, op. cit., p. 51.

72   A.R. Williams, *Durch die russische Revolution,* Berlin, 1922, pp. 233-234.

73   Bothmer, op. cit., p. 62.

74   *Illustrierte Geschichte der russischen Revolution,* Berlin, 1928, p. 539.

75   On 17 November 1918, 'Admiral Kolchak ... was declared 'Supreme Ruler of all Russia' ... The British and French representatives approved of the coup ... The Socialist Revolutionaries, in hiding in Ufa, disowned the Corps but were unable to do much more. Some of them made precarious peace with the Communists; the Socialist

Revolutionary members of the Directory, Zenzinov and Avksentiev, were forced to emigrate; and Chernov eventually escaped abroad.' Leonard Shapiro, *The Russian Revolution of 1917*, New York, Basic Books, 1984, p. 175.

76   The term 'White' is used to refer to the counter-revolutionaries, as opposed to the 'Reds'. A White general is thus a general from the counter-revolutionary army.

77   John Rees, 'In Defence of October', *International Socialism*, No 52, Autumn 1991.

78   Zvi Gitelman, *A Century of Ambivalence - The Jews of Russia and the Soviet Union*, New York, Yivo, 1988, pp. 99-106.

79   Bruce Lincoln, *Red Victory*, New York, Simon and Schuster, 1989, pp. 184-85.

80   Salo W. Baron, *The Russian Jew under Tsars and Soviets*, New York, Schocken Books, 1987, pp. 184-85.

81   Quoted in the book by P. Price, correspondent in Russia for the liberal British daily Manchester Guardian, *Die russische Revolution*, Hamburg, 1921, p. 456.

82   André Morizet, *Chez Lénine et Trotsky*, Paris, La Renaissance du Livre, 1922, p. 129.

83   Leonard Shapiro, op. cit., pp. 176, 184.

84   Chamberlin, op. cit., pp. 14, 19.

85   Contrary to what is generally thought, the Kerensky regime was very repressive, although in a less bloody fashion than the Ebert Noske regime. Just before the October revolution there were more than 10,000 Bolshevik prisoners in Kerensky's prisons, most of them soldiers.

86   Dan, op. cit., pp. 305-6.

87   Babeuf was a political figure in the French Revolution of 1789. On the left of democratic radicalism, he formulated a communist point of view. He was guillotined in 1797.

88   Marc Raeff, *Comprendre l'Ancien régime russe*, Paris, Editions du Seuil, 1982, p. 176.

89   I have dealt with these problems, including that of the specific nature of the Soviet Thermidor, in my latest book *Power and Money - A Marxist Theory of Bureaucracy*, London, Verso Press, 1992. The term 'Thermidor' originally indicated a political counter-revolution, during the French Revolution of 1789-1815. Starting in 1794 ('thermidor' was the name of a month in the revolutionary calendar) this counter-revolution dismantled the democratic and popular forms of organization created in the rising against the *Ancien régime*, without challenging its bourgeois character. By analogy, the 'Soviet Thermidor' refers to the Stalinist counter-revolution which eliminated socialist democracy and introduced a bureaucratic dictatorship without re-establishing capitalism in the USSR.

90   The historian Marc Ferro gives the following figures which illustrate the transformation of the CPSU: between the first half of 1924 and the second half of 1925, the number of workers among the candidate members of the party fell from 64.5 per cent to 43.8 per cent. Is this not eloquent? (M. Ferro, op. cit., p. 246). This was only an indication of even deeper transformations that were to come.

91   Leon Trotsky, *The Revolution Betrayed*, New York, Pioneer Publishers, 1945, p. 105.

92   Leon Trotsky, 'The Death Agony of Capitalism and the Tasks of the Fourth International' in *The Transitional Programme for Socialist Revolution*, New York, Pathfinder Press, 1973, pp. 145-6.

93   Rosa Luxemburg, *Rosa Luxemburg speaks*, New York, Pathfinder Press, 1970, p. 391. Rosa Luxemburg was a Polish revolutionary leader and Marxist theorist. She was very active in the German workers' movement. She was assassinated by reactionary forces in 1919.

94   Ibid., pp. 393-94. Kautsky was the best-known theorist and leader of German social democracy and the Second International. He became a reformist.

95   'War Communism' is the name given to the politico-economic policy applied during the Civil war (1918-1920). It was characterized by radical 'statization' and exceptional

measures such as forced requisition of food from the peasants.

96   Trotsky, after the failure of his premature proposal of the NEP for a while defended an alternative proposal of the 'militarization of labour'. This was unanimously approved by the Ninth Party Congress. The NEP – or New Economic Policy – was introduced in 1921. It represented a profound break with the command economy of War Communism, introducing a liberalization of the market and peasant production, encouraging a certain development of small private industry and proposing to accept foreign investment.

97   Roy Medvedev, *La Révolution d'octobre*, Paris, Albin Michel, 1973, p. 210. In March 1917, the garrison in Kronstadt, a port on the Baltic rebelled. The negotiations started with the regime. Having failed, the rebellion was crushed by the Red Army. I do not intend in this essay to analyse more deeply the problem posed by the Kronstadt revolt and its repression by the Soviet regime. It is my opinion, given that the Civil War had not yet ended, that we are dealing here with a question of political judgement, of tactics, and not of principle. The difficulty in the discussion lies in the fact that most of those who criticise the decision of the Bolsheviks base their judgement on specifically political assessments, the nature of the demands, the nature of the political forces present, etc. But, in our opinion, in a situation of civil war it is the nature of the social forces (and their 'logic') which is decisive. But on this question, the information available does not make it possible to reach definite conclusions. According to some people, particularly anarchists, the Kronstadt sailors were basically workers, like those of 1917-18. Their revolt was an extension of the workers' protest in Petrograd and elsewhere. So what was posed was the question of soviet, proletarian democracy. According to others, particularly Trotsky, the proletarian sailors of 1917-18 had largely disappeared. They had died at the front or had been absorbed by the Red Army or state apparatus. The 1921 sailors were the sons of middle or well-off peasants. Their revolt reflected the peasants' rejection of 'War communism' and the requisitions of wheat. It was necessary to negotiate with them but not to give in to a social dynamic, which could strengthen the counter-revolutionary threat that hung over Petrograd, a national and international threat, because the thawing of the ice floes could open the port of Kronstadt to the White fleet in the Baltic.

98   Chamberlin, op. cit., Vol. 2, p. 108.

99   L. Kritsman, *Die heroische Periode der grossen russichen Revolution,* Wien-Berlin, 1929.

100   Marx and Engels warned against this primitive 'communism of misery' which would only generalize poverty and lead inevitably to the renaissance of all the 'old shit'.

101   The Hohenzollern and the Habsburg: ruling families of Germany and Austro-Hungary.

102   Lenin, 'Speech at a joint meeting of the Petrograd Soviet of Workers' and Soldiers' Deputies and delegates from the fronts November 4 (17), 1917', *Collected Works,* Vol. 26, p. 295.

103   A.R. Williams, op. cit., pp. 112 ff.

104   Ibid., p. 126.

105   Morizet, op. cit., p. 429.

106   Chamberlin, op. cit., p. Vol. 2 p. 71.

107   George Leggett, *The Cheka: Lenin's political police,* Oxford, Clarendon, 1981, p. 171.

108   Stephen F. Cohen, 'Bolshevism and Stalinism' (in Robert C. Tucker, *Stalinism – Essays in Historical Interpretation,* New York, Norton, 1977) cites a large number of authors who have this judgement. The sources are too numerous to be reproduced here. We can simply note as examples; Merle Fainsod, Hannah Arendt, Robert V, Daniels, Micheal Karpovitch, Ulam, Barrington Moore, Arthur P. Mendel, Zbigniev Brzesinki, Robert H. McNeal, Alexander Solzhenitzyn. One quotation is enough to sum up their thinking. It comes from Merle Fainsod: 'Out of the totalitarian embryo would come

totalitarianism full-blown.'
109 Nikolai Valentinov, *Encounters with Lenin*, Oxford, Oxford University Press, 1968.
110 Lev Kamenev, *Lenins literarisches Erbe*, Hamburg, Hoym, 1924.
111 Mitchell, op. cit., pp. 152 and 156.
112 Ronald W. Clark, *Lenin, the Man Behind the Mask*, London, Faber and Faber, 1988, pp. 207, 239-240.
113 Ibid., p. 227.
114 Moynahan, op. cit., pp. 19-201 and Chamberlin op. cit., Vol. 1.
115 Moynahan, op. cit., p. 143.
116 Fritz Plattten (general secretary of the Swiss Socialist Party), *Lénine, de l' émigration en Russie*, Moscow, 1925.
117 Moyhahan, op. cit., p. 143.
118 Moyhanan, op. cit., p. 161.
119 In fact, it is almost forgotten that it was the Mensheviks and not Lenin who formulated the concept of democratic centralism.
120 Lenin, Preface to the Collection 'Twelve Years', *Collected works*, Vol. 13, p. 104.
121 Lenin, 'What is To Be Done?', *Collected Works*, Vol. 5, p. 477.
122 Claudio Sergio Ingerflom, *Le Citoyen impossible – Les racines russes du Léninisme*, Paris, Payot, 1988.
123 Lenin, 'Preface to the Collection 'Twelve Years', *Collected Works*. Vol. 13, pp. 103-104. In 1905-1907, Russia experienced an important wave of revolutionary struggles. This was a major experience for all the organizations, a test for the validity of their programmes and the quality of their structures. The later evolution of these organizations – like that of the Tsarist regime – was deeply marked by these key years. See in particular Teodor Shanin, *The Roots of Otherness: Russia's Turn of Century*, Volume 2, Russia, 1905-07, Revolution as a Moment of Truth, London, Macmillan, 1985.
124 Lenin, 'Our tasks and the Soviet of Workers' Deputies', *Collected Works*, Vol. 10, pp. 20. 'Black Hundreds' is the name usually given to the Association of Russian People, one of the main far-right organizations founded during the 1905-07 revolution to attack the revolutionary forces. These organizations also wanted to reverse the constitutional reforms made under the pressure of the events in October 1905.
125 Lenin, 'Appeal to the Party by Delegates to the Unity Congress who belonged to the former 'Bolshevik' group', *Collected works*, Vol. 10, pp. 314.
126 Lenin, 'Freedom to Critisize and Unity of Action', *Collected Works*, Vol. 10, p. 443.
127 Lenin, 'Let the Workers Decide', *Collected Works*, Vol. 10, pp. 502-03.
128 Louis Fischer, *Lénine*, Paris, Bourgeois, 1966.
129 It was at the time of the 'Moscow Trials' during the 1930s, that Stalin had the majority of the Communist Party Cadres condemned and liquidated, in order to consolidate the role of the bureaucracy.
130 Fischer, op. cit., p. 462.
131 Haimsom goes into the claimed relationship between the positions of Lenin and those of the populist/terrorist Thachev. But he does not say a word about the positions of Victor Adler and Karl Kautsky on the need to introduce of socialist consciousness from the outside, that is to say from the intellectuals, into the working class. It can however be demonstrated that this is the real origin of the so much criticized passage in 'What is to be done' (see Leopold Haimson, *The Russian Marxists and the Origins of Bolshevism*, Boston, Beacon, 1966, p. 16).
132 This episode, which is not very well-known, deserves to be explained in detail:
     When the Second Congress of the Soviets ratified the Bolshevik seizure of power on 25 October, it was broadly assumed even among the Bolsheviks that the new government would include representatives of all the soviet parties. Martov's proposal that the

congress should immediately consider the establishment of such a regime was seconded by Lunacharsky and passed by the delegates unanimously ...

The secondary Bolshevik leadership was strongly in favour of coalition. Nein was rebuffed in Petrograd, and the Moscow city organization, led by Rykov and Nogin, openly backed Zinoviev and Kamenev. Even the Moscow Regional Bureau, distinguished by its left-wing coloration, resolved to accept coalition if the Bolsheviks had a majority cabinet posts. On 2 November, the coalition issue began to come to a head when a resolution was passed by the Central Executive Committee insisting that Lenin and Trotsky be included in any cabinet and that at least half the portfolios go to the Bolsheviks. In opposition to this minimal condition, the whole Bolshevik Right voted against the party – Kamenev ... Zinoviev, almost half in the Council of People's Commissars (Rykov, Lunacharsky, Nogin, Miliutin, Teodorovich) and others including Lozovsky and the ex-Mensheviks Ryazanov and Yurenev ...

... On 4 November the crisis erupted. The Central Executive Committee was discussing the moves made by the government to muzzle the non-socialist press, and the representative of the Bolshevik Opposition, apprehensive over the possibility of dictatorial rule, joined in condemning restraints on newspapers which were not actually calling for rebellion. Larin... offered a resolution to this effect. It failed, twenty-two to thirty-one, with a number of abstentions ...

All five of Lenin's critics left the Central Committee – Zinoviev, Kamenev, Rykov, Miliutin, and Nogin. Collectively they declared '... Long live the government of the Soviet Parties!'...

Shliapnikov, the Commissar of Labour, joined this group in a declaration to the Central Executive Committee: 'We take the stand that it is necessary to form a socialist government of all parties in the soviet ...'

From Robert Daniels, *The Conscience of the Revolution*, Boulder, Westview, 1988 pp. 64-66.

133   See Thomas F. Remington, op. cit., on the running conflict and debate on the question of industrial administration inside the Bolshevik Party.

134   Cited in S. Farber, op. cit., p. 206.

135   A. F. Ilyin Zhenevsky, *The Bolsheviks in power – Reminiscences of the year 1918,* London, New Park, 1984, pp. 48-51.

136   Marcel Liebman, op. cit., P. LeBlanc, *Lenin and the Revolutionary party,* New Jersey, Humanities Press, 1990, S. Cohen, op. cit.

137   According to Leopold H. Haimson, Lening more than Marx and the 'orthodox Marxists', was convinced the 'passions' played a central role in individual and social choices. But he deeply distrusted these passions, including his own. This led to his ideological intransigence. He had been traumatized by some personal disappointments, particularly in his relations with Plekhanov, (op. cit., pp. 139, 186-187). But Haimson himself recognized that at the end of the Second Congress of the RSDLP, Lenin had adopted a very conciliating attitude to the Mensheviks, particularly Martov. He was ready to withdraw his proposals to change the editorial board of Iskra. It was Martov's intransigence and not Lenin's, which provoked the split. (Ibid., pp. 182-183).

138   It was the first sentence of his 'Note' of 30 December 1922, on the question of 'The question of nationalities or 'autonomization'' where he violently criticizes Stalin's policy on this question *(Collected Works,* Vol. 36, p. 605). On this period see Moshe Lewin, *Lenin's Last Struggle,* Ann Arbor, University of Michigan Press, 2005.

139   On the overwhelmingly working-class composition of the Bolshevik Party see *The Workers' Revolution in Russia – The view from Below,* op. cit.

140   Cited by P. Le Blanc, op. cit., pp. 60 and 126.

141   B. Williams, op. cit., pp. 28-29.

142   L. Trotsky, *History of the Russian Revolution,* New York, 1980, p. xix.

143   Nadeja Krupskaya, *Reminiscences of Lenin,* New York, International Publishers, 1970, pp. 124-125.

144   In March 1921 the Tenth Congress of the CP banned factions and reduced the internal democracy of the party. Moreover, the famous 'Lenin promotion' of 1924, a wave of recruitment which brought into the party hundreds of thousands of politically uneducated workers who were not forged in struggle, paradoxically contributed to the de-politicization of the party and proletariat.

145   Agnosticism considers that it is impossible to know what is reality beyond what is apparent (i.e. a doctrine which declares the unknowable inaccessible to human beings) or which considers any metaphysics as useless. Teleology is a set of speculations applied to the question of the purpose of the world, men or, here, of history. It thus tends to interpret the course of history starting from a supposed purpose.

146   The term 'mechanistic' designates a current of materialist thinking which excessively simplifies the interaction between different factors, by defining rigid chains of cause and effects which neglects in particular the historical dimension. Mechanism originates in the natural sciences of the eighteenth century which used extensively comparisons with machines and particularly with a watch mechanism. In a mechanistic conception of historical materialism, of Marxist theory, economic contradictions determine a rigid, unique and inevitable succession of societies (primitive communist, antique slave, feudal, capitalist, socialist). The (more authentic) dialectical conception of historical materialism obviously integrates socio-economic factors and constraints. But it also takes into account the weight of other factors (for example: states, cultures, ideologies, traditions of struggle). In particular it emphasizes the active role of socio-political struggles, the class struggle. This is what makes it possible to understand that the course of history is determined by the interaction between these different factors and not simply the 'iron logic' of economic contradictions.

147   Charles Darwin was an English naturalist and biologist of the nineteenth century, known for his work on the evolution of living species through the process of natural selection. His theories, 'Darwinism', are very rich but have sometimes been interpreted in a very simplistic way (with Neo-Darwinism) and incorrectly transposed into the field of sociology.

148   Rosa Luxemburg, 'The Russian Revolution' in op. cit., 375 and pp. 395.

149   The January 1919 Spartakist uprising in Germany, the attempt led by Bettelheim to take power in Vienna, Austria a little later, and above all the 'March 1921 Action' in Germany as well as the Bulgarian CP's coup against Stambulinsky, fall into this category. Auguste Blanqui, a very important French revolutionary in the nineteenth century, gave his name to 'Blanquism', considered as the desire to conquer power basing oneself on an active minority and using conspiratorial methods.

150   John Rees, 'In Defence of October' in *International Socialism,* No 52.

151   Samuel Farber, *Before Stalinism,* Cambridge, Polity Press, 1990, pp. 159-62.

152   The resolution 'Socialist Democracy and the Dictatorship of the Proletariat' was first presented at the 11th World Congress of the Fourth International in 1979. Adopted first by an indicative vote, it was re-discussed, amended and finally adopted at the 12th World Congress in January 1985. Available online at http://www.internationalviewpoint.org/spip.php?article921.

153   *The Times,* 29 November 1991. A white-collar worker is an office worker, a blue-collar worker is a manual worker.

154   *Sunday Times Magazine,* 1 December 1991.

155   Dan, op. cit., p. 298.

156   Pierre Broué, *Révolution en Allemagne (1917-1923),* Paris, Editions de Minuit, 1971,

publishes a very extensive bibliography of the German Revolution 1918-1919. Here we will only mention the memoirs of Richard Muller, leader of the *Obleute* revolutionaries of Berlin; the memoires of Noske, of Philip ScheIbid.ann, of Severing, of General Groener, the books of Benoist Méchin, Peter Von Oertzen, Paul Frolich, Paul Levi, Franz Borkenau (see bibliography for titles).

157   Pierre Broué, op. cit., p. 173.

158   For the manoeuvres and lies in regard to the population, Ebert denied that he wanted to bring the Army troops into Berlin (the accusation made by the USPD), when he was faced with the first congress of the workers' and soldiers' councils. He said that there was only a question of the troops being brought back from the front which were going to cross Berlin. In fact he really had brought into Berlin the troops of the ten divisions led by General Lequis.

159   Gustav Noske, *Von Kiel bis Kapp*, Berlin, 1920.

160   Cited by Broué, op. cit., p. 273. The Spartakists were the German revolutionary movement.

161   For readers who were not brought up in Roman Catholicism, statements by the Pope ex cathedra (by virtue of his office) are supposed to be infallible, which says a lot about the democratic character of the very Christian Catholic Church.

162   Marx and Engels. 'A. A. Bebel, W. Liebknecht, W. Bracke et autres, Leipzig', *Correspondance*, Paris/Moscou, 1981, pp. 323-324.

163   This is one of Lenin's argument in his polemic with Kautsky: 'The proletarian revolution and the renegade Kautsky', *Collected Works*, Volume 28. Kautsky 's work was published as *The Dictatorship of the Proletariat*, Ann Arbor, University of Michigan Press, 1964. In the section of this text on Russia, Kautsky does not say anything about the dangers of counter-revolution!

164   On the German 'elites' left in place by social democracy, and their role in the rise of Nazism see: Arthur Rosenberg, *Entstehung und Geschichte der Weimarer Republik;* Evelyn Anderson, *Hammer oder Amboss*. The Weimar Republic was established in Germany on November 9, 19 18, after the abdication of Wilhelm II, with the participation of many social democrats. The government, which included the social democrats, sent troops in to Saxony to oust a left social-democrat government which enjoyed broad popular support (op. cit., pp. 774-775). After having repressed the German revolution, this regime turned out to be incapable to dealing with the social and economic crisis. In 1933, it called Hitler to power, who then gradually established the Nazi dictatorship.

165   *The Times,* 17 November 1925.

166   Karl von Bothmer, op. cit., pp. 102, 131, 132.

167   B. Williams, op. cit., p. 80.

168   Ibid., p. 94.

169   André Morizet, op. cit., p. 179.

170   N. Stone, *Sunday Times,* 5 January 1991.

171   V. P. Tomin, *Uroven' obrazovanniya naseleniya SSE,* Moscow, 1981.

172   Karl von Bothmer, op. cit., p. 47.

173   Alfons Goldschmidt, *Moscow, 1920,* Berlin, 1920.

174   It was Paquet who made the well-known and ignoble accusation that the Soviet regime had 'socialized women'. He cited an alleged decree by the anarchists of Saratov, which they immediately denounced as a gross provocation.

175   Alfons Paquet, *Der Geist der russischen Revolution,* Munich, 1920, p. 69.

176   Morizet, op. cit., pp. 194-5.

177   David Mitchell, op. cit., p. 156.

178   B. Williams, op. cit., pp. 92-93.

179   Alfons Paquet, op. cit., pp. 40, 51-2.
180   Alfons Goldschmidt, op. cit., p. 20.
181   Alfons Paquet, *Der Geist der russischen Revolution,* op. cit., p. 75.
182   William G. Rosenberg, 'Russian Labor and Bolshevik power, Social dimensions of protest in Petrograd after October', in *The Workers Revolution in Russia 1917 – The view from Below,* op. cit., p. 98 f.
183   See in particular Ilyin Zheneysky, op. cit., pp. 32-33 and A. Morizet.
184   Alfons Morizet, op. cit., p. 111.
185   William H. Chamberlin, op. cit., Vol. II, p. 34.
186   S. A. Smith, *Red Petrograd,* op. cit., pp. 243-4.
187   Quoted in A. R. Williams, pp. 242-3.
188   Leonard Shapiro, op. cit., p. 219.
189   David Mitchell op. cit., p. 166.

ECONOMIC POWER AND FACTORY COMMITTEES IN THE RUSSIAN REVOLUTION[1]

David Mandel

The movement for workers' control in Russia arose in the wake of the February Revolution and played a central role in the workers' subsequent radicalization leading to the soviet seizure of power in October. Workers' control had not figured in the programmes of any of the socialist parties before the February Revolution. Although it was commonly held that socialism would put an end to authoritarian management, Russia's socialist parties, Bolsheviks included, had considered that the coming revolution would be 'bourgeois-democratic' and not go beyond the bounds of a capitalist democracy. Although it would usher in significant social reform, including the eight-hour day and land redistribution, it would not fundamentally threaten the economic power of the bourgeoisie.

The Bolshevik party reoriented itself in late April 1917 following Lenin's[2] return from exile, when it began calling for the transfer of power from the liberal-dominated Provisional Government to the soviets of workers', soldiers' and peasants' deputies. But the party remained vague about the social programme of future soviet power. In his April Theses Lenin wrote: 'It is not our *immediate* task to 'introduce' socialism, but only to bring social production and the distribution of products at once under the *control* of the Soviets of Workers' Deputies.'[3] The Russian word *kontrol'*[4] implies oversight or regulation, as distinct from administration, and, as such, the formulation could well have been part of a reformist programme (although a quite radical one) of state regulation of a capitalist economy. Nikolai Sukhanov, a Menshevik-Internationalist[5] member of the Petrograd Soviet's Economic Department, observed that, to the extent the Bolsheviks had an economic programme at all, it did not go beyond the Soviet's proposal of May 1917, when it was still dominated by the moderate socialists. In his view, what the Bolsheviks did have was 'in essence far from socialism. [...] True, control was a cardinal point at all workers' meetings. But this 'socialism' was still very timid and modest. It pointed in a different direction but did not go farther than the right-wing Menshevik Groman, with his 'regulation' and 'organization' of the economy and labour.'[6]

Yakov Sverdlov, a member of the Bolshevik leadership, admitted to the party's Petrograd Committee in late September that 'there is insufficient clarification of the economic question, [...] and this is the cause of many complications.' He explained that everyone was too busy with current problems to work on the economic programme. But the fundamental reason was that the Bolsheviks had not yet decided what that programme would be. At the First All-Russian Conference of Factory Committees, just a week before the October Revolution, a Menshevik delegate from Saratov in central Russia complained: 'In order to decide correctly the question of workers' control of production we have to clarify once and for all for ourselves whether the Russian Revolution is a social revolution or not. We constantly pose this fundamental question to the Bolsheviks, but they never give us a serious answer. We say that our revolution is not social but political with a social leavening, so to speak: in it, questions of enormous social significance are posed.'[7] An anarchist delegate from the Schlusselburg Powder Factory outside of Petrograd was equally definite: 'We are living through a social revolution.'[8] But Mykola Skrypnik, a Bolshevik member of Petrograd's Central Council of Factory Committees, would not be pinned down: 'Workers' control is not socialism. It is only one of the transitional measures that bring us nearer to socialism.'[9]

In fact, as Marxists, the Bolsheviks could not be more specific. They recognized that Russia, a poor, overwhelmingly peasant society, albeit with a concentrated and militant working class, lacked the necessary political and economic prerequisites for socialism. However, the world war had created the conditions and the need for the immediate overthrow of capitalism, not only in the developed capitalist countries, but in Russia, too. The generalized crisis meant that Russia's workers and poor peasants could realistically hope for support from socialist revolutions in the developed West. Accordingly, the social content of Russia's revolution, indeed its very survival, depended on the nature and timing of events abroad. Hence the tentative formulation.

This was the theoretical side of the matter. But in the end, it was concrete, practical exigencies that drove the revolution forward. The Bolsheviks' economic programme before October amounted to a form of dual power: the workers' and peasants' government, supported by the factory committees, would 'control' (monitor, oversee, regulate) the capitalists; and the latter would continue to manage their enterprises. But just as dual power in the political sphere, established by the February Revolution, soon proved untenable in face of the propertied classes' refusal to be 'controlled' by the soviets, which they, in fact, wanted to crush under a military dictatorship, so too in the economic sphere dual power would prove illusory. After all, the economic power of the bourgeoisie was its last and most basic line of defence.

Contemporary bourgeois commentators, the moderate socialists, many trade union leaders, including some Bolshevik trade unionists, and later Western historians have portrayed the movement for workers' control as anarchist in inspiration: a spontaneous, rather mindless, revolt aimed at group takeover of the factories.[10] Even historians sympathetic to workers' control often portray the factory committees as an essentially libertarian movement for industrial democracy and so in conflict with central planning and regulation.[11] The reality was, however, more complex.

Of course, it was natural for anarchists to be attracted to the factory committees. But it was, in fact, the Bolsheviks who dominated the committees from the outset almost everywhere, well before they won majorities in the soviets. Anarchist resolutions that skirted the issue of political power never gathered more than a handful of votes at the factory-committee conferences, while the Bolshevik position in favour soviet power and state economic regulation garnered large majorities.

The factory committees were about workers' economic power. But when first formed in the wake of the February Revolution, their goals, at least in private enterprises, did not go much beyond the aspirations of militant trade unions. What distinguished them, as well as analogous organizations in other countries, from trade unions, was, first of all, the fact that they were elected by all the non-managerial personnel of the given enterprise; whereas union membership was usually individual and voluntary. But more important was their ideological orientation: in contrast to most trade unions, even those linked to socialist parties, they did not consider capital's managerial prerogatives either legitimate or inevitable. If they tolerated them, it was because the balance of forces (linked to the level of economic development and so also to workers' managerial capacities) did not yet allow them to go farther.[12] Historically, factory councils have arisen in periods of heightened mobilization and radicalization, very often in opposition to conservative union leadership.[13]

In what follows, I will trace the evolution of the factory committee movement in Russia through its major stages in 1917 and the first part of 1918, with a particular focus on Petrograd, the capital and militant centre of the workers' movement.[14] My basic argument is that the progressive radicalization of the factory committees, while fundamentally a defensive response to the threat to workers' jobs, and thereby also to the revolution, was made possible, and to some degree encouraged, by the committees' strategic view of the power of capitalist management as provisional and conditional. A final section will briefly discuss the fate of the factory committees during the civil war.

The February Revolution and the factory committees

The general strike in Petrograd that soon drew in the garrison to become the February Revolution was at the same time a political mobilization against the autocracy and an economic strike directed at capital. As such, it was in direct continuity with the pre-war labour movement, in which economic and political demands had been inextricably intertwined.[15] After the Tsar's abdication, the workers returned to their factories only long enough to formulate economic demands and to vote to remain on strike until they were won. Most workers ignored the appeal of the Soviet, then led by the moderate socialists (Mensheviks and Socialist Revolutionaries), to resume work on 7 March, since they had not yet won the eight-hour day and wages 'befitting a worker and free citizen.'[16] The minority who did resume work on that date had already introduced the eight-hour day without consulting management.

Besides better wages and shorter hours, the workers expected the democratic revolution to usher in a 'constitutional regime' to the factories.[17] By that they meant an end to the autocratic despotism that had characterized factory administration under the Tsar. A binding convention adopted in 1912 by the St. Petersburg Society of Factory and Mill Owners had ruled out even the minimal shop-level representation allowed by law and rejected any interference by workers' organizations in matters of wages, conditions, hiring and firing, and the factories' internal regime.[18] The outbreak of war had only added new repressive measures to the industrialists' arsenal against the workers, including the loss of military deferral.

When work finally did resume after the February Revolution, one of the workers' first actions was to purge management of its most oppressive members, sometimes carting them out of the gates in wheelbarrows with a sack over their heads, a mark of particular opprobrium. In this, as well as in the workers' independent introduction of the eight-hour day (a phenomenon limited mostly to Petrograd[19]), one has already a glimpse of the workers' conditional attitude towards capital's managerial power, an attitude supported by the sense that they had made the revolution, not the bourgeoisie, whose fear of the masses paralyzed their opposition to the autocracy.

But the central element of the 'constitutional regime' was workers' collective representation in the form of elected factory committees, whose task it was to 'supervise' (*vedat'*) the 'internal regime.' At the Radiotelegraph Factory, for example, the general assembly instructed its committee to work out rules and norms regarding the length of the workday, the minimum wage, the organization of medical care, management of the sick fund (based on a 1912 law), the establishment of a mutual-aid fund, the hiring and firing of workers[20], conflict resolution, labour discipline, rest time, the factory's physical security, the provision of food[21], and the establishment of a permanent, elected factory committee.[22] This was a broad spectrum of activities, some of which were obviously meant to be negotiated with management. But there was no intention here of challenging the administration's basic prerogatives to manage the technical and economic sides of production. Nor did this occur. In the private factories, the demand for 'workers' control,' let alone workers' management, was not heard at this time.

All the same, the inclusion in the committees' purview of protection of the factories' physical integrity and their citing of technical incompetence (though never on its own) as justification for purging certain managers both point to the workers' new sense of responsibility toward production. Still embryonic, it would evolve into more radical positions, as workers saw their jobs and revolution come under threat. N. Kutler, a prominent industrialist and a leader of the Kadet (liberal) party, was not alone in observing a new 'enthusiasm for work' in the first weeks after the revolution.[23] Related to this was a changed attitude to the war, as most workers now felt they had something to defend - their revolution. (The workers' 'revolutionary defensism' would, however, be short-lived, as they soon realized the Provisional Government had no intention of seeking a democratic peace.)

In state-owned plants, on the other hand, workers initially adopted a more radical position, based on the view that workers in a democratic state should participate in the management of the state's enterprises.[24] Added to this was the fact that the top administrators in state plants held military rank and many of them had fled during the revolution. Similar attitudes were in evidence on the predominantly state-owned railroads and at the post and telegraph.[25] But this did not last long. In the state factories the workers soon retreated from claims to an active role in management. A resolution of the conference of factory committees of state plants on 15 April claimed broad rights of control (monitoring), including access to information and documents and the right to dismiss administrators 'who cannot assure normal relations with the workers.' But, 'not wishing to assume responsibility for the technical and administrative organization of production in the given circumstances until the full socialization of the economy, the representatives of the general factory committee have only a consultative voice in management.'[26] The chairman of the committee of the Admiralty shipbuilding factory explained this retreat by the concern not to undermine efficiency, given the complexity of managing the factory and to the workers' inexperience. But his committee did claim the right of control, including the right to demand the removal of managerial staff through arbitration.[27] Between February and October the committees of state factories were able to wield considerably more power than those in the private sector, where workers met strong resistance to the demand for control that arose in the late spring.[28] There were also reports of increased productivity after February in the state sector. At a conference of factories of the Artillery Authority in March the worker delegate even accused the Authority of mismanagement and call for its abolition.[29]

Fears of sabotage and emergence of the demand for workers' control

The more enlightened liberal politicians urged the industrialists not to fear the workers' social demands, now that democracy had been won. The owners should rather make concessions to the workers precisely in order to steer their demands in the appropriate direction and avoid social revolution that was so feared by the bourgeoisie. The industrialists appeared at first to heed this advice. But, in reality, they considered their concessions, and especially the eight-hour day and the recognition of the factory committees, particularly in the area of hiring and firing of workers, as merely temporary until the correlation of class forces allowed them to recoup their losses.

A few weeks only after the victorious revolution, the bourgeois (that is, non-socialist) press began to prepare the ground for such a counter-offensive by launching a campaign against the workers' alleged egoism that, so it was claimed, was harming production for the valiant army. The campaign was clearly aimed at the soldiers in the hope of driving a wedge between them and the workers, whose coalition had made possible the February Revolution. The campaign failed, as the workers invited the soldiers to send delegations to the factories to inspect the situation for themselves. On the other hand, it put an abrupt end to illusions workers had nurtured in the weeks after the revolution about national unity, illusions that had been fostered by the relative ease of the revolution's victory.

It was in the course of this press campaign that workers began to question the explanations offered by the factory management (that most often cited supply problems) for productive capacity standing idle. On 20 March, a delegate to the Petrograd Soviet from the Metallicheskii factory proposed the election of a commission consisting of delegates from the factories 'with a view to control': the commission would conduct inspections to verify the reasons offered by management 'in order to make sure there are no abuses.'[30] Here was already a call to control, in the sense of monitoring, to be carried out by the Soviet.

As the weeks passed, the workers' suspicions grew stronger. In early May, the Menshevik-Internationalist paper observed 'cutbacks in production in a whole series of plants. So far this phenomenon has been limited to medium and small enterprises. But all the same it is beginning to worry workers.'[31] The bourgeois press, on its part, did nothing to reassure the workers. 'Two or three weeks will pass,' wrote the Kadet (liberal party) daily, 'and the factories will start closing one after the other.'[32] Even the newspaper of Menshevik-defencists, whose leaders were now part of a coalition government with the liberals, wrote of an 'Italian' (slowdown) strike, being conducted by the industrialists. It portrayed this as a flanking movement in preparation for an offensive: 'We have before us a different means of struggle – the hidden lockout. At the Labour Department of the Soviet [...], we encounter daily facts that confirm the existence of a definite plan among the industrialists.'[33]

The word *lokaut* was laden with bitter memories for the workers. In only the six months preceding the outbreak of war, Petrograd's workers had been treated to no less than three coordinated lockouts, in the course of which a total of 300,000 had been fired.[34] Lockouts occurred even during the war. Many remembered that the general lockouts of November and December 1905 had dealt a decisive blow to Russia's first revolution.

And as if to confirm the workers' suspicions, the industrialists rejected out of hand proposals for strengthening the state's role in regulating the economy, a policy they themselves had promoted before the revolution to shore up the economy that was cracking under the strain of the prolonged war and tsarist mismanagement. Now, however, they blamed industry's problems exclusively on the workers' 'inordinate demands.' In mid-May, the Petrograd Soviet, which was still controlled by the moderate socialists (Menshevik-Defensists and Socialist Revolutionaries), adopted a rather modest plan for state economic regulation that had been prepared by its economic commission. Two days later, the Minister of Trade and Industry, A.I. Konovalov, an industrialist who was considered to be on the left flank of his class, resigned, citing specifically the Soviet's plan for economic regulation and the excessive demands of the Left. He warned ominously that 'if in the near future a sobering of minds does not occur, we will witness the closing of tens and hundreds of enterprises.'[35]

Opposition to state regulation of the economy was also the leitmotif of the All-Russian Congress of Representatives of Trade and Industry in early June.[36] P. P. Ryabushinskii, another 'left-wing' capitalist, explained that state regulation was possible in the West because there the state was independent and in full control. But in Russia such regulation was out of the question, as the government itself was 'under control' (of the soviets.)[37] Implicit was the fear that economic regulation would turn against the industrialists' interests.

On 19 May, the Petrograd Committee of the Bolshevik party issued for the first time an appeal for workers to establish commissions in the factories with a view to 'control', in the Russian sense of monitoring management's activities. The wording of the appeal makes clear that the party was responding to the workers' own initiatives: 'In response to a series of declarations from factory committees on the need for control and its establishment, it was decided to recommend to comrade workers to create control commission in the enterprises from representatives of the workers.'[38]

The movement for workers' control thus originated 'from below.' It was a response to perceived threats to production and not inspired by anarchist ideals or any other ideological motivations. The committee of the Putilov factory, Russia's largest industrial enterprise explained that:

> When our factory committee arose, it was handed neither a programme of action nor a charter to guide its activity. As the functions of the committee developed, its own practical measures became the basis for its guiding principles. In this way, the factory committee had the best teacher – life itself.[39]

The conflict at the Langezipen machine-building factory[40] illustrates the motives behind the push for workers' control. On 27 April, the factory committee posted guards at the gates and refused to allow managerial personnel, including the director, to leave before the end of their workday. According to the province's Senior Factory Inspector, the workers suspected that the administration was purposely holding back production.[41] A joint commission made up of representatives of the Petrograd Soviet and of the employers' association failed to resolve the dispute. Then on 2 June, the director announced that the factory would close, citing losses of the value of ten million roubles incurred on defence contracts that were the result of rising costs and a decline of two thirds in output as a result of the eight-hour day. He cited a 50 per cent decline in labour productivity, in addition to problems obtaining fuel and material.

The workers turned for help to the Central Soviet of Factory Committees, recently elected at citywide conference of factory committees, held on 30 May–3 June. The Central Soviet's investigation uncovered a long and suspicious chain of stock transfers. Suddenly, the director announced that he had 'by chance' come up with 450,000 roubles, loaned from an acquaintance, and that production could go ahead at full steam.[42] But in the meanwhile, the workers had decided to set up control. On 5 June, the factory committee announced that no goods or materials could leave the factory without its authorization; that its orders were binding on the personnel; that management's orders required its validation; and that no documents could be destroyed without first being reviewing by the committee.[43]

In claiming such powers, this committee was clearly going beyond the initial conception of workers' control as monitoring. (It is not clear how successful the committee was in exercising its claimed powers.) But the defensive nature of its motivation is still evident. In a declaration from 5 June, it explained that the workers had been 'placed before the necessity' of adopting these measures because of the administration's decision to shut the factory, by its refusal to respect an arbitration decision concerning the salaries of the office personnel, and by its refusal to recognize the workers' control commission.

Izvestiya, the newspaper of the Soviet, which was controlled by the moderate socialists, described this conflict as characteristic of a whole series of announcements of factory closures that were reaching the Central Soviet of factory committees. Most of these reports gave as reasons financial losses incurred to the enterprise and a lack of funds. 'But,' continued the paper, at the first attempt of the workers' organizations to verify the reasons offered by the entrepreneurs, they very often uncover the most complex and crafty machinations aimed at a lockout by the capitalists.'[44] (After the October Revolution the same moderate socialists would claim that the Bolsheviks' claims of economic sabotage were mere inventions.)

Nor was this limited to Petrograd. In the textile centre of Ivanovo-Voznesensk, the 'Russian Manchester', several mills did not reopen after the Easter holidays. The owners cited supply problems. But when the local soviet, which wielded very significant power in this working-class town, decided that the idle workers would receive full wages and established an industrial control commission, the owners immediately announced the reopening of the mills.[45]

Workers' control and political power

The idea to convene a citywide conference of factory committees at the end of May came from the realization that the balance of power in individual factories, as well as the committees' lack of expertise, did not allow the workers to establish effective control over management. Meanwhile, the threat of a general industrial collapse was becoming increasingly real. V.M. Levin, a left SR member of the conference's organizing committee, opened the conference with the following words:

> Whether they want to or not, the factory committees have to intervene in the economic life of their factories – otherwise they will shut down. All the factories in Petrograd are in crisis. But management has not been active in securing the supply of materials and fuel. The workers have to be become active where the industrialists aren't. [...] This is an entirely new task that the revolution has placed before us. The theoretical task of the conference is to define how to accomplish that. The practical task is to create a powerful centre of factory committees to lead and generate the maximum of working-class influence in an economy that has been completely ruined by the imperialist war and by the rapacious banditry of the big bourgeoisie.[46]

Choosing to ignore the industrialists' opposition to state regulation that had effectively paralyzed his government's action in the area of economic regulation, the right-wing Menshevik Minister of Labour, Matvey Skobelev, reminded the conference that Russia was experiencing a bourgeois revolution and that regulation of industry was not the concern of any single class, but of the state.[47] To this the delegate from the 1886 Electric Lighting Company replied:

> To us workers, it is clear that the bourgeoisie, by undermining production, is [...] very skilfully, at first glance imperceptibly, organizing a counterrevolution. [...] Sabotage in the Donbass, in the textile industry, in a whole series of Petrograd factories, requires the organized intervention of the working class in the form of the immediate establishment of workers' control. [...] Otherwise, all the workers' organizations will be destroyed. And unemployed, hungry workers don't think about organization. [...] It is naive to think the Provisional Government will set up control over its own capitalists. All the more should we strive for control with representatives of workers and workers' organizations in the factories and locally. [...] Life itself has put forth the demand for workers'

control of production, but it will be realized fully not under a bourgeois government but under a government of revolutionary democracy [i.e. of representatives of the workers and peasants]. Until then, the factory committees will have a great role to play in carrying out workers' control and saving the country.[48]

The conference adopted two resolutions by overwhelming majorities. The first called for a two-thirds majority of worker representatives in all-important state economic bodies and for the right of the workers' committees, soviets and trade unions to participate in control in the factories. This control should 'gradually and carefully, but without undue delay,' develop into full regulation of production and distribution by workers.[49] The other resolution called for the transfer of state power to the soviets. This was the first city-wide assembly of worker delegate to adopt that demand. Levin explained the relationship between workers' control and the demand for soviet power: 'The factory committees will play a great role, but not without the support of truly revolutionary state power. And the government of revolutionary Russia will find itself in a hopeless situation unless it can rely on authoritative workers' shop-floor organizations.'[50]

Where was all this leading? 'No one knows how this revolution will end up,' continued Levin, 'At the least, it will deprive capital of some of its rights; at the most, who can say whether from a Russian revolution it will not become a world revolution.'[51] Only some anarchist delegates called for the workers to take over the factories. To this a Bolshevik delegate answered: 'Control is not yet socialism, nor even taking of production into our hands. But it already goes beyond the bourgeois framework. [...] Having taken power into our hands, we should direct capitalism along a path such that it will outlive itself. [...] Having taken control into our hands, we will learn in a practical way to work actively in production and we will direct it toward socialist production in an organized manner.'[52]

Capital's response

This gradualist approach to the question of power in the factories was based upon the assumption that the industrialists would continue to manage their factories under the 'control' of the workers. But this was far from evident. In the aftermath of the July Days[53], when the moderate socialists in the coalition government sanctioned repressive measures against workers and the left-wing parties, the industrialists, sensing the shift in correlation of class forces, became more aggressive. On the economic front, with the government's support, they forbade factory committees from meeting during work hours and refused to pay wages to their members or to allow them any say in the area of hiring and dismissal. They also refused access to their factories to representatives of the Central Soviet of factory committees.[54]

They became more brazen in openly brandishing the spectre of industrial collapse. On 3 August, Ryabushinksii, in a speech to the Congress of Commerce and Industry that subsequently became notorious among workers, reaffirmed his rejection of state economic regulation. The revolution, he declared, was 'bourgeois,' and those at the helm of the state should act accordingly. The soviets were driving the country into an abyss, and, 'unfortunately, the long bony hand of hunger and national impoverishment will have to seize the false friends of the people by the throat, the members of the various soviets and committees, before they come to their senses.'[55] This speech drew a 'thunder of applause' from the assembled captains of industry. They leaped to their feet to hail the orator. But the workers considered the speech an open admission that a hidden lockout was in progress,[56] a view supported by the increasing number of announcements, now coming even from larger factories, of impending cuts to production and even closures.[57]

Parallel to this was the ominous rise to prominence of General Kornilov, newly appointed commander-in-chief of the armed forces. Kornilov was enthusiastically welcomed among the propertied classes as the saviour of Russia. In accepting his command, the Cossack general demanded extension of the death penalty to the rear (in June it had been restored at the front)[58] as well as complete freedom of action. He declared himself responsible solely to his 'own conscience and to the entire people.'[59] At the end of August, with the barely concealed support of the liberals, whose ministers had only just resigned from the coalition government, Kornilov marched on Petrograd in the avowed aim of crushing the workers' organizations and establishing a military dictatorship. But his troops melted on the way route thanks to sabotage by of railroad workers and the influence of worker-agitators who rushed out from Petrograd to meet the troops.

But Kornilov's defeat only strengthened the industrialists' aggressiveness in the factories - their economic power was their last line of defence. In a note from early September, the Committee of United Industry demanded from the government a guarantee of their exclusive power over hiring and firing; their right to discipline workers up to and including dismissal; a complete prohibition of any interference in management by workers' organizations; elimination of any obligation of the owners to the workers' organizations; and the dismissal of workers whose productivity fell below the previous year's level. And the note concluded: 'Without these measures to influence the worker masses, industry is threatened with a complete shutdown.'[60]

Given the defensive nature of workers' control and the employers' resistance to it, that had the government's backing, a serious struggle for workers' control did not develop in all, or even most, factories prior to the October insurrection. It developed where workers perceived the imminent threat of mass layoffs or closure. At the Rozenkrantz copper-rolling mill, for example, it was only in September that the factory took decisive steps in response to 'attempts by the administration to sabotage, and with the acting Ministry of Trade and Industry himself threatening to come and shut down the factory.'[61]

But even when so provoked, effective control in the private factories very often eluded the committees. On the eve of the October insurrection, a delegate from the Putilov shipyards told a conference of factory committees that:

We know how often the factory committees turn out to be helpless – they know how to prevent the stoppage of production in the factories but they have no possibility of intervening. [...] Both private and state administrations are sabotaging production and cite [the decisions of] the Society of Factory and Mill Owners. They [the owners] are still strong. The conference must first of all point out the obstacles that prevent people of action from saving the country. These obstacles are being put before us by the bourgeois government. Only reorganization of state power can make it possible to develop our activity.[62]

Moving beyond 'control': the issue of class collaboration

The most common form of incursion into managerial prerogatives was, in fact, not 'control' but the committees' efforts to find fuel and raw materials for their factories, and sometimes also orders and financing. Even before their first conference of factory committees at the end of May, the committees had organized a meeting on supply problems. Some sent delegations as far away the Donbass coalfields in eastern Ukraine.[63] A delegate to the conference observed:

Strangely, after the first weeks of the Revolution,', 'in one plant after the other, there was no fuel, no raw materials, no money. More important, management took no steps to procure what was needed. Everyone saw this as an Italian strike. The factory committees sent representatives all over in search of fuel – to other factory committees, to railroad junctions, warehouses, etc. [... and] as a result of their activity, oil, coal, money, orders were found.[64]

Some committees went farther. At the Vulkan machine-building factory, the committee responded to an announced cutback in production and possible closure by setting up a commission of inquiry. The commission proposed measures aimed at reducing defective output, strengthening labour discipline, as well as a series of technical improvements. These recommendations were endorsed by the workers' general assembly, which also decided to allow overtime when production required it. The administration accepted the first set of proposals but it would not consider the technical recommendation and it announced 640 layoffs, promising more to follow. Meanwhile, it cut by half the wages that it had been paying to the eleven full-time members of the factory committee and forbade the office employees from giving them any information. Ignoring the factory committee's warning to exercise caution, a workers' general assembly gave the director 48 hours to resign. If he did not, the workers would 'relieve the factory committee of any responsibility for actions the workers might take.' With the support of the Central Soviet of factory committees, Vulkan's committee was able to convince the government to set up its own control over management. The committee admitted that this was merely a palliative, that the workers put little store in control by that government and without the establishment of workers' control on the national level.[65]

At the New Parviainen machine-building factory, the committee, also with the help of the Central Soviet of factory committees, was able to prevent 1,630 announced layoffs by proposing measures that reduced fuel consumption by 30 per cent. Even so, management had agreed to implement these measures only under pressure.[66] At the state-owned Sestroretsk rifle factory, when fuel began to run out in August, the factory committee initiated the digging a canal to a source of waterpower on a nearby estate. The left SR daily reported this under the title: 'What Would Happen to the Factories without the Factory Committees?'[67]

These examples show that some workers were moving beyond 'control,' in its original sense of monitoring the administration's activity, a goal that often remained elusive. These committees were moving directly into the sphere of activity of management. A delegate to a factory-committee conference in August explained: 'They tell us to control [in the sense of monitoring]. But what will we control when we have nothing left but walls, bare walls?'[68] Nevertheless, the goal remained officially 'control' in the sense of monitoring. The rapporteur on workers' control at the All-Russian factory committee conference in October noted that 'many comrades pointed out that the executive functions of the factory committees were not made clear in the reports. This was done on purpose, since economic functions are only an inevitable evil that should not be erected into a system.'[69]

The committees' incursion into managerial functions in a capitalist system raised the question of class collaboration. The workers' aspiration to independence from the owners, both on the level of the factories and in the broader political arena, where they rejected any alliance with the liberals, had been a defining trait of the Russian labour movement since the Revolution of 1905. It was also a defining element Bolshevism, which had become the dominant political current among workers in the labour upsurge of 1912-14. Now, the Mensheviks and some of the more moderate Bolsheviks, often people with links to the trade unions, used this as an argument against the factory committees. At the national conference of factory committees in October, the moderate Bolshevik David Ryazanov remarked that 'the trade union movement does not bear the stain of the entrepreneur. But it is the misfortune of the committees that they are an integral part of the administration. The trade union opposes itself directly to capital, but a member of a factory committee involuntary turns into an agent of the entrepreneur.'[70] The Bolshevik Aleksei Gast'ev, a leader of the Petrograd Metalworkers' Union, similarly remarked on the 'touching solidarity [of the committees] with management.' He told how committees in the provinces factories sent representatives to Petrograd to praise their factories in support of the owners' requests for government contracts and subsidies.[71] These same critics accused the committees of anarchism, of pursuing the narrow interests of their factory's workers at the expense of the general class interest.

But such criticism was largely unfounded, as the factory committees were the first to call for soviet power and for national economic regulation. Underlying the criticism was opposition to incursions into the rights of private property in the context of a bourgeois-democratic revolution, since, in the view of these critics, the revolution in backward, peasant Russia could not go beyond that limit with incurring defeat.

At one of the early conferences, Lenin also criticized the committees for acting as 'errand boys for the capitalists.' But he was coming from a different angle than the moderate socialists: he was arguing that only soviet power and worker majorities in the state's regulatory bodies would ensure that the factory committees' efforts served the workers' interests and not those of capital. But, in fact, the vast majority of the delegates to that conference were in agreement. However, they had no choice but to act at once to defend workers' jobs and the factories. A delegate from the New Arsenal factory responded to Lenin: 'The factory committees had to obtain raw materials. This is not 'running errands'. If we didn't support the factories in this way, who knows what would happen?'[72]

Workers were prepared to cooperate with management to save jobs, but only if they were convinced of management's good faith. To this end they insisted on workers' control, in the sense of access to information. At the Baltic wagon factory, management announced that losses were forcing it to close the automobile department. When the factory committee questioned the figures management was citing, the director agreed to keep the department open on condition that the workers maintained productivity at a level that made production profitable. The workers agreed to that but demanded in turn the right of control. Management rejected that as 'having no precedent.'[73]

The factory committees' incursions into management prerogatives were often made reluctantly by the committee members, under pressure from workers, concerned about their jobs. N. Skrypnik, a member of the Central Soviet of factory committees reported to the Bolsheviks' Central Committee on the eve of the October insurrection that 'everywhere one observes the desire for practical results. Resolutions no longer satisfy. It is felt that the leaders do not entirely express the mood of the masses. The former are more conservative. One notices an increase in the influence of anarchists in the Moscow and Narva Districts.'[74] Anarchists were proponents of 'direction action' in the factories.

The 'conservatism' of the factory committees reflected their reluctance to assume responsibility for managing the factories. They did not feel technically prepared for that, especially in the conditions of deepening economic dislocation and a hostile government. Rank-and-file workers were more distant from these problems and so more tempted by calls to direct action. Meanwhile, as the economic situation deteriorated, the administration of state factories, and even that some private enterprises, began in the autumn to offer the committees a minority participation in management. This was overwhelmingly rejected by the All-Russian conference of factory committees in October, which called instead to continue the struggle for control through commissions that were separate from management.[75] Vlas Chubar, a member of the Central Council, explained: 'The members of the factory committee would turn into pushers, whom management would use as extra help, itself remaining inactive. Such phenomena are already observed in state factories. Besides, [...] in a critical moment [...] the workers will direct all their discontent at the factory committee. [...]'[76] A similar position was adopted by committees in the state-owned factories, which reaffirmed at the same time their right to be present at management meetings and to obtain exhaustive answers to their questions.[77]

A long and painful discussion on this issue took place in late September in the committee of the Putilov factory. It was facing the layoff of 10,000 workers, a third of its workforce, because of a shortage of fuel. The Minister of Trade and Industry, well-known as a friend of capital and an opponent of workers' control, had offered the committee a minority voice in a joint commission with management. The committee members had no doubt that the intention was to shift responsibility onto it for the factory's disastrous situation. But it was not being given any real power to act. 'The entrepreneurs are presently seeking any means to make the workers whip themselves. [...] When it turned out that the government could not do without us and that things were in a bad way, it came to us for help.' All the same, the committee decided that it could not pass up any opportunity to defend the workers. And so it accepted the offer but only with a view to 'control', explicitly rejecting any responsibility for managing the enterprise.[78]

All political power to the soviets! But how much economic power?

The factory committees were not blind to these contradictions. And everyone, except the anarchists (and not all of them) saw the soviet seizure of political power and the exclusion of the propertied classes from influence on government policy as the only way to resolve them. 'Our conference said from the start that under a bourgeois government we would not be able to realize consistent control,' explained Skrypnik to the national conference of factory committees in October. 'To speak of a [national] controlling body under a bourgeois government is impossible. Therefore, the working class cannot bypass the question of state power, as [anarchist] comrade Renev recommends [...].'[79]

For rank-and-file workers, the looming economic crisis was the most urgent and potent argument for an insurrection. On 15 October, a joint meeting of Petrograd's trade union leaders with the Central Soviet of factory committees discussed the food and employment situations. There was a common sense that the economic dam was about to burst. The Provisional government was subjected to withering criticism for its inaction and for aggravating the situation when it did act. The conference declared that soviet power was an 'indispensable condition for the successful struggle against economic dislocation and the food crisis.' Among its tasks would be to establish workers' control on a national scale, to organize the demobilization of industry, and to promote public works.[80] Around this time, V. Schmidt, a Bolshevik trade union leader, reported to his party's central committee that 'In light of the specific economic conditions, one can expect colossal unemployment in the nearest future. In connection with that, the [workers'] mood is hesitant [*vyzhidatel'noe* - wait-and-see.] All agree that outside the struggle for power there is no way out of the situation. They demand power to the soviets.'[81]

But where would soviet power take the factory committees? On this question, the position remained unchanged. 'Workers' control is not socialism,' Skrypnik told the national conference of factory committees on the eve of the October insurrection. 'It is only one of the transitional measures that bring us closer to socialism.'[82] D. Evdokymov, another Bolshevik member of the Central Soviet of factory committees, turning to the anarchists, stated that 'to demand the transfer of all factories to the workers is premature. That means transition to a socialist system. But the time for socialism in Russia has not yet arrived. Our revolution is not socialist but transitional. The most numerous class in Russia is the peasantry, and the peasantry, a petty bourgeoisie, is individualistic.'[83] Yet already in August, Levin, also a member of the Central Soviet of factory committees, had warned that 'It is possible that we stand before a general strike of capitalists and industrialists. We have to be ready to take the enterprises into our hand to render harmless the hunger upon which the bourgeoisie is counting so much as a counterrevolutionary force.'[84]

Once the soviets had taken power, the factory committees abandoned their reluctance to assume responsibility for managing the factories. The Central Soviet's draft guidelines on workers' control read:

> Workers' control of industry, as an integral part of control of the entire productive life of the country, must not be conceived in the narrow sense of inspection [*reviziya*] but, on the contrary, in the broadest sense of *intervention* into the disposition by the entrepreneur of capital, inventory, raw materials and finished goods that belong to the enterprise; as the *active* monitoring of the correct and rational fulfillment of [the enterprise's] orders, the utilization of energy and the labour force, and as *participation in the organization of production itself* on a rational basis, etc., etc.[85]

These guidelines included the committees' right to issue orders that would become binding on management after three days, until which management could appear the order to a higher body of workers' control.

But 'this is not socialism,' Skrypnik insisted at a conference of factory committees on 15 November. 'It is a first step. [...] We are linked to other countries. [...] The torch that our revolution has raised will ignite the proletariat of Western Europe. [...] Socialism is not created at once but by the gradual restructuring of all economic and political life. We have entered the first period of that restructuring. [...] Our foundation is all power in the hands of the soviets of workers' and soviets' deputies. Not all power to the soviet but to the soviets, including the soviets in the factories and the villages.'[86]

This 'active' interpretation of control on the part of the factory committees was opposed by 'comrades on the right' (so designated by factory-committee activists), who had the backing of the All-Russian Trade Union Council and subsequently of the All-Russian Trade Union Congress. They called for only 'passive' control, in the sense of monitoring.[87] Their draft instruction on workers' control read: 'The control commission does not participate in management of the enterprise and does not bear responsibility for its work and activity, which remain that of the owner.' Only government and higher trade union bodies would be able to countermand the factory administration's orders. And the document also provided for penalties for the factory committees – up to two years imprisonment and confiscation of property – in cases of violations of the instruction or seizure of factories.[88] It was argued that to give the committees broad powers to intervene in management would encourage their allegedly anarchist tendencies, as each committee pursued the interests of the workers' of its own factory at the expense of the common class interest.

This argument was to a very significant degree disingenuous, since all the factory committee conferences both before and after October insisted that workers' control could be effective only within a framework of systematic national regulation. The urgency of centralism to combat the growing economic chaos, to distribute scarce fuel, raw materials, and contracts, and to organize conversion to peacetime production - was a leitmotif of the sixth Petrograd conference of factory committees, held in January 1918. At the gathering, the Central Soviet's proposal to create regional economic councils (*sovnarkhozy*) 'was met with the warmest sympathy.'[89] Yet, according to this proposal, decisions of the *sovnarkhozy* would be binding on all local institutions, including factory committees.[90] (The Central Council itself eventually merged into the *Sovnarkhoz* of the Northern Region.[91]) The guidelines on workers' control adopted by the conference stated that, while factory committees execute the will of their plants' general assemblies, 'at the same time they carry out all instructions, guidelines [...] and measures of higher state economic bodies and answer to the state authority for the strictest order and rationality of management of the enterprise, in accordance with the needs of the entire toiling people, and answer also for the integrity the enterprise's property.'[92] Other resolutions of the conference called for the centralization of distribution of production contracts and fuel.[93]

Both the discussion at the conference and the guidelines it adopted on workers' control (with only three dissenting votes[94]) made clear that orders from above that might require the sacrifice of local group interests had to be obeyed.[95] To the argument of an anarchist delegate that centralization would inevitably lead to 'some kind of autocracy,' another replied:

> The factories have to coordinate their activity. Who can do that? Only a higher organization that [...] has all the information, distributes the contracts, and knows what each plant is doing. We control directly in the factory; we [...] inform of what we need. But distribution has to be centralized. [...] We need organization, centralization, like oxygen. [...] Otherwise we will be lost and never get out of the present mess.[96]

Another delegate observed that the anarchists, for all their criticism, failed to explain how they would organize the economy and that, to be consistent, they should also oppose the factory committees too, since they limit the freedom of individual workers.[97] Fears of bureaucratic despotism were undoubtedly allayed by the provision that the higher economic bodies would be elected and would function according to principles of democratic centralism.[98]

Besides that, the 'comrades on the right' who criticized the factory committees' conception of active control, were choosing to ignore the reality: workers could not stand by passively awaiting the organization of effective centralized economic regulation. They had to act immediately to save their factories and jobs. By 1 January 1918, the employed industrial workforce of Petrograd had shrunk to 339,641 from 406,312 a year before, most of that decline occurring after the October insurrection. (By May 1918, only 142,915 would remain.)[99] Responding to critics, F. Katyn', a member of the Central Soviet of factory committees, wrote in January 1918:

> [...The factory committees] see themselves as the basic units of the higher regulating institutions of the economy and are doing everything in their power to follow the path laid out by these organs and institutions. And it is not their fault that all these institutions do not yet exist, or that everywhere they are packed with the tsarist bourgeoisie and conciliators

of our bourgeois revolution, so that no one can make head or tail of them and they are themselves incapable of productive action. It is not the factory committees' fault that, faced with total uncertainty in this or that matter, circumstances and a lack of time sometimes force them to act at their own risk and on their own responsibility...[100]

As noted earlier, the opponents of 'active control' were in reality less concerned with alleged anarchist tendencies than with the prospect of the Russian revolution going beyond capitalism. They believed such radicalization would doom the revolution to defeat, since the political and material conditions for socialism were lacking in Russia. Not surprisingly, the factory owners preferred the position of these 'comrades on the right.' A report to the All-Russian Society of Leather Manufacturers on 25 January 1918 noted the existence of two currents within the workers' movement: 'an anarchistic current represented by the factory committees' and a 'thought-out system of gradual transition to state socialism on the basis of the existing capitalist system [...], supported by all active members of the union movement.' It considered trade union members the only allies of industry. The report approvingly cited an article published in a Menshevik newspaper that argued that the revolution was bourgeois and that private property, therefore, had to be respected. The meeting unanimously endorsed the guidelines for 'passive' control, as 'something we can live with.'[101] The official position of the Petrograd Society of Factory and Mill Owners' was that its members should abandon their enterprises if faced with attempts to impose 'active' control.[102]

However, not all union leaders opposed 'active' control. The more left-wing unions, in particular the Petrograd Union of Metalworkers, had no trouble endorsing the factory committees' position.[103] On the other hand, the Mensheviks, who opposed soviet power[104], argued, along with the Bolshevik 'comrades on the right,' that 'active' control would 'rivet the workers' horizon to *their own* enterprise.' Ignoring their own earlier reports of a disguised lockout aimed at crushing the workers' movement, the moderate Menshevik press now termed talk of sabotage a 'demagogic fantasy.'[105]

Despite the fears of the socialist moderates, the factory committees themselves were concerned not to needlessly alienate owners and their administrators by insisting on 'active' control when the latter were acting in good faith. In a mid-January 1918, the Putilov factory committee reported that 'in defending the workers' interests, the committee not only adhered to the principle of resolving conflicts between capital and labour, but tirelessly pursued the tendency of intervening in the economic life of the factory, doing that, as far as possible, by assuming only control, not executive functions. All the results in that area, all the control positions assumed by the committee were won without open conflict with the representatives of capital, without summoning the masses to defend these positions, exclusively through verbal negotiation and similar measures.'[106]

Around this time, the committee of the Erikson telephone factory, long a Bolshevik stronghold, reported that management agreed to cooperate with it in obtaining fuel and materials, as it did not perceive that sort of activity by the committee as a threat to its prerogatives. But it rejected control over finances and refused to provide the committee with information, threatening the resignation of the entire administrative staff if the committee insisted. The committee decided, therefore, not to press the matter 'in order to avoid premature complications that could lead to a temporary stoppage.'[107] Similarly, at the Tentelevskii chemical factory the administration agreed to 'passive' control in return for the committee's pledge to respect management's executive powers.[108] When the head of the control commission at the Novaya Bumagopryadil'naya cotton-spinning mill provoked the owner's departure by insisting on verifying the validity of expenses before countersigning checks, she was immediately replaced by the factory committee and told: 'Don't you know we can't manage without a specialist!'[109]

These examples argue against the view of workers' control as motivated primarily by ideology or some sort of anarchist impulses rather than by the concrete interest in defending production and jobs. It is the case that the guidelines for the regional *sovnarkhozy* drafted by the Central Soviet of factory committees initially provided for their election solely by the committees themselves. Such a position might be viewed as syndicalist. However, the Central Soviet readily accepted the amendments proposed by the Supreme *Sovnarkhoz* that added representatives of the local soviets (local government), cooperatives, as well as of the technical-managerial personnel to the composition of the regional *sovnarkhozy*.[110]

The call for nationalization

In whichever of its versions, active or passive, workers' control implied a form of dual power in the factories. As such, it was a compromise between antagonistic interests and, by its very nature, an unstable and necessarily temporary relationship, similar to dual power in the political arena. Workers' control was premised on the industrialists' interest in continue to run their factories. But the factory committees were demanding control precisely because they could not take that for granted. And while the Petrograd Society of Factory and Mill Owners, ignoring its official position, instructed its members not to abandon factories that still represented value to the owners, this was becoming less and less the case. Even leaving aside politically-motivated sabotage and fear of workers taking over, factory owners could not help being pessimistic about prospects of making money from their enterprises in the foreseeable future, given the termination of military orders, the cost and complexity involved in converting to peacetime production, and the transport crisis that made supplying fuel and materials a huge problem. It was the owners' loss of interest in maintaining production that drove workers' committee to move beyond control and to press the Soviet state for nationalization.

This logic was clearly laid out in a letter from March 1918 to the *sovnarkhoz* of the Northern Region, written by the committee of the Vulkan machine-building factory:

> The entire policy of management [...] has been conducted with a definite view toward closing, [...and] if the factory has not already been shut, the credit belongs to the factory committee, whose entire policy, in face of never-ending and insurmountable obstacles, was aimed at maintaining the life of the factory. [...] The kind of control that management is willing to accept is only a palliative, since it will continue to be the master of the enterprise, while responsibility [...] will lie entirely with the control commission, and, consequently, dual power will not be eliminated. [...] The only way out is nationalization, and with the present petition we once again affirm this.[111]

Even the 'comrades on the right' among the Bolsheviks finally had to accept this logic. Yu. Larin, a former Menshevik and co-author of the draft decree on 'passive' control in November 1917, told the congress of the Metalworkers' Union in January 1918 that 'we tried in many cases to put off the moment of full management of the enterprises and to restrict ourselves to control. But all our efforts came to naught. In the present situation none of the existing forces can – and sometimes they do not even want to – manage the economy. Example: the Volga merchant fleet, where the industrialists have stopped repairing the ships and have ceased activity in general. [...] Either we move forward or we go down. Like it or not, we have to abandon the idea of workers' control and shift to a system of full management of the enterprises and direction of the country's economy.'[112]

Nationalization was the major point on the agenda of the sixth

Petrograd conference of factory committees in 22-27 January 1918. The only dispute arose over how fast it could be carried out, with anarchists demanding immediate and complete takeover of the factories by the workers. The resolution, adopted unanimously, recognized that immediate nationalization of all industry was impossible without the creation beforehand of an 'organized technical apparatus, corresponding to the interests of the proletariat,' that would work under direction of the Supreme *Sovnarkhoz*. But it did call for immediate nationalization of enterprises whose management refused to recognize workers' control, that openly or secretly sabotaged, or refused to continue production.

At the same time, the conference sounded a new note in calling for immediate nationalization of factories that were in good physical and financial condition and immediately suited for peacetime production, 'since the proletarian Republic takes from the hands of the predators not only the ruined economy that will be a burden on the people's finances, but also enterprises that can function intensively, providing the people with economic resources, and so helping to restore the health of the people's property.'[113] This was a break with the hitherto predominantly defensive view of workers' control (and secondarily portrayed as school for a future socialism) as forced upon workers by the threat to their jobs and to the revolution.

But this shift did not reflect any new chiliastic mood. Everyone who spoke at this conference painted a very bleak picture of the economic situation: 'We have heard here reports of such ruin, of such a horrible reality, one that, in fact, we ourselves have already been experiencing.'[114] Nor did the delegates spare from criticism the performance of their own class organizations. But the task had changed. 'Every one of us knows that our industrial life is coming to a standstill and that the moment when it dies is coming soon. We are now living through its death spasms,' declared one delegate. 'Here the question of control is no longer relevant. You can control only when you have something to control. [...] Everyone, from the left to the right wing, agrees on one thing: we have to rebuild economic life itself on a new basis [...].' This was echoed in the resolution on demobilization, 'a tremendously difficult task [...] that only the proletariat can realize on a national scale and in a planned, organized way.'[115]

But if the mood was sombre, it was nevertheless determined. Delegates evoked the Revolution of 1905, defeated by mass lockouts.[116] They were not going to let that happen again. In calling for nationalization, members of the Central Council observed that committees were increasingly coming to it with demands for the state to take over their factory. 'Thus,' stated the

Council's paper, 'unexpectedly arises the practical question of nationalizing production.'[117]

In practice, nationalization proceeded slowly over the next months and on an individual enterprise basis, as either a punitive measure or to prevent closure, and mostly in sectors of metallurgy and metalworking.[118] After the merchant fleet, which workers spent several months repairing without pay, the first complete sector to be nationalized was sugar in May 1918, followed by oil in June, and by what still remained private in the metal sector.[119]

As in the case of workers' control, nationalization was primarily viewed as being imposed by objective circumstances. In a pamphlet from 1918 entitled *From Workers' Control to Workers' Management*, I. Stepanov, a prominent Bolshevik, wrote: 'Yes, 'socialist experiments', as our opponents chuckle. [... But] this is not a 'fantastic theory' nor 'free will.' *We have no choice.* And since it is done by the working class and in the course of the revolutionary struggle the capitalists are removed, it has to be socialist regulation.' As Marxists, the Bolsheviks, no less than the Mensheviks, recognized that the material and political conditions for socialism were absent in an isolated Russia.[120] 'Will this be another Paris Commune or will it lead to world socialism?' Stepanov asked. 'That depends on international circumstances. But we have absolutely no choice.'[121]

After nationalization

The factory-committee conference in January 1918 called for the committees to assume management of enterprises that would be nationalized, since 'a government of workers, soldiers and peasants is strong inasmuch as it rests on the confidence of the toilers and their organizations. [...] The workers' committees should be at the head of these enterprises locally, working under the leadership of the *sovnarkhozy*.'[122] To the suggestion that the committees not assume responsibility for managing the enterprises but limit themselves to delegating two or three members with only a consultative voice, M. Zhivotov, a Bolshevik member of the Central Soviet retorted: 'That is extremism; that, it seems, is a deformed version of Bolshevism. [...] The factory committees must absolutely stand at the head of the factories, [...] subordinated, of course, to the state regulating organization, the *sovnarkhoz*, [...since] the committees know best the situation at their factory and the workers have confidence in them.' And if the factory committees find they lack expertise, nothing stops them from inviting members of the technical staff.[123]

But in March 1918, the Supreme *Sovnarkhoz* issued a decree that fell far short of committees' position, although it did not entirely exclude worker representation in management. It provided for the appointment by its *glavky* (industrial branch directorates) of a commissar to each of the factories under their supervision, as well as one technical and one administrative director. The technical director could be overruled only by the commissar or by the branch directorate. The administrative director, on the other hand, would work under supervision of an economic administrative council, consisting of representatives of the workers, white-collar and technical staff, the trade union, and the local soviet. But workers' and white-collar employees would constitute no more than half of the council's members. As for the factory committees, they could not independently issue orders but had to pass through economic administrative councils.[124]

The push for centralism at the expense of meaningful worker participation in management would only increase in the following months, as the outbreak of full-scale civil war, backed by foreign intervention, and continued economic decline forced the Soviet state into a desperate survival mode that would last for the next several years. These conditions strengthened the hand of the advocates of authoritarian management, and leaders like Lenin and Trotsky, who had formerly adopted left positions, rallied to their side.[125] (The Mensheviks, as before, limited themselves to the demand for trade union autonomy.) Within the Bolshevik party, the cause of the factory committees was defended by the Left Opposition and, later towards the end of the civil war, by the Workers' Opposition, which defended a syndicalist platform.

There is an obvious contradiction between centralism, an essential element of planning, and, therefore, of socialism, and self-management, also an essential ingredient of socialism, since the more power is concentrated in the centre, the less room there is for workers to participate meaningfully in managing the enterprises. This contradiction can, however, be managed (it need not be 'antagonistic') and can even become a positive factor, if certain conditions are present. In particular, the degree and scope of central control has to be limited and the economy must ensure the workers needs for material security at a minimally decent standard. In the absence of these conditions, self-management cannot be meaningful, nor can workers develop the consciousness necessary for them to willingly to sacrifice local group interests to the more general class interests. In conditions of civil war, industrial collapse, and severe food shortage, the Soviet state could meet none of these conditions.

Another important condition is a working class capable of defending self-management against centralizing tendencies of the state, even its own state. At the January 1918 factory-committee conference, an anarchist delegate proposed amending the proposed guideline that obliged factory committees to submit to orders emanating from superior bodies by adding the proviso that such orders 'not violate the interests of the proletariat.' If they did, the committees need not submit. The rapporteur for the Central Soviet, a Bolshevik worker, answered that the presidium had, in fact, considered such a reservation, but decided not to include it, since:

> the *sovnarkhoz*, that we are ourselves organizing, will not turn against us, as it is not a bureaucratically constituted organ but one elected by us and composed of people whom we can recall. [...] Don't forget that the *sovnarkhoz* is a class organ. If we adopt an attitude of mistrust from the outset, then these organs will scarcely be able to function correctly. [...] Only an anarchist who in general rejects and mistrusts any superior leadership (*verkhy*) could propose such an amendment. But we, the proletariat, [...] construct leadership on the principle of complete democratism. [...] If these organs really do turn away from the masses, then, of course we will have to introduce that amendment. Indeed, we will have to overthrow those organs, and perhaps make a new revolution. But so far we feel that the Soviet of People's Commissars [the central government] is our soviet and the institutions it creates are fully in accord with us.[126]

This response reflected the confidence of workers whose class had led two, for some of them - three, revolutions. But conditions were fast undermining the independent power of the working class. Its members were being scattered by unemployment, war, and needs of state building. The minority that remained in the factories was being demoralized by hunger. At the same January conference, another delegate made a proposal that was the opposite to the anarchist's: the responsibility of committees to their general assembly be limited when the general assembly's decision contradicted the more general interest. To this another member of the Central Soviet retorted that:

> it would be out of place for us, who base ourselves on the support of these proletarian masses, to introduce such an element that portrays them beneath any criticism. [...] For as long as I have observed workers in the factories, I can say, comrades, that we can consider them a conscious

element that will always take the right decision, and not some sort of ugly mass that does not know what it is doing, barbarians or a children, as comrade Gorky says.[127] [...] In their decisive majority they will be conscious enough not to adopt decisions that their factory committee cannot carry out because they contradict the interests of the country.[128]

Yet the discussion at the conference presented several examples that contradicted that claim. Responding to the anarchists, a delegate from the Metallicheskii factory observed that:

Some factories are not needed and have to be shut. Here you need a state apparatus that can sort this out. [...] Comrade Bleikhman [an anarchist] says: 'Take [the factories] into our hands, and basta!' [...] I'd like to ask these comrade anarchists [...] how they presently conduct themselves in the factories with their unconscious masses. Do they speak openly to them? I don't know how to talk to masses that are demanding money. I wasn't at the conference yesterday and I came late today because things aren't very good at my factory: we are laying off a hundred people. There you have anarchy, [...] and not the kind of well being in the ultimate sense of anarchy, about which comrade Bakunin wrote. That would be heaven on earth. But until then, we have to live through all these misunderstandings, [...] when each worker wants only to obtain, not merely a month and a half [of severance pay], but to grab two or three months' worth [...].[129]

Some argued that such happened mostly when the workers were recent arrivals to industry from the countryside. The urbanized proletariat was conscious and responded reasonably when the situation was explained to them.[130] However, discussion of the conflict that had arisen between the committee of the Treugol'nik rubber factory, which had reserves of fuel beyond the three-month limit that the Central Soviet had set, and the Putilov factory committee, which was preparing for conversion to peace production and lacked fuel, showed that the problem went beyond wartime recruits to industry. The Treugol'nik committee had agreed to give up its surplus fuel only at an exorbitant price that would cover complete amortization of fuel tanks that would be left standing empty. 'The factory committee was so stubborn that it openly declared that 'you, the Putilov workers, failed to act in time and now you want to take fuel from our workers and leave them without work. You have to fend for yourselves; but we won't give.' This might be patriotic and very good for the workers of Treugol'nik,' commented this rapporteur on the fuel crisis. 'Maybe the factory committee of Treugol'nik is really trying for its workers. But it's not good for the country and not for the working class that is struggling in desperation to revive industry.'[131] The conference decided that all fuel beyond two-month's supply should be put under the sole control of the regional *sovnarkhoz*.[132]

This contradiction would only become more acute as the economic and military situations deteriorated. In a June 1918 report, the metal section of the *Sovnakhoz* of the Northern Region complained that:

> the committees, ignoring everything, defend the interests of their own parish, trying to obtain subsidies and advances, even though this money is allocated only after the most careful investigation. The committees try to revive the operation of closed enterprises even when there is no objective basis. [...] The data we receive from them [...] are always one-sided. [...They] very often besieged the authorities, snatched up contracts, obtained advances, [...] and without the approval of the *sonvarkhoz*, reopened their factories. Unfortunately, the majority of such contracts objectively could not be fulfilled, not to mention the fact that they very much disorganize the work of our section, [...which] will have to take all contracts under its control and reorganize them in the interests of the general state mechanism. This will not happen without a struggle of the workers' government against the workers' organizations.[133]

The Left Opposition at the First Congress of *Sovnarkhozy* in 26 May-6 June 1918 defended the cause of the factory committees. Nikolaï Osinski, who had himself briefly headed the Supreme *Sovnarkhoz*, began by emphasizing the 'absolute decline of the material productive forces that is reaching the extreme point when an economy starts to die.' They had therefore, to shift into a basic survival mode, adopt a 'miserly' economic policy, with the state monopolizing the existing productive forces and with the strictest accounting and expenditure of the scarce resources. But if this analysis seemed to argue in favour of centrally appointed commissars to run the factories, Osinskii went on to call for worker management (at least two-thirds representation in management). He rejected the argument that this inevitably led to the defence of group interests against those of the whole, citing his recent experience in the Donbass: 'It is all a question of the general conditions of the enterprise - whether it has bread and money, whether its managerial staff is well-chosen and maintains close relations with the regulating centre.' If there is no bread and money, then the work proceeds badly even under commissars, who 'are themselves forced to trade in monopolized goods or factory property' in order to feed the workers.[134]

But in painting so bleak, if realistic, a picture and in calling to shift the economy to a strict survival mode, Osinskii inadvertently gave fuel to the advocates of management by commissar and tighter centralization. Alexis Rykov, the current chair of the Supreme *Sovnarkhoz* and an opponent of self-management, cited an article by Osinksii himself:

> The preservation of existing productive forces [...] is possible only by means of their most systematic concentration; the most effective utilization of the available technical forces makes completely inevitable the nationalized management of these forces from a single centre.[135]

Osinskii again inadvertently gave comfort to his opponents when he opposed the introduction of piece rates in an effort to raise labour discipline and labour intensity. He argued that such measures would further undermine solidarity and foster petty-bourgeois attitudes at time when 'one observes a severe degradation, a major class decomposition of the proletariat as a result of unemployment.'[136] G. Lomov was caught in the same contradiction. He argued that 'the use of commissars of all kinds not only does not arouse local energies to increase production and strengthen productive forces, but, on the contrary, it decreases and destroys local energies.' But then, virtually in the same breath, he observed that 'workers and peasants at present, like worms, are becoming entwined in their domestic shells and show signs of life only insofar as it is necessary to satisfy their own personal needs. Everything is broken. We have totally suppressed the vital, creative forces in the country. Everything is going underground and existing only for itself.'[137]

In fact, the argument could be, and was, made both ways. But with the immediate survival of the revolution at stake and the social base of the advocates of democratic management increasingly dispersed and demoralized[138], the odds favoured the supporters of more centralization and of authoritarian management. When Osinksii declared that there was really no solution for the Russian revolution except for revolutions in the West to end the world war and come to Russia's aid, he was voicing a widely shared view.[139] For him, this was an argument against sacrificing socialist principles for the sake of survival. But others drew the opposite conclusion: since defeat of the revolution in Russia would deal a major blow to the revolutionary movements in the West, it was better temporarily to sacrifice principle. Aid from the West would permit the correction of the distortions. Very few believed the revolution in Russia would survive without that support.

The evolution of factory management during the civil war awaits further research. A recent study, based on archives of the committees of twelve of Petrograd's largest factories, not only confirms workers' continued attachment to participation in management but also the continued practice of such participation, in some cases even the wielding of full managerial power by the committees as late as 1920, in spite of spite official policy. The same was true of the practice of collegial management (which normally meant a strong factory-committee presence in the administration), which also contradicted the official policy of one-person management.[140]

Eventually, however, with the introduction of bureaucratic planning in the late 1920s, even the circumscribed trade union rights of the New-Economic-Policy (1921-28) era were suppressed. And yet, official Soviet ideology never ceased to present workers' participation in management as an integral element of socialism and of Soviet reality. Near the end of the Soviet Union's existence, in an effort to win workers to his reforms and to activate 'the human factor' in the economy, Gorbachev tried to breathe some life into this ideology, albeit in a limited and contradictory manner. A 1987 Law on Enterprises provided for the election of works councils and directors. However, it was only after Gorbatchev annulled this law in 1989, having decided to restore capitalism, that a genuine movement for self-management arose.[141] That movement, however, was cut short by the collapse of the Soviet Union and the ensuing 'revolution from above.'

NOTES

1   This is an expanded and revised version of David Mandel, 'Workers Control and Factory Committees in the Russian Revolution 1917-18,' in Immanuel Ness and Dario Azzellini, eds., Ours to Master and to Own: Workers' Control from the Commune to the Present Paperback, Chicago, Haymarket, 2011.

2   When exactly during the war Lenin himself changed position is not entirely clear.

3   V.I. Lenin, Polnoe sobranie sochinenii, 5 ed., Moscow, 1962, vol. 31, p. 116.

4   In this text, the word 'control' will be used in the Russian sense.

5   The Internationalists formed the left wing of the Menshevik Party. Sukhanov is the author of a valuable seven-volume chronicle of the revolution.

6   N. Sukhanov, Zapiski o revolyutsii, Moscow-Berlin-Petrograd, 1923, vol. 7, pp. 24-26.

7   Oktyabr'skaya revolyutsiya i fabzavkomy, Moscow, 1927, vol. II, p. 182

8   Op. cit., p. 183.

9   Op. cit., p. 184.

10   In his classic work on the revolution, E.H. Carr wrote: 'The mounting tide of anarchy in the factories served their [the Bolsheviks'] purposes. They could not have dammed it even had they desired to; but they could partly steer it so long as they were prepared to ride with it. It was this situation which involved them in accepting and acclaiming as their own practices which were anarchist and syndicalist rather than Bolshevik.' (The Bolshevik Revolution 1917-23, Baltimore, Penguin, 1966, vol. 2, pp. 63-64). Sukhanov in similar fashion wrote that behind the Bolshevism of 1917 'was an unbridled anarchistic

petty bourgeois storm that was eliminated only when Bolshevism no longer had any masses behind it.'(Sukhanov, op. cit.,vol. 6, pp. 192-193.)

11   See, for example, D. O. Churakov, *Fabzavkomy v bor'be   za proizvodstvennuyu demokratiyu*, Moscow, Prometei, 2005, pp. 255-57.

12   This outlook was clearly expressed, for example, in a pamphlet written by two leaders of the workshop movement on the Clyde in England in 1917: 'There must be never be alliance or compromise with the employer. We shall be obliged, indeed, to negotiate with him through his representatives on the daily routine of the workshop, but not to espouse his interests or to advance them in any way when it lies in our power to do otherwise. Our policy is that of invaders in our native province. Industry, now in the hands of an arrogant and tyrannical usurper, and that which we win in our advance we control *exclusively* and *independently*.' (W. Gallacher and J. Paton, 'Towards Industrial Democracy,' Paisely Trades and Labour Council, 1917, cited in G.D.H. Cole, *Workshop Organization*, Oxford, Clarendon Press, 1923, pp. 171-172.)

13   Unions, of course, are also a form of dual power, in as much as they pose limits on managerial absolutism. But they are typically organized to represent workers as sellers (or leasers) of their labour power. They, therefore, rarely pose a radical challenge to capital's fundamental power to decide how, what, when, or whether to produce. That is how Gramsci explained the conservatism of Italy's unions in 1919. He contrasted their conservatism to the revolutionary spirit of the factory councils that represented workers as producers. ('Syndicalisme et conseil,' *Ordine Nuovo*, 8 November 1919, in E. Mandel, *Contrôle ouvrier, conseils ouvriers, autogestion*, Paris, Maspero, 1973, vol. 2, p. 68.)

14   According to the former leaders of the factory-committee movement, compilers of three volumes of documents on the committees in 1917-18, 'Petrograd was the main centre of the factory-committee movement that set the tone for the whole periphery,' and the documents of the central organizations for Russia and Petrograd 'undoubtedly provide a general canvass and outline of the revolutionary activity of the factory committees in 1917-18.' (*Oktyabr'skaya revolyutsiya i fabzavkomy*, Moscow, vol. III, 1929, p. 4).

15   The employers' position during this pre-war labour upsurge mirrored that of the workers', with management actively collaborating with the police in putting down political strikes. Indeed, the authorities sometimes had to restrain the industrialists' zeal in fining workers for participation in political protests, since they feared it would pour oil on the flames. (E. Kruze, *Peterburgskie rabochie v 1912-14*, Moscow, 1961, p. 98.) The most striking manifestation of the fusion of political and economic protest was the workers' widespread and insistent strike demand for 'polite address' (second person plural) from management, a demand that V.I. Timiryazev, Minister of Trade and Industry, himself an entrepreneur, qualified in 1912 as political. (L.M. Kleinbort, *Ocherki rabochei intelligentsii, 1906-16*, Petrograd, 1923, vol. I, p. 11.)

16   From the textile workers' union paper, cited in P.V. Volobuev, *Proletariat i buzhuaziya v 1917g.*, Moscow, 1964, p. 64.

17   E. Maevski, *Kanun revolyutsii*, Petrograd 1918, p. 43.

18   Kruze, *Peterburgskie rabochie ...*, pp. 99-100.

19   On 10 March, the Petrograd Soviet concluded a general agreement with the Petrograd Society of Factory and Mills owners that included the eight-hour day. This took much longer in Moscow and the provinces, and in smaller plants workers were often unable to obtain it at all. The Provisional Government, although supposedly under the Soviet's 'control', never made it law.

20   Like the other measures, this was aimed at preventing managerial abuses and ensuring justice. Of particular concern to workers was the presence in their midst of well-to-do

elements hiding from the draft.

21   Mainly through consumer cooperatives.

22   *Revolyutsionnoe dvizhenie v Rossii posle sverzheniya samoderzhaviya*, Moscow, 1957, oc. cit., pp. 491-492.

23   P.V. Volobuev, *Proletariat i burzhuaziya v 1917g*, Moscow, 1964, p. 157.

24   *Rabochii kontrol' i natsionalizatsiya promyshlennykh predpriyatii Petrgorada v 1917-19 gg.*, Leningrad, vol. 1, p. 179.

25   K. Bazilevich, *Professional'noe dvizhenie rabotnikov svyazi*, Moscow, 1927, p.40; A. Tanyaev, *Ocherki po istorii zheleznodorozhnikov v revolyutsii 1917 goda*, Moscow-Leningrad, 1925, p. 53.

26   *Revolyutsionnoe dvizhenie v Rossii v aprele 1917g.*, Moscow, 1958, pp. 383-386.

27   TsGASPb (Central State Archive of St. Petersburg, formerly LGAORSS), f. 9391, op. 1, d. 11, l. 4.

28   *Oktyabr'skaya revolyutsiya i fabzavkomy*, Moscow, 1927, vol. I, p. 100. For a view of the range of the comittees' activities in state enterprises, see the minutes of the committees of five large state plants in *Fabrichno-zavodskie komitety Petrograda v 1917g., protokoly*, Moscow, 1979.

29   TsGASPb, f. 4601, op. 1., d. 10, l. 33.

30   Op. cit., f. 1000, op. 73, d. 16, l. 6.

31   *Novaya zhizn'*, 10 May 1917.

32   *Rech'*, 13 May 1917.

33   *Rabochaya gazeta*, 20 May 1917.

34   Kruze, *Peterburgskie rabochie...*, p. 328.

35   *Novaya zhizn'*, 19 and 20 May 1917.

36   Op. cit., 2 June 1917; *Revolyutsionnoe dvizhenie v Rossii v mae-iyune 1917g.*, Moscow, 1959, p. 197.

37   *Izvestiya moskovskogo voenno-promyshlennogo komiteta*, no. 13, 1917, p. 15.

38   *Pravda*, 21 May 1917.

39   *Putilovtsy v trekh revolyutiyakh*, Leningrad 1933, p. 431.

40   This plant, with some 1,200 workers in 1917, had seen 31 strikes in 1912-14, for a total of 103,970 lost worker-days. Kruze, op. cit., pp. 73 and 323.

41   *Revolyutsionnoe dvizhenie v Rossii v aprele...*, p. 444.

42   *Oktyabr'skaya revolyutsiya i fabzavkomy*, vol. I, p. 182; *Izvestiya*, 17 June 1917; *Novaya zhizn'*, 19 June 1917.

43   *Rabochii kontrol' i natsionalizatsiya....*, vol. I, 1949, p. 104.

44   *Izvestiya*, 17 June 1917.

45   *Utro Rossii*, 27 April 1917.

46   *Oktyabr'skaya revolyutsiya i fabzavkomy*, vol. I, p. 81.

47   Op. cit., p. 84.

48   Op. cit., p. 105.

49   Op. cit., p. 86.

50   Op. cit., p. 114.

51   Op. cit., p. 113.

52   Op. cit., p. 126.

53   Massive, but peaceful, demonstrations by workers and soldiers in Petrograd on 1 and 2 July aimed at pressuring the Central Executive Committee of Soviets, then led by moderate Mensheviks and SRs, to abandon the socialist-liberal coalition government and take power on its own.

54   *Oktyabr'skaya revolyutsiya i fabzavkomy*, vol. 1, p. 193.

55   *Ekonomicheskoe polozhenie Rossii nakanune Velikoi oktyabr'skoi sotsialisticheskoii revolyutsii*, Moscow-Leningrad, 1957, pp. 196, 200-201.

56 To workers, Ryabushinksii became the personification of the 'capitalist-lokautchik.' 'Thanks for the truth,' commented the Bolshevik paper. 'The conscious workers and peasants can only thank Rybushinksii. The only question remains: whose hand will grasp whom by the throat?' (*Proletarii*, 10 August 1917.)

57 Z.V. Stepanov, *Rabochie Petrograda v period podgotovki i provedeniya Oktyabr'skogo vooruzhennogo vosstaniya, avgust-sentyabr' 1917g.*, Leningrad, 1965, pp. 140-41; *Izvestiya*, 18 August 1917.

58 The death penalty had been abolished after the February Revolution. But in June, the Provisional government restored it at the front in conjunction with its new military offensive, launched under pressure from the Allies. This offensive, which broke the de facto cease-fire at the front, was roundly denounced by the soldiers and workers.

59 Sukhanov, *Zapiski...*, vol. 8, p.110.

60 *Rech'*, 10 September 1917.

61 *Revolyutsionnoe dvizhenie v Rossii nakanune Oktyabr'skogo vooruzhennogo vosstaniya v Petrograde*, 1962, pp. 286-287.

62 *Oktyabr'skaya revolyutsiyai i fabzavkomy*, vol. II, p. 121.

63 *Rabochii kontrol' i natsionalizatsiya...* vol. I, pp. 70, 75, 80; *Putilovtsy v trekh revoyutsiyakh*, p. 337.

64 *Oktyabr'skaya revolyutsiya i fabzavkomy*, vol. II, p. 121.

65 Stepanov, *Rabochie Petrograda...*, 216; *Rabochii put'*, 8 October 1917; *Znamya truda*, 30 September 1917; *Revolyutsionnoe dvizhenie v Rossii v sentyabre 1917g.*, Moscow, 1962, p. 326-27. John Reed reported a conversation with the owner of this factory, who vowed never to tolerate factory committees or give workers a say in management. He said he was counting on international intervention to put an end to ideas of 'social revolution.' But even without that, 'the factories are closing and the Germans are advancing. Starvation and defeat may bring the Russian people to their senses.' (J. Reed, *Ten Days that Shook the World*, N.Y., Vintage, 1960, p. 8).

66 *Rabochii put'*, 8 September 1917; *Oktyabr'skaya revolyutsiya i fabzavkomy*, vol. II, p. 17.

67 *Znamya truda*, 1 October 1917.

68 *Oktyabr'skaya revolyutsiya i fabzavkomy*, vol. I, p. 269.

69 *Oktyabr'skaya revolyutsiya i fabzavkomy*, vol. II, p. 184.

70 Op. cit., vol. 2, p. 192.

71 *Pervaya vserossiiskaya tarifnaya konferentsiya rabochikh metallistov*, Petrograd, 1918, p. 7.

72 *Oktyabr'skaya revolyutsiya i fabzavkomy*, vol. I, pp. 91-92, 100.

73 *Izvestiya*, 17 June 1917. It is not clear how this conflict ended.

74 *Oktyabr'skoe vooruzhennoe vosstanie v Petrograde*, Moscow, 1957, p. 52.

75 *Oktyabr'skaya revolyutsiya i fabzavkomy*, vol. 2, p. 192.

76 Op. cit., pp. 174.

77 *Oktyabr'skoe vooruzhennoe vosstanie...*, pp. 110, 127.

78 *Rabochii kontrol' i natsionalizatsiya...*, vol. 1, p. 205; *Putilovtsy v trekh revolyutsiyakh*, pp. 386-91; *Fabrichno-zavodskie komitety Petrograda v 1917g.*, pp. 483-87,494-97. The Putilov factory had been sequestered and placed under state management in 1915, although it remained privately owned and the stockholders on the board of directors continued to keep a close watch over its affairs.

79 *Oktyabr'skaya revolyutsiya i fabzavkomy*, vol. II, p. 121.

80 *Revolyutsionnoe dvizhenie v Rossii nakanune...*, pp. 119-125.

81 *Oktyabr'skoe vooruzhennoe vosstanie...*, p. 53.

82 *Oktyabr'skaya revolyutsiya i fazvakomy*, vol. II, pp. 184-85.

83 Op. cit., vol. 2, p. 43.

84 Op. cit., vol I, p. 269.

85   *Natsionalizatsiya promyshlennosti SSSR*, Moscow, 1954, p. 78, *Izvestiya*, 7 December 1917; *Oktyabr'skaya revolyutsiya i fabzavkomy*, vol. III, Moscow, 1929, pp. 167-79; vol. IV, St. Petersburg, 2002, vol. IV, p. 416.

86   *Oktyabr'skaya revolyutsiya i fabzavkomy*, vol. III, p. 36.

87   For the attitudes of various unions and union leaders to control, see *Oktyabr'skaya revolyutsiya i fabzavkomy*, vol. III, pp. 115-31.

88   *Oktyabr'skaya revolyutsiya i fabzavkomy*, vol. III, pp. 93-95; *Izvestiya*, 17 December 1917; *Rabochii kontrol' i natsionalizatsiya...*, vol. I, p. 341.

89   *Rabochii put'*, no. 6-8, 1918. The full protocols of the conference are published in *Oktyabr'skaya revolyutsiya i fabzavkomy*, vol. IV.

90   *Oktyabr'skaya revolyutsiya i fabzavkomy*, vol. IV, p. 439.

91   Op. cit., vol. III, pp. 128, 286; vol. IV, pp. 26, 34. For the Council's efforts to organize the supply and distribution of fuel and raw materials, see op. cit., vol. III, pp. 253-77.

92   Op. cit., vol. IV, pp. 417.

93   Op., cit, pp. 443-444.

94   Op. cit., p. 200.

95   Op. cit., p. 158.

96   Op. cit., p. 180.

97   Op. cit., p. 187.

98   Op. cit., p. 421.

99   *Materialy po statistike truda severnoi oblasti*, vyp. V, Petrograd, 1918, p. 33.

100   N. Katyn', 'Ot rabochego kontrolya k organizatsii i regulirovaniyu proizvodstva,' *Novyi put'*, no. 1-2 (5-6), 14 January 1918.

101   *Natsionalizatsiya promyshlennosti SSSR*, pp. 82-86; *Rabochii kontrol' i natsionalizatsiya...*, vol. 1, pp. 345-47; *Novaya zhizn'*, 5 December 1917. This was essentially the position adopted by the St. Petersburg Society of Factory and Mill Owners, too. (*Oktyabr'skaya revolyutsiya i fabzavkomy*, vol. III, p. 106.).

102   *Rabochii kontrol' i natsionalizatsiya...*, vol. 1, pp. 346-47.

103   *Metallist*, no. 1, 1918, p. 13. For more material on the attitudes of union to control, see *Oktyabr'skaya revolyutsiya i fabzavkomy*, vol. III, pp. 115-31.

104   Their position changed only after the German Revolution began in November 1918, but even so their support was grudging. The party's right wing did not follow this turn and even supported armed opposition.

105   *Rabochaya gazeta*, 12 November 1917.

106   *Oktyabr'skaya revolyutsiya i fabzavkomy*, vol. III, pp. 216-17.

107   *Rabochii kontrol' i natsionalizatsiya...*, pp. 325-26

108   Op. cit., p. 285.

109   V. Perazich, *Tekstili Leningrada v 1917g.*, Leningrad, 1927, p. 142.

110   *Oktyabr'skaya revolyutsiya i fabzavkomy*, vol. IV, pp 437-479.

111   *Natsionalizatsiya promyshlennosti SSSR*, p. 351.

112   *Novaya zhizn'*, 21 January 1918.

113   *Novyi put'*, nos. 4-5(8-9), 1918, pp. 13-14; nos. 6-8 (10-12), pp. 22-24.

114   *Oktyabr'skaya revolyutsiya i fabzavkomy*, vol. IV, pp. 241.

115   Op. cit., pp. 241, 446. That spring, Larin, as head of the Supreme Economic Council, announced several ambitious economic projects, which, however, had to be shelved when the civil war soon after forced the Soviet state into survival mode for the next three years. (*Byulleten' Vysshego soveta narodnogo khozyaistva*. no. 1, April 1918, pp. 23-24.)

116   *Oktyabr'skaya revolyutsiya i fabzavkomy*, vol. IV, pp. 241, 174-77.

117   Op. cit, pp. 5, 290; *Novyi put'*, nos. 6-8 (10-12), p. 24.

118   *Trudy I Vserossiiskogo s'ezda sovetov narodnogo khozyaistva*, Moscow, 1918, pp. 53, 91-

92.
119   Carr, *The Bolshevik Revolution*, vol. II, p. 189.
120   In May 1918, Lenin told the Congress of *sonvarkhozy* that 'We do not close our eyes to the fact that we cannot by ourselves carry through a socialist revolution, even if Russia were much less backward, even if we were in better circumstances than after four years of a painful, harsh, ruinous war – in one country you cannot fully, by your own forces, carry out a socialist revolution.' But implicitly addressing the Mensheviks, he continued: 'He who turns away from the socialist revolution that is occurring in Russia, pointing to the obvious lack of correspondence of forces, is like a person frozen in a case, who cannot see past his nose and forgets that no historical revolution of any significant proportions occurs without a whole series of non-correspondences of forces. Forces grow in the process of struggle as the revolution grows. [...] The [concrete] experience [of the workers in organizing the economy], whatever happens, as difficult as the various turns of the Russian Revolution and of the international socialist revolutions might be, this experience cannot be taken away. It has entered history as a conquest of socialism, and on the basis of that experience the future international revolution will build its socialist edifice.' (*Trudy I Vserossiiskogo s'ezda sovetov narodnogo khozyaistva*, p. 5)
121   I. Stepanov, *Ot rabochego kontrolya k rabochemu upravleniyu v promyshlennosti i zemledelii*, Moscow, 1918, pp. 4, 13-14.
122   *Oktyabr'skaya revolyutsiya i fabzavkomy*, vol. IV, p. 443.
123   Op. cit., pp. 293-94, 255-56.
124   Carr, p. 92.
125   Lenin's position remained contradictory. In a January 1919 speech to a national congress of trade unions, he forcefully insisted that socialism meant that the workers themselves, not bureaucrats, run the economy and the state and that the role of the trade unions was to educate workers for this and draw them into these functions. He condemned the 'harmful prejudice that management of the state is for the privileged, a special art.' Only if the mass of workers themselves actually managed could the revolution be secure against capitalism. And their education could not be theoretical, not through books, lectures or meetings, but through actual practice. Yet in practically the same breath, he warned against the trade union's taking on state functions 'without authorization' (*samochinno* – on their own). 'We are coming to it but we have not reached it.' It was, thus, not the workers themselves, but the ruling party, the conscious elements of the proletariat, who would control the educational process and decide how and when the mass of workers could manage economic and political affairs on their own. Lenin was undoubtedly not unaware of the contradiction, but he, like most Bolsheviks, viewed it as the temporary product of a situation in which 'the new class, because of the vicious opposition of the exploiters against one of the weakest and least prepared countries, as Russia is, when the union of toilers has had to make its revolution with mad rapidity, in conditions that force it to think not so much about the smooth development of the revolution but about holding on until the proletariat of Western Europe begins to awake.' (Lenin, *Polnoe sobranie sochinenii*, vol. 37, pp. 435-453.) After the revolutionary wave in the West had been beaten back, making Russia's isolation a long-term prospect, this contradiction took on a permanent character.
126   *Oktyabr'skaya revolyutsiya i fabzavkomy*, vol. IV, pp. 316, 323-24.
127   Op. cit., p. 320. Maksim Gorky, along with others contributors to the left-Menshevik *Novaya zhizn'*, were writing articles critical of the workers' efforts to build a new state and organize the economy. The tone of the articles was often condescending, even mocking, which worker activists found deeply insulting, all the more so as most of the left intelligentsia, including Gorky himself, were opposed to the soviet seizure of power

and stood by the side lines. (See my 'The Working Class and the Intelligentsia in 1917,' *Critique*, no. 14, 1981, pp. 67-87.)

128   Op. cit., pp. 318-19.

129   Op. cit., p. 284.

130   Op. cit, pp. 237, 319.

131   Op. cit., 338-339, 354-56; *Novaya zhizn'*, 28 January 1918.

132   *Novyi put'*, no.s 4-5 (8-9), 1918, p. 14.

133   *Natsionalizatsiya prommyshlennosti i organizatsiya sotsialisticheskogo proizvodstva v Petrograde*, vol. I, Leningrad, 1958, p. 99.

134   *Trudy I Vserossiiskogo s'ezda sovetov narodnogo khozyaistva*, pp. 57-66.

135   Op. cit., p. 98.

136   Op.cit., p. 66.

137   Op. cit., pp. 74-5.

138   An insightful recent study of these processes in Petrograd's industrial working class during the civil war concluded: 'In the period of civil war and war communism the revolutionary passion of the workers of Petrograd faded rapidly. Its numbers significantly declined because of the economic crisis, the collapse of the financial system, the breakdown of military industry. Very many left the factories. The decline in numbers affected more the most politicized circle of workers, those capable of developing independent consciousness. A part of it that supported the new regime transferred into the institutions. Others took shelter in the villages or scattered among the craft workshops. The change in numbers and composition of the workers very much weakened their capacity for self-organization, which undoubtedly favoured the monopolization of power by the Bolsheviks. In 1918-1919, the Petrograd workers avoided politics and were preoccupied with survival in conditions of growing crisis.'A.V. Gogolevskii, *Revolyutsiya i psikhologiya: politicheskie nastroeniya rabochikh Petrograda v usloviyakh bol'shevistskoi monopolii na vlast' 1918-1920*, St. Petersburg, University of St. Petersburg, 2005, p. 216.

139   *Trudy I Vserossiiskogo s'ezda sovetov narodnogo khozyaistva*, p. 60.

140   Gogolevskii, op. cit., ch. 6. This does not necessarily mean, however, that the committees were still under control of the factory general assemblies, another question that needs to be researched.

141   On this, see my "Destatization' and the Struggle for Power in the Soviet Economy: A New Phase in the Soviet Labour Movement,' in R. Miliband & L. Panitch, eds., *The Socialist Register 1991*, London, Merlin Press, 1991, pp. 95-127.

THE LEGITIMACY OF THE OCTOBER REVOLUTION[1]

David Mandel

To argue in support of the historical legitimacy of the October Revolution and of the suppression of capitalism that followed goes is to go against the currently dominant viewpoint in the historiography of the revolution, as well as the position of the present Russian government. Of course, to defend the historical legitimacy of October is not to claim it was inevitable. Nothing in the history of a people is inevitable. There are always alternative paths of development, especially in periods of revolutionary crisis. But a liberal-democratic path of development – and that was the aim of the February Revolution, even among workers – was not a choice available to Russian society. Yet, that is the argument, explicit or implicit, of those who would deny legitimacy to the October Revolution.

What does one mean by 'historical legitimacy'? Above all it means that October was not an arbitrary act organized behind the back of Russian society by a group of Marxist ideologues who were bent on carrying out, at any price, a 'socialist experiment'. That is how the October Revolution is presented in a draft 'Concept of the New Educational-Methodological Complex on National History,' ordered by the present Russian government. In that document one can read, for example, that 'The Great Russian Revolution that occurred in 1917, and also the 'Soviet experiment' that began in October 1917, by their impact on world processes, are recognized as some of the most important events of the twentieth century.'[2] The February Revolution is still thus considered 'great' (although it did overthrow the Tsar, whom the present-day Russian Church has elevated to sainthood, while among the people, sinful as it was, he was daubed 'Nikolai the Bloody). But October is reduced to an 'experiment,' in other words to an arbitrary act that deviated Russia from its natural path of development, presumably one of capitalist democracy.

My own research into the revolutionary period[3] supports the conclusion that October was indeed a popular revolution. For workers and peasants, its aim was to save February's democratic revolution from the threat of counterrevolution at the hands of the propertied classes, the bourgeoisie and the aristocratic landowners. And since this second revolution was directed against those classes and was led by the workers' movement, it unleashed economic and political dynamics that led to the suppression of capitalism.

The historical experience of capitalist democracy shows that a necessary condition is that the bourgeoisie not consider that its socio-economic dominance – or any other interest that it might consider vital in the given circumstances – is threatened by the democratic freedoms. There is involved, therefore, a certain subjective element: the perception on the part of the bourgeoisie of the degree of threat to what it considers vital to its dominance. Be that as it may, this condition was absent in Russia of the early twentieth century. The Russian bourgeoisie, and the nobility even more, feared remaining face to face with the toiling classes, the workers and peasants, without the support of the repressive apparatus of the autocratic state.

Russian society was deeply split, polarized between the propertied classes, on the one hand, and the toiling classes, on the other. This polarization, this irreconcilable opposition had deep roots in the history and social structure of Russian society. It was not something that the Bolsheviks created in October 1917. 'We are accused of sowing civil war,' said a Bolshevik worker at the conference of worker and Red-army delegates of the First City District of Petrograd in May 1918. 'There is here a big mistake, if not a lie... Class interests are not created by us. They are a question that exists in life, a fact, before which all must bow.'[4]

Fear of the people explains the cowardly, fundamentally impotent opposition to the autocracy even among the most radical elements of the propertied classes. The Kadet (Constitutional Democrat - liberal) Vasily Maklakov expressed this graphically in a famous article entitled 'A Tragic Situation', published in 1915. He used a metaphor to explain his point. An automobile is travelling along a mountain road, and the driver is obviously crazy. The threat of a catastrophe is great. There are people sitting in the car (read: liberal political actors) who know how to drive. But their action is paralyzed by the fear that in the course of the struggle to get control of the steering wheel, the car will fall into the abyss. And your mother (Russia, clearly identified with the social dominance of the propertied classes) is seated in the back. This fear paralyzes the action of those 'who know how to drive.'[5] Maurice Paleologue, French ambassador to Russia during the war, recalled a conversation in June 1915 with the prominent banker and industrialist Aleksei Ivanovich Putilov. The latter described the coming revolution as 'horrifying anarchy, endless anarchy... anarchy for ten years.'[6]

When the workers of Petrograd, supported by the garrison, overthrew the autocracy in February 1917, the propertied classes at first, so it seemed, welcomed the revolution. Their members came out into the streets sporting red ribbons in their lapels. But in their hearts, they were deeply alarmed. V.V. Stankevich, a Popular (right-wing) Socialist, military commissar under the Provisional Government in 1917 and an acute observer of the political scene, recalled of that period: 'Officially they were jubilant. They praised the revolution, shouted 'hurray' for the fighters for freedom, decorated themselves with ribbons and marched under red banners. They are said 'we', 'our' revolution, 'our' victory. But in their hearts, in intimate conversation, they were horrified, they shuddered and felt themselves captives of hostile elemental forces that were going along some unforeseeable path.'[7]

A fundamental condition of liberal democracy was thus missing: the propertied classes were too afraid of the popular masses. Did they have anything to fear? The landed aristocracy without question did. The peasants' conception of land reform – and peasants constituted the overwhelming majority of the population – would put an end to their existence, not only as a dominant class, but as a class per se. But neither could the bourgeoisie be indifferent to the perspective of land reform as the peasants wanted it – without compensation – since it would violate the sacrosanct inviolability of private property, even if the property in question was feudal in origin. Besides, by 1917 a very significant part of landlord's land was mortgaged to the banks, a fact that brought the two propertied classes even closer together.[8]

But the workers, including the most radical ones, members of the Bolshevik party, were not aiming at the overthrow capitalism in February 1917. That revolution was supposed to be liberal-democratic. Its popular goals were: a democratic republic; an energetic diplomacy aimed at rapidly concluding a democratic, just peace; the eight-hour workday; and land reform. The last two goals were without doubt social. And they were not the only ones. As one of the Petrograd Soviet's agitators explained in March 1917: 'The workers can't obtain freedom and not use it to ease their burden of labour, to fight capital.'[9] Besides the introduction of the eight-hour workday, in the days after the February Revolution, the workers purged the factory administrations of their most odious members (under the Tsar, the factory administration had collaborated intimately with the civil and political police and was notoriously despotic); they sought increases to their wages (which had been seriously eroded by wartime inflation); they sought the right to elect representatives to permanent factory committees that would represent them in dealings with the administration (the owners had stubbornly resisted permanent collective representation of the workers in their factories), and they obtained the right of their elected factory committees to 'oversee the internal work rules' in the factories. Finally, hiring and dismissal of workers were to be carried out with the consent of the factory committee – this had been another area of unbridled managerial arbitrariness before the revolution.

This was undoubtedly a lot, especially for Russia. But workers were not thinking to threaten capitalism with these measures. Neither the workers, nor the Bolsheviks put forth the demand for workers' control (with the partial exception of workers in state-owned enterprises.) And when they did later do that, they were demanding access to information, not participation in management of the factories.

The more enlightened representatives of the bourgeoisie understood that. Speaking to a meeting of the Council of Private Railroads in March 1917, Nikolai Nekrasov, Minister of Railways and a leftist among liberals, tried to calm the fears of the assembled:

> There is no need to fear the fact that social elements are now beginning to appear. One should rather strive to direct these social elements in the right direction… A rational combination of the social moment with the political is essential, and in no circumstances to deny the social moment, to fear it… That which we need to achieve is not a social revolution, but the avoidance of social revolution through social reform.[10]

At first, it seemed that the industrialists were prepared to heed this advice. But, in fact, they considered the concessions they had made in the wake of the revolution to be only temporary, until the workers' revolutionary ardour cooled and the concessions could be taken back. Only a few weeks after the revolution, the bourgeois (non-socialist) press began to write of the workers' 'excessive demands' that were threatening supplies to the valiant soldiers in the trenches. Workers immediately saw in this an attempt to drive a wedge between them and soldiers – it was the worker-soldier alliance that had made possible the February Revolution. They began to suspect that, behind increasingly frequent production problems, a hidden, creeping lockout was being put into effect. Before the revolution, lockouts had been a favourite weapon of the industrialists against the workers' movement. The general lockout in St. Petersburg in November and December 1905 had dealt a decisive blow to Russia's first revolution.

The workers suspicions only grew stronger when they saw the Provisional Government refuse to adopt any serious measures to combat the growing economic dislocation caused by the war and Tsarist incompetence. The Minister of Trade and Industry, Alexander Konovalov, himself an industrialist, resigned in protest against a rather modest plan for state economic regulation that had been drafted by the Economic Commission of the Petrograd Soviet, controlled at the time by the moderate socialists, the Mensheviks and the Socialist Revolutionaries (SRs). These parties strongly advocated the political alliance with the liberal bourgeoisie. A few weeks later, in a speech to a Congress of the War-Industry Committees, Konovalov complained about of the workers' 'excessive demands' and warned that 'if in the nearest future a sobering of minds does not occur, we will witness the closure of tens and hundreds of enterprises.'[11] And Konovalov was known as a 'leftist' among industrialists.

And so already from the late spring of 1917, workers were becoming increasingly convinced that the bourgeoisie was conducting a hidden lockout, hoping to suppress the workers' movement with 'the bony hand of hunger', as the liberal banker and industrial magnate Pavel Ryabushinskii so graphically put it at the Second All-Russian Congress of Trade Industry Congress in early August 1917. Against the threat of advancing economic collapse and mass unemployment, the workers tried to introduce control of the administration, in the sense of access to information in order to verify the causes cited by management for production problems. But they soon realized that such control would evade them unless the bourgeoisie was removed from influence in the government. And so it was no accident that the first citywide assembly of workers' representatives in the capital to vote for the transfer of power to the soviets was the Conference of Factory Committees that met at the beginning of June.

The transfer of power to the soviets meant for the workers the removal of the propertied classes from influence over state policy. Workers were increasingly convinced that the propertied classes were bent on counterrevolution. The Provisional Government, a coalition of representatives of those classes with the moderate socialists, during the eight months of its existence failed to carry out a single one of the objectives that popular classes had sought in the February Revolution: not land reform, not a peace policy, not convocation of a constituent assembly; not the adoption of a law on the eight-hour workday. (The latter was introduced in the capital by the workers on their own initiative, but a law was never adopted.) Instead, the Provisional Government, pressed by the Allies, launched a new offensive at the front in June. It rejected state economic regulation and fought against workers' control. And it abetted and facilitated a generals' conspiracy at the end of August 1918 aimed at suppressing popular organizations, the soviets first of all.

Russia's workers fully supported the October insurrection and the transfer of power to the soviets. In the removal of the propertied classes from any influence on government policy, they saw the only possibility of avoiding a counterrevolution and realizing the promise of the February Revolution. They did not expect miracles from the transfer of power to the soviets. They saw that industrial collapse and hunger were approaching. And the Bolsheviks, on their part, did not promise miracles.

In the Russian capital, the workers, and first of all Bolshevik workers, who numbered more than 30,000 in October 1917 – understood that they would have ranged against them not only the propertied classes, but also most of the intelligentsia, the educated elements of society, including the socialist intelligentsia. The latter, with significant but too few exceptions, turned its back on the people at the very moment it dared to straighten its bent back and stand at full height. But the transfer of power to the soviets offered at least a chance to save the revolution. And there was also the hope that Russia's example would inspire revolutions in Western countries, and that the latter would come to the aid of Russia's revolution.

The Bolsheviks are often condemned for organizing the October insurrection and for unleashing civil war, when, in fact, they deserve praise for their action in October. As a workers' party, they honestly carried out their duty – they did not abandon the people at the most critical moment, leaving it without leadership. In contrast, the left Mensheviks, who shared basically the Bolsheviks' view of the counterrevolutionary aspirations of the propertied classes, decided to stand aside, since they did not believe that a government based solely on the soviets, that is, on the workers and peasants, and without participation of the middle strata of society, would be viable. But these middle strata in 1917, and most importantly their educated element, the intelligentsia, had chosen the side of bourgeoisie, or else they vainly tried to stand above the fray. As for the right-wing Mensheviks and SRs, they continued to insist on including in power, in one form or another, representatives of the bourgeoisie. After all, they argued, it was a bourgeois-democratic revolution, the only one possible in backward Russia - closing their eyes to the counterrevolutionary aspirations of the propertied classes.

Those who consider the Bolsheviks a group of ideologues and usurpers have trouble explaining how such a group, without any experience in state or economic administration, without the support of the bulk of the educated part of society, without an army (at least in the first several months), was able to hold onto power against the propertied classes not only of Russia, but of all the more developed capitalist countries, and even some undeveloped ones.

In fact, the Bolshevik party of 1917 was flesh of the flesh of the working class. That was the secret of its success. It was very far from the later image of a 'Leninist party,' portrayed as an authoritarian, strictly hierarchical organization of professional revolutionaries. If the party had been such in October 1917, there never would have been a second revolution. Only the pressure of the party's lower and middle strata forced the reluctant Central-Committee majority to act in October. The Central Committee went so far as to burn Lenin's letters demanding preparation of the insurrection!

Three quarters of the Bolshevik party membership in Russia's capital (40,000 members in October 1917) were workers.[12] The members of the district and city committees were overwhelmingly workers. These Bolshevik workers were the most active, politically aware and determined part of the working class. They were that part of the working class that dared to take on the leadership of the revolution, knowing that the chances of victory were not great. They had above all a strongly developed sense of dignity - human and class dignity – and they were determined not to yield without giving battle.

It was to these Bolsheviks that Lenin appealed in October against the majority of the party's Central Committee. The latter preferred to wait for the constituent assembly (elections to which were finally organized by the Soviet government in November), as if that assembly could magically cure the profound split in Russian society. The Kornilov uprising at the end of August 1917, sympathy for which the Kadet party, which was hegemonic among the propertied classes in 1917, did not conceal, demonstrated clearly the kind of regime that latter desired.

One often encounters the claim in the historiography that the roots of Stalinist totalitarianism were already present in the 'Leninist' conception of the party. But the party in 1917 was an open, democratic organization. The capital's Bolsheviks more than once rejected positions adopted by the Central Committee and supported by Lenin.

As for the totalitarian tendencies ascribed to the party, one need only recall the unanimous support among Petrograd's Bolsheviks on the morrow of the October insurrection in favour of the formation of a broad coalition of all the socialist parties, from the Bolsheviks on the left to the Popular Socialists on the right. How does this fit with the claim that the Bolsheviks aspired to a one-party dictatorship? If that coalition was not formed, it was because the moderate socialists rejected the principle of a government accountable to the soviets, representative organizations of the workers and peasants, to the exclusion representation of the propertied classes. They insisted on including, in one form or another, representatives of the latter and on limiting the Bolsheviks to a minority status in the government, even though the Bolsheviks had constituted the majority at the recent Congress of Soviets of Workers' and Soldiers' deputies. The Mensheviks and SRs were demanding, in effect, to annul the October insurrection and to restore the status quo ante, which had been the reason for the insurrection. When the workers saw that to be the case, they lost interest in the proposed coalition.

But when subsequently the Left SRs decided to participate in the Soviet government and the Peasant Congress decided to merge with the Central Executive Committee of worker and soldier deputies, there was jubilation among workers, including the Bolshevik workers, who were very conscious of the danger of their political isolation and of the tremendous difficulties that confronted the Soviet government. Despite this, the Mensheviks and the SRs, from the very first days of the Soviet government, referred to it only as 'the Bolshevik dictatorship'.

In actual fact, the Bolshevik organization in the capital almost disappeared in the year following the October insurrection. The politically active workers – and most of these were organized in the Bolshevik party – felt that, now that the people had taken power in its hands, the task was to work in the soviets, in the economic administrations, to organize the Red Army. This is how Konstantin Shelavin, a member of Petrograd's Bolshevik Committee, recalled that period:

> A series of responsible, highly qualified comrades who had gone through the school of illegality became infected with an exclusively 'soviet' spirit, not to speak of the masses of the younger generation. Even if these comrades did not give full expression to what they were thinking, all of them, nevertheless, had a certain difficulty imagining what, in essence, was left for the party organizations to do after the victory of the proletariat. Some thought that there at least remained agitation and propaganda activities. But they still felt that the real activity now is, for example, to organize the district soviet of the national economy, and certainly not to 'ferment' in the district party committee. Indeed, around them everything was churning; the old was being destroyed and the new was being built; sabotage was being fought; the first new soviet state forces were being recruited; the districts were being organized like independent republics with their own commissars – of labour, of education, etc.; the best party forces were being thrown into this whirlwind of construction… When the Vasileostrovskii district soviet moved into a new building on Srednii Prospekt from the 16th Line, they relegated the district party committee to the fifth floor, and their thinking went something along the lines: what sort of particular work can they possibly have now? [13]

This was clearly not the behaviour of a party bent on establishing its totalitarian power.

It is always tempting to read history backwards, in this case from Stalin's totalitarian regime to the October insurrection, or perhaps even farther – to Lenin's brochure *What Is To Be Done?*[14] Stalinism did not arise, of course, out of nowhere, but out of the social and political conditions that preceded it. But if the Communist party eventually replaced the soviets already during the civil war as the real centre of power, the explanation should be sought in the social and political conditions of that period, and not in some kind of ideological DNA of the Bolshevik party.

Victor Serge, a Belgian anarchist who arrived in Petrograd in 1919 and quickly became a supporter of the Soviet government (after the civil war, in the 1920s, he was active in the left opposition to rising Stalinism), wrote the following in 1920 in a letter to his anarchist comrades back home:

> The suppression of so-called freedoms; dictatorship backed up if necessary by terror; the creation of an army; centralization for war purposes of industry, food supplies and administration (whence state control and bureaucracy); and finally, the dictatorship of a party. In this fearsome chain of necessities, there is not a single link that is not rigorously conditioned by the one that precedes it and which does not in turn condition the one that follows it.

Serge recognized that such a state, however justified by the goal of saving the revolution, could generate powerful vested interests that would want to maintain it even after the threat of counterrevolution had passed. His response was a call for vigilance, and he expressed the hope that the revolutionary struggle in more developed countries would not be as difficult and as drawn out as in Russia, a country already devastated by the world war, especially if the following revolutions could rely on the support of an already established revolutionary state in Russia. At the same time, he recognized that in the eventual struggle against the power of the bureaucracy in Russia, 'the Communists may need to resort to profoundly revolutionary activity which will be long and difficult.'[15]

Serge's words find surprising echo in those of a Bolshevik worker at a conference of factory committees in Petrograd in January 1918. The industrial situation was already approaching catastrophic, particularly the shortages of fuel and raw materials. The delegates to the conference were unanimous about the need to centralize economic authority so that the scarce resources and the industrial orders could be allocated in a rational manner according to the most urgent needs of the young Soviet state. The Economic Soviet of the Northern Commune had only just been created, and the conference was to consider proposed regulations, according to which orders emanating from that body would be binding on the factory committees. In the course of the discussion, an anarchist delegate proposed an amendment: the orders would be binding, 'except in cases where the order contradicts the interests of the working class.' To this, the chairperson of the presidium, a Bolshevik worker, answered:

At the time, when we were examining these regulations, we saw the corresponding point and we wanted to insert exactly that reservation. We thought about it. But we didn't insert it into the charter, thinking that the *sovnarkhoz* [economic council] that we are organizing will not move against us, because it is not a bureaucratically created organ, not appointed from above, but an organ that we ourselves have chosen, that we can recall, and it consists of people that we can remove from their activity... Don't forget that the *sovnarkhoz* is a class body, based on the class of the proletariat and the poorest peasants, and it seems to us that it is hardly necessary, by inserting such a reservation, to express that kind of lack of confidence in them. If we adopt an attitude of mistrust from the very beginning, then these organs will hardly be able to function correctly... And I think that only an anarchist could propose such an amendment, as they reject any sort of leaders and have absolutely no confidence in them... [But] if these organs really do thus part ways with the masses, then, of course, we will have to introduce such an amendment. And that will not be enough - we will have to overthrow those organs and perhaps make a new revolution. But it seems to us that, for now, the Soviet of People's Commissars is our soviet, and the institutions that it has established are functioning harmoniously together.[16]

What Serge and these workers feared might eventually happen did happen. But when the time came to make a new revolution, the working class, which had already led three revolutions, could not find the strength for a fourth. The decisive factor in the authoritarian development of the Soviet regime was, without doubt, the dispersal of the working class after the October Revolution, something that occurred surprisingly quickly in the very first months after the insurrection. For a quarter century prior to that, the urban working class had been the vanguard of the struggle for democracy in Russia. Not long after October, it practically ceased to exist as an independent political force. The Communist party claimed to represent the working class. And, at least in the first years, it did have in its ranks the best forces of that class. But the party could not substitute itself for the social class as an active socio-political force, one capable of exercising effective control over the state it had brought into existence.

NOTES

1   This text is based on a talk by David Mandel in May 2016 in Moscow to introduce *The Petrograd Workers in the Russian Revolutions of 1917: February 1917 - June 1918*, to be published by Brill in the Netherlands and Haymarket in the USA.

2   http://rushistory.org/wp-content/uploads/2013/11/2013.10.31-Концепция_финал. pdf. (site of the Russian Historical Society, consulted 2 February 2014.)

3   This text is largely based on D. Mandel, *The Petrograd Workers in the Revolutions of 1917 (February 1917-June 1918)*, Brill and Haymarket Press, to appear in 2017.

4   *Pervaya konferentsiya rabochikh I krasngvardveiskikh deputatov 1-go gorodksovo raiona*, Petrgorad, 1918, p. 248.

5   *Russkie vedomosti*, no, 221, 1915.

6   Cited in M. Mitel'man, B. Glebov, and A. Ulyanskii, *Istoriya Putilovskogo zavoda 1801- 1917 gg.*, Leningrad, 1926, p. 33.

7   V.V. Stankevich, *Vospominaniya 1914-1919 gg.*, Leningrad, 1926, p. 33.

8   By the start of 1917, the banks held as much in mortgages to the landowners as they had loaned out to all of industry. T.V. Osipova, *Rossiskoe kres'yanstvo v revolyutsii I grazhdanskoi voiny*, Moscow, Streletz, 2001, pp. 7-8.

9   *Pravda*, 17 March 1917.

10   *Rech'*, 29 March 1917.

11   *Novaya zhizn'*, 19 May 1917.

12   The following is largely based on my forthcoming *The Petrograd Workers.*

13   Shelavin, 'Iz istorii Peterburgskogo komiteta bol'shevikov v 1918 godu', *Krasnaya letopis'*, no. 2 (26) (1928) p. 111.

14   On the latter, the book by Lars Lih, *Lenin Rediscovered: What Is To Be Done in Context* (http://ouleft.org/wp-content/uploads/lenin-rediscovered.pdf) is highly recommended. Lih convincingly shows that the ideas in this pamphlet were widely share in social-democratic circles across Europe.

15   Victor Serge, *Revolution in Danger, Writings from Russia, 1919-1921*, Chicago, Haymarket, 2011, pp. 142-143; 150.

16   *Oktyabr'skaya revolyutsiya i fabzavkomy*, vol. IV., St. Petersburg, 2002, pp. 323-24.

THE OLD MOLE

Rosa Luxemburg

The outbreak of the Russian Revolution has brought an end to the historical standstill engendered by the continuation of the world war and the simultaneous failure of working-class struggle. It is as if a window had suddenly been opened in a Europe whose musty air has been nearly suffocating everyone for three years, admitting a fresh and invigorating breeze. Everyone has started breathing deeply and vigorously again. The eyes of the 'German liberators' in particular are anxiously fastened on the drama of the Russian Revolution. The grudging respect the German and Austro-Hungarian governments accord to the 'scroungers and plotters' and the anxious attention that is paid to anything said on the question of war and peace by Cheidze or by the workers' and soldiers' councils offer tangible confirmation of a fact that was only yesterday uncomprehendingly denied even by the oppositional socialists of the A. G.[1]: the fact that only the revolutionary action of the proletariat – and not any diplomatic 'agreements' or Wilsonian declarations – offers a way out of the dead end of the world war. The victors of Tannenberg and Warsaw[2] now nervously await their own 'liberation' from the throttling noose of war by the Russian proletariat, by the "masses on the street"!

Yet this noose cannot be loosened by the proletariat of one country alone, however heroic. The Russian Revolution itself is becoming an international problem. For the Russian workers' efforts for peace bring them into sharp conflict not only with their own bourgeoisie, whom they well know how to control, but also with the English, French and Italian bourgeoisies. The growling of the bourgeois press in all the countries of the Entente – *The Times, Le Matin, Corriere della Sera*, etc. – shows that the capitalists of the West, the doughty champions of 'democracy' and the rights of the 'small nations', are witnessing with ever-increasing, teeth-grinding rage the advances of the proletarian revolution that has put an end to the glorious age of imperialism's undivided rule in Europe. The capitalists of the Entente are now the strongest support of the Russian bourgeoisie against whom the

Russian proletariat has risen up in the struggle for peace. They are able to exert the greatest pressure on Russia in every way – diplomatic, financial, commercial – and are surely already doing so. A liberal revolution? A provisional government of the bourgeoisie? Fine! These will be officially recognized without delay, and welcomed as a guarantee of Russia's military serviceability as an obedient tool of international imperialism. But not a step further! Should the Russian Revolution insist on its intrinsically proletarian character, should it, in all logic, turn against war and imperialism, then its dear allies will show their teeth and seek to curb it by all means possible. The socialist proletariat of England, France and Italy is thus now duty bound to raise the banner of revolt against war. Only by vigorous mass action in their own countries, against their own ruling classes, can they avoid simply betraying the Russian revolutionary proletariat, and prevent it bleeding to death in an unequal struggle against not only the Russian but also the Western bourgeoisie. The Entente powers' present intervention in the domestic affairs of the Russian Revolution requires that the workers of those countries, as a matter of honour, provide cover to the Russian Revolution by attacking their ruling classes' flank and so compelling them to make peace.

And what now of the German bourgeoisie? With one eye smiling sourly and the other weeping bitterly, it observes the deeds of the Russian proletariat and the power it has gained. Accustomed, like a spoiled child, to treat its own working masses as mere military and political cannon fodder, the German bourgeoisie might well hope to use the Russian proletariat to get the war off its back as soon as possible. In the greatest of difficulties both in the West and in Asia Minor, and at its wits' end with food supply problems at home, a hard-pressed German imperialism would like to extricate itself as quickly as possible, and with some semblance of decorum, so as to be able to repair and equip itself in peace for further wars. The Russian Revolution will serve the purpose, precisely by virtue of its proletarian and socialist inclination to peace. Both German imperialism and the Entente powers are thus trying to think how they can profit from the revolution, only from opposite sides. The Western powers want to hitch the bourgeois-liberal tendency of the revolution to the wagon of imperialism, so as continue the war until the defeat of their German rival. German imperialism would like to exploit the proletarian tendency of the revolution to escape the imminent threat of military defeat. Well, why not, gentlemen? German Social Democracy has served so excellently well to disguise the unleashing of mass-murder as an 'act of liberation' against Russian Tsarism, so why shouldn't Russian Social Democracy help free 'liberators' ensnared in the difficulties of a war gone wrong? The German workers helped wage war when it suited imperialism; the Russian workers might be expected to make peace in the same helpful fashion.

Cheidze, however, is not so childishly easy to deal with as is little Scheidemann. A hasty 'announcement' in the *Norddeutsche Allgemeine* and Scheidemann's speedy despatch to Stockholm for 'negotiations' will get them at best a kick in the pants from Russian socialists of all shades. And as for a quickly cobbled together backstairs deal – the eleventh-hour separate peace with Russia that the German 'liberators' so hanker for – it can't be done. If the Russian proletariat is to see its peace tendency win out, the class as a whole has to achieve an increasingly powerful position in the country, its class action has to become colossal in scope, energy, depth and radicalism, so that Social Democracy either sweeps along or sweeps aside the still undecided classes duped by bourgeois nationalism. With barely concealed horror, the German 'liberators' now find themselves faced with this clearly visible, inevitable and yet most frightful obverse of the peace tendency in Russia. They fear, and with good reason, that the Russian Moor, unlike his German counterpart, will not want to 'go' when his work is done. They fear that sparks might fly onto East Prussian barns from the fire next door. They fully understand that only the unfolding of the most extreme revolutionary energy in an all-encompassing class struggle for political power in Russia can bring the struggle for peace to a successful conclusion, yet at the same time they long for the fleshpots of Tsarism, for their 'centuries-old, abiding friendship with our Eastern neighbour', Romanov absolutism. *Tua res agitur!* This concerns you! The Prussian minister's warning against the Russian Revolution still rings in the mind of the German ruling classes, and the heroes of the Königsberg Trial[3] are all 'as fair as on the primal day'. A republic, let alone one freshly established and controlled by the revolutionary-socialist proletariat, is the last thing the East-Prussian police and military State can be expected to tolerate on its flank. And its East-Prussian police soul is compelled to acknowledge its secret horror of the open market. The German 'liberators' have today to raise their hands and swear in public that they have no intention of strangling the revolution and restoring the dear old snub-nosed Nicholas to the Tsarist throne! It was the Russian Revolution that compelled the German 'liberators' to give themselves this resounding box on the ears in front of the whole world, and in doing so it brusquely wiped from the slate of history the whole monstrous lie on which German Social Democracy and the official mythology of German militarism had sustained themselves for three years. This is how the storm of revolution cleanses, sanitizes, does away with lies; this is how it suddenly sweeps away with ruthless broom the dung-pile of official hypocrisy that has accumulated since the onset of the world war and the stilling of class struggle in Europe. The Russian Revolution tore the mask of 'democracy' from the face of the Entente bourgeoisie, and from German militarism it tore away the mask of the would-be liberator from Tsarist despotism.

Yet for the Russian proletariat the question of peace is not quite as simple as would suit Hindenburg and Bethmann. The victory of the revolution and its further tasks require that a secure position be maintained in future. The outbreak of the revolution and the commanding position achieved by the proletariat immediately transformed the imperialist war in Russia into what the mendacious clichés of the ruling classes would have us believe it is in every country, a war of national defence. Milyukov and his associates saw their fair dreams of Constantinople and world-beguiling plans for 'national-democratic' reapportionment thrust back down their throats by the masses of workers and soldiers, and the slogan of national defence implemented in practice. However, the Russian proletariat can end the war and make peace with a clear conscience only when its achievements – the inception of the revolution and its consequent unimpeded progress – are secured. They, the Russian proletariat, are today the only ones who truly defend the cause of freedom, progress and democracy. And these have to be defended not only today, against the chicanery, the pressure and the war mania of the Entente bourgeoisie, but also tomorrow, most especially against the 'fists' of the German 'liberators'. A semi-absolutist police and military state is no good neighbour for a young republic wracked by internal struggles, and an imperialist soldiery tried and tested in blind obedience is no good neighbour for a revolutionary proletariat embarking upon the boldest of class struggles, of vast scope and long duration.

Even now, the German occupation of unhappy 'independent Poland' represents a severe blow against the Russian Revolution. The operational base of the revolution is thereby reduced, a country that has always been one of the brightest-burning torches of the revolutionary movement, a country that politically marched in the van of the Russian Revolution of 1905, has been neutralised, transformed, socially, into a graveyard, politically into a German barracks. Who can now guarantee that tomorrow, when peace has been made, as soon as German militarism has freed its clawed paw from the trap, it will not strike the Russian proletariat in the flank to prevent a dangerous destabilisation of the German semi-absolutist regime?

The strangled 'assurances' of yesterday's heroes of Königsberg are not enough to allay such fears. The example of the Paris Commune is too fresh in the mind. In general, cats don't leave mice alone. The world war has unleashed such an orgy of reaction in Germany, revealed such an ascendancy of militarism, exposed the German working class as so feeble behind its mighty façade, and showed the foundations of so-called 'political freedom' in Germany to be so flimsy and fragile that the prospects on that quarter have become a severe and tragic problem. The 'danger of German militarism' to imperialist England or France is of course humbug, war propaganda, the huckster cry of Germany's competitors. The danger of German militarism to revolutionary, republican Russia, on the other hand, is very real. The Russian proletarians would be the most reckless of politicians if they did not ask themselves whether the German cannon-fodder that today allows imperialism to lead it to slaughter on every field of battle will not tomorrow allow itself to be ordered against the Russian Revolution. Scheidemann, Heilmann and Lensch would of course provide a 'Marxist' theory for it, and Legien and Schlicke would draw up the contract for the slave-consignment, true to the patriotic tradition of the German princes who sold their countrymen for cannon-fodder abroad.

In the face of these self-evident apprehensions regarding the future of the Russian Revolution, there can be only one safeguard: the awakening of the German proletariat, the attainment of a position of power in their own country by the *German* 'workers and soldiers', the conduct of a revolutionary struggle for peace by the *German* people. For the Russian revolutionary soldiers, making peace with Bethmann and Hindenburg would be a damnably sticky business and a very dubious proposition. With the German 'workers and soldiers', peace would be concluded immediately and upon solid foundations.

The question of peace is thus in reality bound up with the most unimpeded, most radical development of the Russian Revolution, this however being dependent on the parallel revolutionary struggles for peace by the French, English, Italian and, especially, the German proletariat.

Is the international proletariat to leave the conflict with the bourgeoisie of Europe to the workers of Russia alone, abandoning them to the imperialist fury of the Anglo-Franco-Italian bourgeoisie, to the lowering reaction of the German? This is how now the question of peace must be formulated.

The conflict between the international bourgeoisie and the Russian proletariat thus reveals the current world situation in the form of a dilemma: either world war until all have been bled white, or proletarian revolution – imperialism or socialism.

Here we are again confronted by our old, forsaken slogans of revolution and socialism, words a thousand times repeated in our agitational work that we neglected to invoke on the outbreak of war, when the time came to give them substance. They presented themselves anew, quite logically, to every thinking socialist as the long and hopeless mass-murder dragged on. They were evoked once again, in the negative, by the wretched fiasco of bourgeois pacifism and of diplomatic efforts to reach agreement. Today again they stand before us in the positive, given substance by the deeds, the destiny and the future of the Russian Revolution. Despite betrayal, despite the general failure of the working masses, despite the collapse of the Socialist International, the great law of history is making headway – like a mountain stream that has been diverted from its course and which, having plunged into the depths, now re-emerges, spurting bright, in an unexpected place.

History, you old mole, you have done your work well! There now resounds through the international and the German proletariat a slogan, an admonition, only ever called up by great turning points in world history: Imperialism or Socialism! War or Revolution! There is no third way!

Spartacus No. 5 May 1917
Reprinted in *Spartakusbriefe* (Berlin: Dietz Verlag, 1958)
Translated by Dafydd Roberts, July 2016

NOTES

1   The *Sozialdemokratische Arbeitsgemeinschaft* [Social Democratic Working Group] were the anti-war opposition within the parliamentary SPD who would go on to form the USPD.
2   The Battle of Tannenberg (26-30 August 1914) saw the almost complete destruction of the Russian Second Army; a year later, Germany occupied Warsaw.
3   The Königsberg Trial in July 1904 saw nine members of the SPD who had smuggled revolutionary writings into Russia accused of attempted high treason, insulting the Tsar and association with illegal secret societies; in their generally successful defence, their lawyers argued that the Russian Social Democrats opposed revolutionary terrorism and posed no threat to Germany.

TO THE POPULATION

Lenin

Comrades—workers, soldiers, peasants and all working people!

The workers' and peasants' revolution has definitely triumphed in Petrograd, having dispersed or arrested the last remnants of the small number of Cossacks deceived by Kerensky. The revolution has triumphed in Moscow too. Even before the arrival of a number of troop trains dispatched from Petrograd, the officer cadets and other Kornilovites in Moscow signed peace terms—the disarming of the cadets and the dissolution of the Committee of Salvation.[1]

Daily and hourly reports are coming in from the front and from the villages announcing the support of the overwhelming majority of the soldiers in the trenches and the peasants in the uyezds[2] for the new government and its decrees on peace and the immediate transfer of the land to the peasants. The victory of the workers' and peasants' revolution is assured because the majority of the people have already sided with it.

It is perfectly understandable that the landowners and capitalists, and the *top groups* of office employees and civil servants closely linked with the bourgeoisie, in a word, all the wealthy and those supporting them, react to the new revolution with hostility, resist its victory, threaten to close the banks, disrupt or bring to a standstill the work of the different establishments, and hamper the revolution in every way, openly or covertly. Every politically-conscious worker was well aware that we would inevitably encounter resistance of this kind. The entire Party press of the Bolsheviks has written about this on numerous occasions. Not for a single minute will the working classes be intimidated by this resistance; they will not falter in any way before the threats and strikes of the supporters of the bourgeoisie.

The majority of the people are with us. The majority of the working and oppressed people all over the world are with us. Ours is the cause of justice. Our victory is assured.

The resistance of the capitalists and the high-ranking employees will be smashed. Not a single person will be deprived of his property except under the special state law proclaiming nationalisation of the banks and syndicates. This law is being drafted. Not one of the working people will suffer the loss of a kopek; on the contrary, he will be helped. Apart from the strictest accounting and control, apart from levying the set taxes in full the government has no intention of introducing any other measure.

In support of these just demands the vast majority of the people have rallied round the Provisional Workers' and Peasants' Government.

Comrades, working people! Remember that now you yourselves are at the helm of state. No one will help you if you yourselves do not unite and take into *your* hands *all affairs* of the state. *Your* Soviets are from now on the organs of state authority, legislative bodies with full powers.

Rally around your Soviets. Strengthen them. Get on with the job yourselves; begin right at the bottom, do not wait for anyone. Establish the strictest revolutionary law and order, mercilessly suppress any attempts to create anarchy by drunkards, hooligans, counter-revolutionary officer cadets, Kornilovites and their like.

Ensure the strictest control over production and accounting of products. Arrest and hand over to the revolutionary courts all who dare to injure the people's cause, irrespective of whether the injury is manifested in sabotaging production (damage, delay and subversion), or in hoarding grain and products or holding up shipments of grain, disorganising the railways and the postal, telegraph and telephone services, or any resistance whatever to the great cause of peace, the cause of transferring the land to the peasants, of ensuring workers' control over the production and distribution of products.

Comrades, workers, soldiers, peasants and all working people! Take all power into the hands of your Soviets. Be watchful and guard like the apple of your eye your land, grain, factories, equipment, products, transport— all that from now onwards will be entirely your property, public property. Gradually, with the consent and approval of the majority of the peasants, in keeping with their *practical* experience and that of the workers, we shall go forward firmly and unswervingly to the victory of socialism—a victory that will be sealed by the advanced workers of the most civilised countries, bring the peoples lasting peace and liberate them from all oppression and exploitation.

V. Ulyanov (Lenin)
Chairman of the Council of People's Commissars
5 November 1917, Petrograd
Originally published: *Pravda* No. 4, 19 November 1917

Resistance Books and the IIRE are grateful to the Marxist Internet Archive for placing this text in the public domain. The online version is at: https://www.marxists.org/archive/lenin/works/1917/nov/05.htm. Translated and edited by Yuri Sdobnikov, George Hanna, and George Hanna from the original (Lenin's *Collected Works*, Moscow, Progress Publishers, Volume 26, 1972, pp. 297-299). Transcription & HTML mark-up by Charles Farrell and David Walters.

NOTES

1   *Committee of Salvation* (Committee of Public Safety) was set up on 25 October (7 November) 1917, by the Moscow City Council to fight the Soviets in Moscow, and led the counter-revolutionary revolt of officer cadets which broke out on 28 October (10 November). The revolt was crushed on 2 November (15 November), and the Committee capitulated to the Moscow Revolutionary Military Committee.
2   An uyezd was an administrative subdivision in the Russian Empire.

LETTER TO AMERICAN WORKERS[1]

Lenin

Comrades! A Russian Bolshevik who took part in the 1905 Revolution, and who lived in your country for many years afterwards, has offered to convey my letter to you. I have accepted his proposal all the more gladly because just at the present time the American revolutionary workers have to play an exceptionally important role as uncompromising enemies of American imperialism – the freshest, strongest and latest in joining in the worldwide slaughter of nations for the division of capitalist profits. At this very moment, the American multimillionaires, these modern slave-owners have turned an exceptionally tragic page in the bloody history of bloody imperialism by giving their approval – whether direct or indirect, open or hypocritically concealed, makes no difference – to the armed expedition launched by the brutal Anglo-Japanese imperialists for the purpose of throttling the first socialist republic.

The history of modern, civilised America opened with one of those great, really liberating, really revolutionary wars of which there have been so few compared to the vast number of wars of conquest which, like the present imperialist war, were caused by squabbles among kings, landowners or capitalists over the division of usurped lands or ill-gotten gains. That was the war the American people waged against the British robbers who oppressed America and held her in colonial slavery, in the same way as these 'civilised' bloodsuckers are still oppressing and holding in colonial slavery hundreds of millions of people in India, Egypt, and all parts of the world.

About 150 years have passed since then. Bourgeois civilisation has borne all its luxurious fruits. America has taken first place among the free and educated nations in level of development of the productive forces of collective human endeavour, in the utilisation of machinery and of all the wonders of modern engineering. At the same time, America has become one of the foremost countries in regard to the depth of the abyss which lies between the handful of arrogant multimillionaires who wallow in filth and luxury, and the millions of working people who constantly live on the verge of pauperism. The American people, who set the world an example in waging a revolutionary war against feudal slavery, now find themselves in the latest, capitalist stage of wage-slavery to a handful of multimillionaires, and find themselves playing the role of hired thugs who, for the benefit of wealthy scoundrels, throttled the Philippines in 1898 on the pretext of 'liberating' them, and are throttling the Russian Socialist Republic in 1918 on the pretext of 'protecting' it from the Germans.

The four years of the imperialist slaughter of nations, however, have not passed in vain. The deception of the people by the scoundrels of both robber groups, the British and the German, has been utterly exposed by indisputable and obvious facts. The results of the four years of war have revealed the general law of capitalism as applied to war between robbers for the division of spoils: the richest and strongest profited and grabbed most, while the weakest were utterly robbed, tormented, crushed and strangled.

The British imperialist robbers were the strongest in number of 'colonial slaves'. The British capitalists have not lost an inch of 'their' territory (i.e., territory they have grabbed over the centuries), but they have grabbed all the German colonies in Africa, they have grabbed Mesopotamia and Palestine, they have throttled Greece, and have begun to plunder Russia.

The German imperialist robbers were the strongest in organisation and discipline of 'their' armies, but weaker in regard to colonies. They have lost all their colonies, but plundered half of Europe and throttled the largest number of small countries and weak nations. What a great war of 'liberation' on both sides! How well the robbers of both groups, the Anglo-French and the German capitalists, together with their lackeys, the social-chauvinists, i.e., the socialists who went over to the side of '*their own*' bourgeoisie, have 'defended their country'!

The American multimillionaires were, perhaps, richest of all, and geographically the most secure. They have profited more than all the rest. They have converted all, even the richest, countries into their tributaries. They have grabbed hundreds of billions of dollars. And every dollar is sullied with filth: the filth of the secret treaties between Britain and her 'allies', between Germany and her vassals, treaties for the division of the spoils, treaties of mutual 'aid' for oppressing the workers and persecuting the internationalist socialists. Every dollar is sullied with the filth of 'profitable' war contracts, which in every country made the rich richer and the poor poorer. And every dollar is stained with blood – from that ocean of blood that has been shed by the ten million killed and twenty million maimed in the great, noble, liberating and holy war to decide whether the British or the German robbers are to get most of the spoils, whether the British or the

German thugs are to be *foremost* in throttling the weak nations all over the world.

While the German robbers broke all records in war atrocities, the British have broken all records not only in the number of colonies they have grabbed, but also in the subtlety of their disgusting hypocrisy. This very day, the Anglo-French and American bourgeois newspapers are spreading, in millions and millions of copies, lies and slander about Russia, and are hypocritically justifying their predatory expedition against her on the plea that they want to 'protect' Russia from the Germans!

It does not require many words to refute this despicable and hideous lie; it is sufficient to point to one well-known fact. In October 1917, after the Russian workers had overthrown their imperialist government, the Soviet government, the government of the revolutionary workers and peasants, openly proposed a just peace, a peace without annexations or indemnities, a peace that fully guaranteed equal rights to all nations – and it proposed such a peace to *all* the belligerent countries.

It was the Anglo-French and the American bourgeoisie who refused to accept our proposal; it was they who even refused to talk to us about a general peace! It was *they* who betrayed the interests of all nations; it was they who prolonged the imperialist slaughter!

It was they who, banking on the possibility of dragging Russia back into the imperialist war, refused to take part in the peace negotiations and thereby gave a free hand to the no less predatory German capitalists who imposed the annexationist and harsh Brest Peace upon Russia!

It is difficult to imagine anything more disgusting than the hypocrisy with which the Anglo-French and American bourgeoisie are now 'blaming' us *for* the Brest Peace Treaty. The very capitalists of those countries which could have turned the Brest negotiations into general negotiations for a general peace are now our 'accusers'! The Anglo-French imperialist vultures, who have profited from the plunder of colonies and the slaughter of nations, have prolonged the war for nearly a whole year after Brest, and yet they 'accuse' *us*, the Bolsheviks, who proposed a just peace to all countries, they accuse *us*, who tore up, published and exposed to public disgrace the secret, criminal treaties concluded between the ex-tsar and the Anglo-French capitalists.

The workers of the whole world, no matter in what country they live, greet us, sympathise with us, applaud us for breaking the iron ring of imperialist ties, of sordid imperialist treaties, of imperialist chains – for breaking through to freedom, and making the heaviest sacrifices in doing so – for, as a socialist republic, although torn and plundered by the imperialists, keeping *out* of the imperialist war and raising the banner of peace, the banner of socialism for the whole world to see.

Small wonder that the international imperialist gang hates us for this, that it 'accuses' us, that all the lackeys of the imperialists, including our Right Socialist-Revolutionaries and Mensheviks, also 'accuse' us. The hatred these watchdogs of imperialism express for the Bolsheviks, and the sympathy of the class-conscious workers of the world, convince us more than ever of the justice of our cause.

A real socialist would not fail to understand that for the sake of achieving victory over the bourgeoisie, for the sake of power passing to the workers, for the sake of *starting* the world proletarian revolution, we *cannot* and must *not* hesitate to make the heaviest sacrifices, including the sacrifice of part of our territory, the sacrifice of heavy defeats at the hands of imperialism. A real socialist would have proved by *deeds* his willingness for 'his' country to make the greatest sacrifice to give a real push forward to the cause of the socialist revolution.

For the sake of 'their' cause, that is, for the sake of winning world hegemony, the imperialists of Britain and Germany have not hesitated to utterly ruin and throttle a whole number of countries, from Belgium and Serbia to Palestine and Mesopotamia. But must socialists wait with 'their' cause, the cause of liberating the working people of the whole world from the yoke of capital, of winning universal and lasting peace, until a path without sacrifice is found? Must they fear to open the battle until an easy victory is 'guaranteed'? Must they place the integrity and security of 'their' bourgeois-created 'fatherland' above the interests of the world socialist revolution? The scoundrels in the international socialist movement who think this way, those lackeys who grovel to bourgeois morality, thrice stand condemned.

The Anglo-French and American imperialist vultures 'accuse' us of concluding an 'agreement' with German imperialism. What hypocrites, what scoundrels they are to slander the workers' government while trembling because of the sympathy displayed towards us by the workers of 'their own' countries! But their hypocrisy will be exposed. They pretend not to see the difference between an agreement entered into by 'socialists' with the bourgeoisie (their own or foreign) *against the workers*, against the working people, and an agreement entered into *for the protection* of the workers who have defeated their bourgeoisie, with the bourgeoisie of one national colour *against the bourgeoisie* of another colour in order that the proletariat may take advantage of the antagonisms between the different groups of bourgeoisie.

In actual fact, every European sees this difference very well, and, as

I shall show in a moment, the American people have had a particularly striking 'illustration' of it in their own history. There are agreements and agreements, there are *fagots et fagots*, as the French say.

When in February 1918 the German imperialist vultures hurled their forces against unarmed, demobilised Russia, who had relied on the international solidarity of the proletariat before the world revolution had fully matured, I did not hesitate for a moment to enter into an 'agreement' with the French monarchists. Captain Sadoul, a French army officer who, in words, sympathised with the Bolsheviks, but was in deeds a loyal and faithful servant of French imperialism, brought the French officer de Lubersac to see me. 'I am a monarchist. My only aim is to secure the defeat of Germany,' de Lubersac declared to me. 'That goes without saying (*cela va sans dire*),' I replied. But this did not in the least prevent me from entering into an 'agreement' with de Lubersac concerning certain services that French army officers, experts in explosives, were ready to render us by blowing up railway lines in order to hinder the German invasion. This is an example of an 'agreement' of which every class-conscious worker will approve, an agreement in the interests of socialism. The French monarchist and I shook hands, although we knew that each of us would willingly hang his 'partner'. But for a time our interests coincided. Against the advancing rapacious Germans, *we*, in the interests of the Russian and the world socialist revolution, utilised the equally rapacious counter-interests of *other* imperialists. In this way we served the interests of the working class of Russia and of other countries, we strengthened the proletariat and weakened the bourgeoisie of the whole world, we resorted to the methods, most legitimate and essential in *every* war, of manoeuvre, stratagem, retreat, in anticipation of the moment when the rapidly maturing proletarian revolution in a number of advanced countries *completely matured.*

However much the Anglo-French and American imperialist sharks fume with rage, however much they slander us, no matter how many millions they spend on bribing the Right Socialist-Revolutionary, Menshevik and other social-patriotic newspapers, *I shall not hesitate one second* to enter into a *similar* 'agreement' with the German imperialist vultures if an attack upon Russia by Anglo-French troops calls for it. And I know perfectly well that my tactics will be approved by the class-conscious proletariat of Russia, Germany, France, Britain, America – in short, of the whole civilised world. Such tactics will ease the task of the socialist revolution, will hasten it, will weaken the international bourgeoisie, will strengthen the position of the working class which is defeating the bourgeoisie.

The American people resorted to these tactics long ago to the advantage of their revolution. When they waged their great war of liberation against the British oppressors, they had also against them the French and the Spanish oppressors who owned a part of what is now the United States of North America. In their arduous war for freedom, the American people also entered into 'agreements' with some oppressors against others for the purpose of weakening the oppressors and strengthening those who were fighting in a revolutionary manner against oppression, for the purpose of serving the interests of the oppressed *people*. The American people took advantage of the strife between the French, the Spanish and the British; sometimes they even fought side by side with the forces of the French and Spanish oppressors against the British oppressors; first they defeated the British and then freed themselves (partly by ransom) from the French and the Spanish.

Historical action is not the pavement of Nevsky Prospekt, said the great Russian revolutionary Chernyshevsky.[2] A revolutionary would not 'agree' to a proletarian revolution only 'on the condition' that it proceeds easily and smoothly, that there is, from the outset, combined action on the part of the proletarians of different countries, that there are guarantees against defeats, that the road of the revolution is broad, free and straight, that it will not be necessary during the march to victory to sustain the heaviest casualties, to 'bide one's time in a besieged fortress', or to make one's way along extremely narrow, impassable, winding and dangerous mountain tracks. Such a person is no revolutionary, he has not freed himself from the pedantry of the bourgeois intellectuals; such a person will be found constantly slipping into the camp of the counter-revolutionary bourgeoisie, like our Right Socialist-Revolutionaries, Mensheviks and even (although more rarely) Left Socialist-Revolutionaries.

Echoing the bourgeoisie, these gentlemen like to blame us for the 'chaos' of the revolution, for the 'destruction' of industry, for the unemployment and the food shortage. How hypocritical these accusations are, coming from those who welcomed and supported the imperialist war, or who entered into an 'agreement' with Kerensky who continued this war! It is this imperialist war that is the cause of all these misfortunes. The revolution engendered by the war cannot avoid the terrible difficulties and suffering bequeathed it by the prolonged, ruinous, reactionary slaughter of the nations. To blame us for the 'destruction' of industry, or for the 'terror', is either hypocrisy or dull-witted pedantry; it reveals an inability to understand the basic conditions of the fierce class struggle, raised to the highest degree of intensity that is called revolution.

Even when 'accusers' of this type do 'recognise' the class struggle, they limit themselves to verbal recognition; actually, they constantly slip into the philistine utopia of class 'agreement' and 'collaboration'; for in revolutionary epochs the class struggle has always, inevitably, and in every country, assumed the form of *civil war*, and civil war is inconceivable without the severest destruction, terror and the restriction of formal democracy in the interests of this war. Only unctuous parsons – whether Christian or 'secular' in the persons of parlour, parliamentary socialists – cannot see, understand and feel this necessity. Only a life less 'man in the muffler'[3] can shun the revolution for this reason instead of plunging into battle with the utmost ardour and determination at a time when history demands that the greatest problems of humanity be solved by struggle and war.

The American people have a revolutionary tradition which has been adopted by the best representatives of the American proletariat, who have repeatedly expressed their complete solidarity with us Bolsheviks. That tradition is the war of liberation against the British in the eighteenth century and the Civil War in the nineteenth century. In some respects, if we only take into consideration the 'destruction' of some branches of industry and of the national economy, America in 1870 was behind 1860. But what a pedant, what an idiot would anyone be to deny on these grounds the immense, world-historic, progressive and revolutionary significance of the American Civil War of 1863-65!

The representatives of the bourgeoisie understand that for the sake of overthrowing Negro slavery, of overthrowing the rule of the slave-owners, it was worth letting the country go through long years of civil war, through the abysmal ruin, destruction and terror that accompany every war. But now, when we are confronted with the vastly greater task of overthrowing capitalist *wage*-slavery, of overthrowing the rule of the bourgeoisie – now, the representatives and defenders of the bourgeoisie, and also the reformist socialists who have been frightened by the bourgeoisie and are shunning the revolution, cannot and do not want to understand that civil war is necessary and legitimate.

The American workers will not follow the bourgeoisie. They will be with us, for civil war against the bourgeoisie. The whole history of the world and of the American labour movement strengthens my conviction that this is so. I also recall the words of one of the most beloved leaders of the American proletariat, Eugene Debs, who wrote in the *Appeal to Reason*,[4] I believe towards the end of 1915, in the article 'What Shall I Fight For' (I quoted this article at the beginning of 1916 at a public meeting of workers in Berne, Switzerland[5]) – that he, Debs, would rather be shot than vote credits for the present criminal and reactionary war; that he, Debs, knows of only one holy and, from the proletarian standpoint, legitimate war, namely: the war against the capitalists, the war to liberate mankind from wage-slavery.

I am not surprised that Wilson, the head of the American multimillionaires and servant of the capitalist sharks, has thrown Debs into prison. Let the bourgeoisie be brutal to the true internationalists, to the true representatives of the revolutionary proletariat! The more fierce and brutal they are, the nearer the day of the victorious proletarian revolution.

We are blamed for the destruction caused by our revolution... Who are the accusers? The hangers-on of the bourgeoisie, of that very bourgeoisie who, during the four years of the imperialist war, have destroyed almost the whole of European culture and have reduced Europe to barbarism, brutality and starvation. These bourgeoisie now demand we should not make a revolution on these ruins, amidst this wreckage of culture, amidst the wreckage and ruins created by the war, nor with the people who have been brutalised by the war. How humane and righteous the bourgeoisie are!

Their servants accuse us of resorting to terror... The British bourgeoisie have forgotten their 1649, the French bourgeoisie have forgotten their 1793. Terror was just and legitimate when the bourgeoisie resorted to it for their own benefit against feudalism. Terror became monstrous and criminal when the workers and poor peasants dared to use it against the bourgeoisie! Terror was just and legitimate when used for the purpose of substituting one exploiting minority for another exploiting minority. Terror became monstrous and criminal when it began to be used for the purpose of overthrowing *every* exploiting minority, to be used in the interests of the vast actual majority, in the interests of the proletariat and semi-proletariat, the working class and the poor peasants!

The international imperialist bourgeoisie have slaughtered ten million men and maimed twenty million in 'their' war, the war to decide whether the British or the German vultures are to rule the world.

If *our* war, the war of the oppressed and exploited against the oppressors and the exploiters, results in half a million or a million casualties in all countries, the bourgeoisie will say that the former casualties are justified, while the latter are criminal.

The proletariat will have something entirely different to say.

Now, amidst the horrors of the imperialist war, the proletariat is receiving a most vivid and striking illustration of the great truth taught by all revolutions and bequeathed to the workers by their best teachers, the founders of modern socialism. This truth is that no revolution can be successful unless *the resistance of the exploiters is crushed.* When we, the workers and toiling peasants, captured state power, it became our duty to crush the resistance of the exploiters. We are proud we have been doing this. We regret we are not doing it with sufficient firmness and determination.

We know that fierce resistance to the socialist revolution on the part of the bourgeoisie is inevitable in all countries, and that this resistance will *grow* with the growth of this revolution. The proletariat will crush this resistance; during the struggle against the resisting bourgeoisie it will finally mature for victory and for power.

Let the corrupt bourgeois press shout to the whole world about every mistake our revolution makes. We are not daunted by our mistakes. People have not become saints because the revolution has begun. The toiling classes who for centuries have been oppressed, downtrodden and forcibly held in the vice of poverty, brutality and ignorance cannot avoid mistakes when making a revolution. And, as I pointed out once before, the corpse of bourgeois society cannot be nailed in a coffin and buried. The corpse of capitalism is decaying and disintegrating in our midst, polluting the air and poisoning our lives, enmeshing that which is new, fresh, young and virile in thousands of threads and bonds of that which is old, moribund and decaying.

For every hundred mistakes we commit, and which the bourgeoisie and their lackeys (including our own Mensheviks and Right Socialist-Revolutionaries) shout about to the whole world, 10,000 great and heroic deeds are performed, greater and more heroic because they are simple and inconspicuous amidst the everyday life of a factory district or a remote village, performed by people who are not accustomed (and have no opportunity) to shout to the whole world about their successes.

But even if the contrary were true – although I know such an assumption is wrong – even if we committed 10,000 mistakes for every 100 correct actions we performed, even in that case our revolution would be great and invincible, and *so it will be in the eyes of world history*, because, *for the first time*, not the minority, not the rich alone, not the educated alone, but the real people, the vast majority of the working people, are *themselves* building a new life, are *by their own experience* solving the most difficult problems of socialist organisation.

Every mistake committed in the course of such work, in the course of this most conscientious and earnest work of tens of millions of simple workers and peasants in reorganising their whole life, every such mistake is worth thousands and millions of 'lawless' successes achieved by the exploiting minority – successes in swindling and duping the working people. For only *through* such mistakes will the workers and peasants *learn* to build the new life, learn to do *without* capitalists; only in this way will they hack a path for themselves – through thousands of obstacles – to victorious socialism.

Mistakes are being committed in the course of their revolutionary work by our peasants, who at one stroke, in one night, 25-26 October (old style), 1917, entirely abolished the private ownership of land, and are now, month after month, overcoming tremendous difficulties and correcting their mistakes themselves, solving in a practical way the most difficult tasks of organising new conditions of economic life, of fighting the kulaks, providing land for the *working people* (and not for the rich), and of changing to *communist* large-scale agriculture.

Mistakes are being committed in the course of their revolutionary work by our workers, who have already, after a few months, nationalised almost all the biggest factories and plants, and are learning by hard, everyday work the new task of managing whole branches of industry, are setting the nationalised enterprises going, overcoming the powerful resistance of inertia, petty-bourgeois mentality and selfishness, and, brick by brick, are laying the foundation of *new* social ties, of a *new* labour discipline, of a *new* influence of the workers' trade unions over their members.

Mistakes are committed in the course of their revolutionary work by our Soviets, which were created as far back as 1905 by a mighty upsurge of the people. The Soviets of Workers and Peasants are a new *type* of state, a new and higher *type* of democracy, a form of the proletarian dictatorship, a means of administering the state *without* the bourgeoisie and *against* the bourgeoisie. For the first time democracy is here serving the people, the working people, and has ceased to be democracy for the rich as it still is in all bourgeois republics, even the most democratic. For the first time, the people are grappling, on a scale involving one hundred million, with the problem of implementing the dictatorship of the proletariat and semi-proletariat – a problem which, if not solved, makes socialism *out of the question.*

Let the pedants, or the people whose minds are incurably stuffed with bourgeois-democratic or parliamentary prejudices, shake their heads in perplexity about our Soviets, about the absence of direct elections, for example. These people have forgotten nothing and have learned nothing during the period of the great upheavals of 1914-18. The combination of the proletarian dictatorship with the new democracy for the working people – of civil war with the widest participation of the people in politics – such a combination cannot be brought about at one stroke, nor does it fit in with the outworn modes of routine parliamentary democracy. The contours of a new world, the world of socialism, are rising before us in the shape of the Soviet Republic. It is not surprising that this world does not come into being ready-made, does not spring forth like Minerva from the head of Jupiter.

The old bourgeois-democratic constitutions waxed eloquent about formal equality and right of assembly; but our proletarian and peasant Soviet Constitution casts aside the hypocrisy of formal equality. When the bourgeois republicans overturned thrones they did not worry about formal equality between monarchists and republicans. When it is a matter of overthrowing the bourgeoisie, only traitors or idiots can demand formal equality of rights for the bourgeoisie. 'Freedom of assembly' for workers and peasants is not worth a farthing when the best buildings belong to the bourgeoisie. Our Soviets have *confiscated* all the good buildings in town and country from the rich and have *transferred* all of them to the workers and peasants for *their* unions and meetings. This is our *freedom* of assembly – for the working people! This is the meaning and content of our Soviet, our socialist Constitution!

That is why we are all so firmly convinced that no matter what misfortunes may still be in store for it, our Republic of Soviets is *invincible.*

It is invincible because every blow struck by frenzied imperialism, every defeat the international bourgeoisie inflict on us, rouses more and more sections of the workers and peasants to the struggle, teaches them at the cost of enormous sacrifice, steels them and engenders new heroism on a mass scale.

We know that help from you will probably not come soon, comrade American workers, for the revolution is developing in different countries in different forms and at different tempos (and it cannot be otherwise). We know that although the European proletarian revolution has been maturing very rapidly lately, it may, after all, not flare up within the next few weeks. We are banking on the inevitability of the world revolution, but this does not mean that we are such fools as to bank on the revolution inevitably coming on a *definite* and early date. We have seen two great revolutions in our country, 1905 and 1917, and we know revolutions are not made to order, or by agreement. We know that circumstances brought *our* Russian detachment of the socialist proletariat to the fore not because of our merits, but because of the exceptional backwardness of Russia, and that *before* the world revolution breaks out a number of separate revolutions may be defeated.

In spite of this, we are firmly convinced that we are invincible, because the spirit of mankind will not be broken by the imperialist slaughter. Mankind will vanquish it. And the first country to *break* the convict chains of the imperialist war was *our* country. We sustained enormously heavy casualties in the struggle to break these chains, but we *broke* them. We are *free from* imperialist dependence, we have raised the banner of struggle for the complete overthrow of imperialism for the whole world to see.

We are now, as it were, in a besieged fortress, waiting for the other detachments of the world socialist revolution to come to our relief. These detachments *exist*, they are *more numerous* than ours, they are maturing, growing, gaining more strength the longer the brutalities of imperialism continue. The workers are breaking away from their social traitors – the Gomperses, Hendersons, Renaudels, Scheidemanns and Renners. Slowly but surely the workers are adopting communist, Bolshevik tactics and are marching towards the proletarian revolution, which alone is capable of saving dying culture and dying mankind.

In short, we are invincible, because the world proletarian revolution is invincible.

Lenin
20 August 1918

First published: *Pravda* No. 178, 22 August 1918

Resistance Books and the IIRE are grateful to the Marxist Internet Archive for placing this text in the public domain. The online version is at: https:// www.marxists.org/archive/lenin/works/1918/aug/20.htm. Translated and edited by Jim Riordan from the original (Lenin's *Collected Works*, Moscow, Progress Publishers, Volume 28, 1965, pages 62-75). Transcription and HTML mark-up by David Walters.

NOTES

1   The dispatch of the letter to America was organised by the Bolshevik M. M. Borodin, who had recently been there. With the foreign military intervention and the blockade of Soviet Russia this involved considerable difficulties. The letter was delivered to the United States by P. I. Travin (Sletov). Along with the letter he brought the Constitution of the RSFSR and the Soviet Government's Note to President Wilson containing the demand to stop the intervention. The well-known American socialist and journalist John Reed secured the publication of all these documents in the American press.
In December 1918 a slightly abridged version of the letter appeared in the New York magazine *The Class Struggle* and the Boston weekly *The Revolutionary Age*, both organs of the Left wing of the American Socialist Party. *The Revolutionary Age* was brought out by John Reed and Sen Katayama. The letter evoked keen interest among readers and it was published as a reprint from *The Class Struggle* in a large number of copies. Subsequently it was published many times in the bourgeois and socialist press of the USA and Western Europe, in the French socialist magazine *Demain* No. 28-29, 1918, in No. 138 of the *Call*, organ of the British Socialist Party, the Berlin magazine *Die Aktion* No. 51-52, 1918, and elsewhere. In 1934 the letter was brought out in New York in the

form of a pamphlet, which contained the passages omitted in earlier publications.

The letter was widely used by the American Left Socialists and was instrumental in aiding the development of the labour and communist movement in the U.S. and Europe. It helped advanced workers to appreciate the nature of imperialism and the great revolutionary changes effected by the Soviet government. Lenin's letter aroused a mounting protest in the U.S. against the armed intervention.

2   Lenin quotes from Chernyshevsky's review of the book by the American economist H. Ch. Carey, *Letters to the President on the Foreign and Domestic Policy of the Union, and its Effects.* Chernyshevsky wrote: 'The path of history is not paved like Nevsky Prospekt; it runs across fields, either dusty or muddy, and cuts through swamps or forest thickets. Anyone who fears being covered with dust or muddying his boots, should not engage in social activity.'

3   *Man in the muffler* – a character from Chekhov's story of the same title, personifying a narrow-minded philistine scared of initiative and new ideas.

4   *Appeal to Reason* – American socialist newspaper, founded in Girard, Kansas, in 1895. The newspaper propagated socialist ideas and was immensely popular among the workers. During the First World War it pursued an internationalist policy. Debs's article appeared in the paper on 11 September 1915. Its title, which Lenin most probably quoted from memory, was 'When I Shall Fight'.

5   Speech Delivered at an International Meeting in Berne; https://www.marxists.org/archive/lenin/works/1916/feb/08.htm.

IN DEFENCE OF OCTOBER

Leon Trotsky

Speech delivered by Leon Trotsky to an audience of Social Democratic students in Copenhagen, 27 November 1932

The first time that I was in Copenhagen was at the International Socialist Congress and I took away with me the kindest recollections of your city. But that was over a quarter of a century ago. Since then, the water in the Ore-Sund and in the fjords has changed over and over again. And not the water alone. The war has broken the backbone of the old European continent. The rivers and seas of Europe have washed down not a little blood. Mankind and particularly European mankind has gone through severe trials, has become more sombre and more brutal. Every kind of conflict has become more bitter. The world has entered into the period of the great change. Its extreme expressions are war and revolution.

Before I pass on to the theme of my lecture, the Revolution, I consider it my duty to express my thanks to the organisers of this meeting, the organisation of social-democratic students. I do this as a political adversary. My lecture, it is true, pursues historic scientific and not political lines. I want to emphasise this right from the beginning. But it is impossible to speak of a revolution, out of which the Soviet Republic arose, without taking up a political position. As a lecturer I stand under the banner as I did when I participated in the events of the revolution.

Up to the war, the Bolshevik Party belonged to the Social-Democratic International. On 4 August 1914, the vote of the German social-democracy for the war credits put an end to this connection once and for all, and opened the period of uninterrupted and irreconcilable struggle of Bolshevism against social-democracy. Does this mean that the organisers of this assembly made a mistake in inviting me to lecture? On this point the audience will be able to judge only after my lecture. To justify my acceptance of the kind invitation to present a report on the Russian Revolution, permit me to point to the fact that during the thirty-five years of my political life the question of the Russian Revolution has been the practical and theoretical axis of my thought and of my actions. The four years of my stay in Turkey were principally devoted to historical elaboration of the problems of the Russian Revolution. Perhaps this fact gives me a certain right to hope that I will succeed in part at least in helping not only friends and sympathisers, but also opponents, better to understand many features of the Revolution which before had escaped their attention. At all events, the purpose of my lecture is to help to understand. I do not intend to conduct propaganda for the Revolution, nor to call upon you to join the Revolution. I intend to explain the Revolution.

Let us begin with some elementary sociological principles which are doubtless familiar to you all, but as to which we must refresh our memory in approaching so complicated a phenomenon as the Revolution.

The materialist conception of history

Human society is a historically-originated collaboration in the struggle for existence and the assurance of the maintenance of the generations. The character of a society is determined by the character of its economy. The character of its economy is determined by its means of productive labour.

For every great epoch in the development of the productive forces there is a definite corresponding social regime. Every social regime until now has secured enormous advantages to the ruling class.

It is clear, therefore, that social regimes are not eternal. They arise historically, and then become fetters on further progress. 'All that arises deserves to be destroyed.'

But no ruling class has ever voluntarily and peacefully abdicated. In questions of life and death, arguments based on reason have never replaced the arguments of force. This may be sad, but it is so. It is not we that have made this world. We can do nothing but take it as it is.

The meaning of revolution

Revolution means a change of the social order. It transfers the power from the hands of a class which has exhausted itself into those of another class, which is in the ascendant. Insurrection constitutes the sharpest and most critical moment in the struggle for power of two classes. The insurrection can lead to the real victory of the Revolution and to the establishment of a new order only when it is based on a progressive class, which is able to rally around it the overwhelming majority of the people.

As distinguished from the processes of nature, a revolution is made by human beings and through human beings. But in the course of revolution, too, men act under the influence of social conditions which are not freely chosen by them but are handed down from the past and imperatively point out the road which they must follow. For this reason, and only for this reason, a revolution follows certain laws.

But human consciousness does not merely passively reflect its objective conditions. It is accustomed to react actively to them. At certain times this reaction assumes a tense, passionate, mass character. The barriers of right and might are overthrown. The active intervention of the masses in historical events is in fact the most indispensable element of a revolution.

But even the stormiest activity can remain in the stage of demonstration or rebellion, without rising to the height of a revolution. The uprising of the masses must lead to the overthrow of the domination of one class and to the establishment of the domination of another. Only then have we achieved a revolution. A mass uprising is no isolated undertaking, which can be conjured up any time one pleases. It represents an objectively-conditioned element in the development of a revolution, just as a revolution represents an objectively-conditioned process in the development of society. But if the necessary conditions for the uprising exist, one must not simply wait passively, with open mouth; as Shakespeare says: 'There is a tide in the affairs of men which taken at the flood, leads on to fortune.'

In order to sweep away the outlived social order, the progressive class must understand that its hour has struck and set before itself the task of conquering power. Here opens the field of conscious revolutionary action, where foresight and calculation combine with will and courage. In other words: here opens the field of action of the Party.

The coup d'état

The revolutionary Party unites within itself the flower of the progressive class. Without a Party which is able to orientate itself in its environment, appreciate the progress and rhythm of events and early win the confidence of the masses, the victory of the proletarian revolution is impossible. These are the reciprocal relations between the objective and the subjective factors of insurrection and revolution.

In disputations, particularly theological ones, it is customary, as you know, for the opponents to discredit scientific truth by driving it to an absurdity. This method is called in logic *Reductio ad absurdum*. We shall start from an absurdity so as to approach the truth with all the greater safety. In any case, we cannot complain of lack of absurdities. Let us take one of the most recent, and crude.

The Italian writer Malaparte, who is something in the nature of a Fascist theoretician – there are such, too – not long ago, launched a book on the technique of the coup d'état. Naturally, the author devotes a not inconsiderable number of pages of his 'investigation' to the October upheaval.

In contradistinction to the 'strategy' of Lenin which was always related to the social and political conditions of Russia in 1917, 'the tactics of Trotsky.' in Malaparte's words, 'were, on the contrary, not at all limited by the general conditions of the country.' This is the main idea of the book! Malaparte compels Lenin and Trotsky in the pages of his book, to carry on numerous dialogues, in which both participants together show as much profundity of mind as Nature put at the disposal of Malaparte alone. In answer to Lenin's considerations of the social and political prerequisites of the upheaval, Malaparte has his alleged Trotsky say, literally, 'Your strategy requires far too many favourable circumstances; the insurrection needs nothing, it is self-sufficing.' You hear: 'The insurrection needs nothing!' That is precisely the absurdity which must help us to approach the truth. The author repeats persistently, that, in the October Revolution, it was not the strategy of Lenin but the tactics of Trotsky which won the victory. These tactics, according to his words, are a menace even now to the peace of the States of Europe. 'The strategy of Lenin' I quote word for word, 'does not constitute any immediate danger for the Governments of Europe. But the tactics of Trotsky do constitute an actual and consequently a permanent danger to them.' Still more concretely, 'Put Poincaré in the place of Kerensky and the Bolshevik coup d'état of October 1917 would have been just as successful.' It is hard to believe that such a book has been translated into several languages and taken seriously.

We seek in vain to discover what is the necessity altogether of the historically-conditioned strategy of Lenin, if 'Trotsky's tactics' can fulfil the same tasks in every situation. And why are successful revolutions so rare, if only a few technical recipes suffice for their success?

The dialogue between Lenin and Trotsky presented by the fascist author is in content, as well as in form, an insipid invention, from beginning to end. Of such inventions there are not a few floating around the world. For example, in Madrid, there has been printed a book, La Vida del Lenin (The Life of Lenin) for which I am as little responsible as for the tactical recipes of Malaparte. The Madrid weekly Estampa published in advance whole chapters of this alleged book of Trotsky's on Lenin, which contain horrible desecrations of the life of that man whom I valued and still value incomparably higher than anyone else among my contemporaries.

But let us leave the forgers to their fate. Old Wilhelm Liebknecht, the father of the unforgettable fighter and hero Karl Liebknecht, liked to say, 'A revolutionary politician must provide himself with a thick skin.' Doctor Stockmann even more expressively recommended that anyone who proposed to act in a manner contrary to the opinion of society should refrain from putting on new trousers. We will take note of the two good pieces of advice and proceed.

The causes of October

What questions does the October Revolution raise in the mind of a thinking man?

- Why and how did this revolution take place? More correctly, why did the proletarian revolution conquer in one of the most backward countries in Europe?
- What have been the results of the October revolution? And finally:
- Has the October Revolution stood the test?

The first question, as to the causes, can now be answered more or less exhaustively. I have attempted to do this in great detail in my History of the Revolution. Here I can only formulate the most important conclusions.

The law of uneven development

The fact that the proletariat reached power for the first time in such a backward country as the former Tsarist Russia seems mysterious only at a first glance; in reality it is fully in accord with historical law. It could have been predicted, and it was predicted. Still more, on the basis of the prediction of this fact the revolutionary Marxists built up their strategy long before the decisive events.

The first and most general explanation is: Russia is a backward country, but only a part of world economy, only an element of the capitalist world system. In this sense Lenin solved the enigma of the Russian Revolution with the lapidary formula, 'The chain broke at its weakest link.'

A crude illustration: the Great War, the result of the contradictions of world imperialism, drew into its maelstrom countries of different stages of development, but made the same claims on all the participants. It is clear that the burdens of the war would be particularly intolerable for the most backward countries. Russia was the first to be compelled to leave the field. But to tear itself away from the war, the Russian people had to overthrow the ruling classes. In this way the chain of war broke at its weakest link.

Still, war is not a catastrophe coming from outside like an earthquake, but, as old Clausewitz said, the continuation of politics by other means. In the last war, the main tendencies of the imperialistic system of 'peace' time only expressed themselves more crudely. The higher the general forces of production, the tenser the competition on the world markets, the sharper the antagonisms and the madder the race for armaments, so much the more difficult it became for the weaker participants. That is precisely why the backward countries assumed the first places in the succession of collapse. The chain of world capitalism always tends to break at its weakest link.

If, as a result of exceptional unfavourable circumstances – for example, let us say, a successful military intervention from the outside or irreparable mistakes on the part of the Soviet Government itself – capitalism should arise again on the immeasurably wide Soviet territory, its historical inadequacy would at the same time have inevitably arisen and such capitalism would in turn soon become the victim of the same contradictions which caused its explosion in 1917. No tactical recipes could have called the October Revolution into being, if Russia had not carried it within its body. The revolutionary Party in the last analysis can claim only the role of an obstetrician, who is compelled to resort to a Caesarean operation.

One might say in answer to this: 'Your general considerations may adequately explain why old Russia had to suffer shipwreck, that country where backward capitalism and an impoverished peasantry were crowned by a parasitic nobility and a decaying monarchy. But in the simile of the chain and it weakest link there is still missing the key to the real enigma: How could a socialist revolution succeed in a backward country? History knows of more than a few illustrations of the decay of countries and civilisations accompanied by the collapse of the old classes for which no progressive successors had been found. The breakdown of old Russia should, at first sight have changed the country into a capitalist colony rather than into a Socialist State.

This objection is very interesting. It leads us directly to the kernel of the whole problem. And yet, this objection is erroneous; I might say, it lacks internal symmetry. On the one hand, it starts from an exaggerated conception of the phenomenon of historical backwardness in general.

Living beings, including man, of course, go through similar stages of development in accordance with their ages. In a normal five-year old child, we find a certain correspondence between the weight, size and the internal organs. But it is quite otherwise with human consciousness. In contrast with anatomy and physiology, psychology, both individual and collective, is distinguished by exceptional capacity of absorption, flexibility and elasticity; therein consists the aristocratic advantage of man over his nearest zoological relatives, the apes. The absorptive and flexible psyche confers on the so-called social 'organisms', as distinguished from the real, that is biological organisms, an exceptional variability of internal structure as a necessary condition for historical progress. In the development of nations and states, particularly capitalist ones, there is neither similarity nor regularity. Different stages of civilisation, even polar opposites, approach and intermingle with one another in the life of one and the same country.

The law of combined development

Let us not forget that historical backwardness is a relative concept. There being both backward and progressive countries, there is also a reciprocal influencing of one by the other; there is the pressure of the progressive countries on the backward ones; there is the necessity for the backward countries to catch up with the progressive ones, to borrow their technology and science, etc. In this way arises the combined type of development: features of backwardness are combined with the last word in world technique and in world thought. Finally the countries historically backward, in order to escape their backwardness, are often compelled to rush ahead of the others.

The flexibility of the collective consciousness makes it possible under certain conditions to achieve the result, in the social arena, which in individual psychology is called 'overcoming the consciousness of inferiority'. In this sense we can say that the October Revolution was an heroic means whereby the people of Russia were able to overcome their own economic and cultural inferiority.

But let us pass over from these historico-philosophic, perhaps somewhat too abstract, generalisations, and put up the same question in concrete form, that is within the cross-section of living economic facts. The backwardness of Russia expressed itself most clearly at the beginning of the twentieth century in the fact that industry occupied a small place in that country in comparison with the peasantry. Taken as a whole, this meant a low productivity of the national labour. Suffice it to say that on the eve of the war, when Tsarist Russia had reached the peak of its well-being, the national income was eight to ten times lower than in the United States. This expresses numerically the 'amplitude' of its backwardness if the word 'amplitude' can be used at all in connection with backwardness.

At the same time however, the law of combined development expressed itself in the economic field at every step, in simple as well as in complex phenomena. Almost without highways, Russia was compelled to build railroads. Without having gone through the European artisan and manufacturing stages, Russia passed directly to mechanised production. To jump over intermediate stages is the way of backward countries.

While peasant agriculture often remained at the level of the seventeenth century, Russia's industry, if not in scope, at least in type, reached the level of progressive countries and in some respects rushed ahead of them. It suffices to say that gigantic enterprises, with over a thousand workers each, employed in the United States less than 18 per cent of the total number of industrial workers. In Russia it was over 41 per cent. This fact is hard to reconcile with the conventional conception of the economic backwardness of Russia. It does not on the other hand, refute this backwardness, but dialectically complements it.

The same contradictory character was shown by the class structure of the country. The finance capital of Europe industrialised Russian economy at an accelerated tempo. The industrial bourgeoisie forthwith assumed a large scale capitalistic and anti-popular character. The foreign stock-holders moreover, lived outside of the country. The workers, on the other hand, were naturally Russians. Against a numerically weak Russian bourgeoisie, which had no national roots, there stood confronting it a relatively strong proletariat with strong roots in the depths of the people.

The revolutionary character of the proletariat was furthered by the fact that Russia in particular, as a backward country, under the compulsion of catching up with its opponents, had not been able to work out its own social or political conservatism. The most conservative country of Europe, in fact of the entire world, is considered, and correctly, to be the oldest capitalist country – England. The European country freest of conservatism would in all probability be Russia.

But the young, fresh, determined proletariat of Russia still constituted only a tiny minority of the nation. The reserves of its revolutionary power lay outside of the proletariat itself-in the peasantry, living in half-serfdom; and in the oppressed nationalities.

The peasantry

The subsoil of the revolution was the agrarian question. The old feudal monarchic system became doubly intolerable under the conditions of the new capitalist exploitation. The peasant communal areas amounted to some 140 million dessiatines. But 30,000 large landowners, whose average holdings were over 2,000 dessiatines, owned altogether 7 million dessiatines, that is as much as some 10 million peasant population. These statistics of land tenure constituted a ready-made programme of agrarian revolt.

The nobleman Bokorin wrote in 1917 to the dignitary Rodsianko, the Chairman of the last municipal Duma: 'I am a landowner and I cannot get it into my head that I must lose my land, and for an unbelievable purpose to boot, for the experiment of the socialist doctrine.' But it is precisely the task of revolutions to accomplish that which the ruling classes cannot get into their heads.

In Autumn 1917, almost the whole country was the scene of peasant revolts. Of the 642 departments of old Russia, 482, that is 77 per cent, were affected by the movements! The reflection of the burning villages lit up the arena of the insurrections in the cities.

But you may argue the war of the peasants against the landowners is one of the classic elements of bourgeois revolution, and not at all of the proletarian revolution!

Perfectly right, I reply – so it was in the past. But the inability of capitalist society to survive in an historically backward country was expressed precisely in the fact that the peasant insurrections did not drive the bourgeois classes of Russia forward but on the contrary, drove them back for good into the camp of reaction. If the peasantry did not want to be completely ruined there was nothing else left for it but to join the industrial proletariat. This revolutionary joining of the two oppressed classes was foreseen by the genius of Lenin and prepared for him long before.

Had the agrarian question been courageously solved by the bourgeoisie, the proletariat of Russia would not, obviously, have been able to arrive at the power in 1917. But the Russian, bourgeoisie, covetous and cowardly, too late on the scene, prematurely a victim of senility, dared not lift a hand against feudal property. But thereby it delivered the power to the proletariat and together with it the right to dispose of the destinies of bourgeois society.

In order for the Soviet State to come into existence, it was consequently necessary for two factors of a different historical nature to collaborate: the peasant war, that is to say, a movement which is characteristic of the dawn of bourgeois development, and the proletarian insurrection, or uprising which announces the decline of the bourgeois movement. There we have the combined character of the Russian Revolution.

Once let the Bear – the peasant – stand up on his hind feet, he becomes terrible in his wrath. But he is unable to give conscious expression to his indignation. He needs a leader. For the first time in the history of the world, the insurrectionary peasants found a faithful leader in the person of the proletariat.

Four million workers in industry and transport leading a hundred million peasants. That was the natural and inevitable reciprocal relations between proletariat and peasantry in the Revolution.

The national question

The second revolutionary reserve of the proletariat was formed by the oppressed nationalities, who moreover were also predominantly peasants.

Closely allied with the historical backwardness of the country is the extensive character of the development of the State, which spread out like a grease spot from the centre at Moscow to the circumference. In the East, it subjugated the still more backward peoples, basing itself upon them, in order to stifle the more developed nationalities of the West. To the 70 million Great Russians, who constituted the main mass of the population were added gradually some 90 millions of other races.

In this way arose the empire, in whose composition the ruling nationality made up only 43 per cent of the population, while the remaining 57 per cent, consisted of nationalities of varying degrees of civilisation and legal deprivation. The national pressure was incomparably cruder than in the neighbouring States, and not only than those beyond the western frontier, but beyond the eastern one too. This conferred on the national problem an enormous explosive force.

The Russian liberal bourgeoisie was not willing in either the national or the agrarian question, to go beyond certain amelioration's of the regime of oppression and violence. The 'democratic' Governments of Miliukov and Kerensky, which reflected the interests of the great Russian bourgeoisie and bureaucracy actually hastened to impress upon the discontented nationalities in the course of the eight months of their existence: 'You will obtain what you can get by force.'

The inevitability of the development of the centrifugal national movements had been early taken into consideration by Lenin. The Bolshevik Party struggled obstinately for years for the right of self-determination for nations, that is, for the right of full secession. Only through this courageous position on the national question could the Russian proletariat gradually win the confidence of the oppressed peoples. The national independence movement as well as the agrarian movement, necessarily turned against the official democracy, strengthened the proletariat, and poured into the stream of the October upheaval.

The permanent revolution

In these ways the riddle of the proletarian upheaval in a historically backward country loses its veil of mystery.

Marxist revolutionaries predicted, long before the events, the march of the Revolution and the historical role of the young Russian proletariat. I may be permitted to repeat here a passage from a work of my own in 1905:

> In an economically backward country the proletariat can arrive at power earlier than in a capitalistically advanced one …

The Russian Revolution creates the conditions under which the power can (and in the event of a successful revolution must) be transferred to the proletariat, even before the policy of bourgeois liberalism receives the opportunity of unfolding its genius for government to its full extent.

The destiny of the most elementary revolutionary interest of the peasantry … is bound up with the destiny of the whole revolution, that is, with the destiny of the proletariat. The proletariat, once arrived at power, will appear before the peasantry as the liberating class.

The proletariat enters into the Government as the revolutionary representative of the nation, as the acknowledged leader of the people in the struggle with absolutism and the barbarism of serfdom.

The proletarian regime will have to stand from the very beginning for the solution of the agrarian question, with which the question of the destiny of tremendous masses of the population of Russia is bound up.

I have taken the liberty of quoting these passages as evidence that the theory of the October Revolution which I am presenting today is no casual improvisation and was not constructed ex-post facto under the pressure of events. No, in the form of a political prognosis it preceded the October upheaval by a long time. You will agree that a theory is in general valuable only in so far as it helps to foresee the course of development and influence it purposively. Therein, in general terms, is the invaluable importance of Marxism as a weapon of social historical orientation. I am sorry that the narrow limits of the lecture do not permit me to enlarge upon the above quotation materially. I will therefore content myself with a brief resume of the whole work which dates from 1905.

In accordance with its immediate tasks, the Russian Revolution is a bourgeois revolution. But the Russian bourgeoisie is anti-revolutionary. The victory of the Revolution is therefore possible only as a victory of the proletariat. But the victorious proletariat will not stop at the programme of bourgeois democracy: it will go on to the programme of socialism. The Russian Revolution will become the first stage of the Socialist world revolution.

This was the theory of permanent revolution formulated by me in 1905 and since then exposed to the severest criticism under the name of 'Trotskyism'.

To be more exact, it is only a part of this theory. The other part, which is particularly timely now, states:

The present productive forces have long outgrown their national limits. A socialist society is not feasible within national boundaries. Significant as the economic successes of an isolated workers' state may be, the programme of 'Socialism in one country' is a petty-bourgeois utopia. Only a European and then a world federation of socialist republics can be the real arena for a harmonious socialist society.

Today, after the test of events, I see less reason than ever to discard this theory.

Prerequisites for October

After all that has been said above, is it still worthwhile to recall the Fascist writer Malaparte, who ascribes to me tactics which are independent of strategy and amount to a series of technical recipes for insurrection, applicable in all latitudes and longitudes? It is a good thing that the name of the luckless theoretician of the coup d'état makes it easy to distinguish him from the victorious practitioner of the coup d'état; no one therefore runs the risk of confusing Malaparte with Bonaparte.

Without the armed insurrection of 7 November 1917, the Soviet State would not be in existence. But the insurrection itself did not drop from heaven. A series of historical prerequisites were necessary for the October Revolution:

1.   The rotting away of the old ruling classes – the nobility, the monarchy, the bureaucracy.
2.   The political weakness of the bourgeoisie, which had no roots in the masses of the people.
3.   The revolutionary character of the agrarian question.
4.   The revolutionary character of the problem of the oppressed nationalities.
5.   The significant social burdens weighing on the proletariat.

To these organic preconditions must be added certain highly important connected conditions:

6.   The Revolution of 1905 was the great school or in Lenin's phrase, 'the dress rehearsal' of the Revolution of 1917. The Soviet's as the irreplaceable organisational form of the proletarian united front in the Revolution were created for the first time in the year 1905.
7.   The imperialist war sharpened all the contradictions, tore the backward masses out of their immobility, and thus prepared the grandiose scale of the catastrophe.

The Bolshevik Party

But all these conditions, which fully sufficed for the outbreak of the Revolution, were insufficient to assure the victory of the proletariat in the Revolution. For this victory one condition more was necessary:

8.   The Bolshevik Party

When I enumerate this condition last in the series, I do it only because it follows the logical sequence, and not because I assign the last place in the order of importance to the Party.

No, I am far from such a thought. The liberal bourgeoisie can seize power and has seized it more than once as the result of struggles in which it took no part; it possesses organs of seizure which are admirably adapted to the purpose. But the working masses are in a different position; they have long been accustomed to give, and not to take. They work, are patient as long as they can be, hope, lose patience, rise up and struggle, die, bring victory to others, are betrayed, fall into despondency, bow their necks, and work again. Such is the history of the masses of the people under all regimes. To be able to take the power firmly and surely into its hands the proletariat needs a Party, which far surpasses other parties in the clarity of its thought and in its revolutionary determination.

The Bolshevik Party, which has been described more than once and with complete justification as the most revolutionary Party in the history of mankind was the living condensation of the modern history of Russia, of all that was dynamic in it. The overthrow of Tsarism had long been recognised as the necessary condition for the development of economy and culture. But for the solution of this task, the forces were insufficient. The bourgeoisie feared the Revolution. The intelligentsia tried to bring the peasant to his feet. The muzhik, incapable of generalising his own miseries and his aims, left this appeal unanswered. The intelligentsia armed itself with dynamite. A whole generation was wasted in this struggle.

On 1 March 1887, Alexander Ulianov carried out the last of the great terrorist plots. The attempted assassination of Alexander III failed. Ulianov and the other participants were executed. The attempt to make chemical preparation take the place of a revolutionary class, came to grief. Even the most heroic intelligentsia is nothing without the masses. Ulianov's younger brother Vladimir, the future Lenin, the greatest figure of Russian history, grew up under the immediate impression of these facts and conclusion. Even in his early youth he placed himself on the foundations of Marxism and turned his face toward the proletariat. Without losing sight of the village for a moment he sought the way of the peasantry through the workers. Inheriting from his revolutionary predecessors their capacity for self-sacrifice, and their willingness to go to the limit, Lenin, at an early age, became the teacher of the new generation of the intelligentsia and of the advanced workers. In strikes and street fights, in prisons and in exile, the workers received the necessary tempering. They needed the searchlight of Marxism to light up their historical road in the darkness of absolutism.

Among the émigrés the first Marxist group arose in 1883. In 1899 at a secret meeting, the foundation of the Russian Social-Democratic Workers Party was proclaimed (we all called ourselves Social-Democrats in those days). In 1903 occurred the split between Bolsheviks and Mensheviks, and in 1912 the Bolshevik faction finally became an independent Party.

It learned to recognise the class mechanics of society in its struggles during the events of twelve years (1905-1917). It educated groups equally capable of initiative and of subordination. The discipline of its revolutionary action was based on the unity of its doctrine, on the tradition of common struggles and on confidence in its tested leadership.

Such was the party in 1917. Despised by the official 'public opinion' and the paper thunder of the intelligentsia Press it adapted itself to the movement of the masses. It kept firmly in hand the lever of control in the factories and regiments. More and more the peasant masses turned toward it. If we understand by 'nation' not the privileged heads, but the majority of the people, that is, the workers and peasants, then the Bolsheviks became during the course of 1917 a truly national Russian Party.

In September 1917, Lenin who was compelled to keep in hiding gave the signal, 'The crisis is ripe, the hour of insurrection has approached.' He was right. The ruling classes faced with the problems of the war, the land and liberation, had got into inextricable difficulties. The bourgeoisie positively lost its head. The democratic parties, the Mensheviks and Social-Revolutionaries, dissipated the last remaining bit of confidence of the masses in them by their support of the imperialist war, by their policy of compromise and concessions to the bourgeois and feudal property owners. The awakened army no longer wanted to fight for the alien aims of imperialism. Disregarding democratic advice, the peasantry smoked the landowners out of their estates. The oppressed nationalities of the far boundaries rose up against the bureaucracy of Petrograd. In the most important workers' and soldiers' Soviets the Bolsheviks were dominant. The ulcer was ripe. It needed a cut of the lancet.

Only under these social and political conditions was the insurrection possible. And thus it also became inevitable. But there is no playing around with insurrection. Woe to the surgeon who is careless in the use of the lancet! Insurrection is an art. It has its laws and its rules.

The party faced the realities of the October insurrection with cold calculation and with ardent resolution. Thanks to this, it conquered almost without victims. Through the victorious soviets the Bolsheviks placed themselves at the head of a country which occupies one sixth of the surface of the globe.

The majority of my present listeners, it is to be presumed, did not occupy themselves at all with politics in 1917. So much the better. Before the young generation lies much that is interesting, if not always easy. But the representatives of the old generation in this hall will certainly remember well how the seizure of power by the Bolsheviks was received: as a curiosity, as a misunderstanding, as a scandal; most often as a nightmare which was bound to disappear with the first rays of dawn. The Bolsheviks would last twenty-four hours, a week, month, year. The period had to be constantly lengthened. The rulers of the whole world armed themselves up against the first workers' state: civil war was stirred up, interventions again and again, blockade. So passed year after year. Meantime, history has recorded fifteen years of existence of the Soviet power.

Can October be justified?

'Yes', some opponents will say, 'the adventure of October has shown itself to be much more substantial than many of us thought. Perhaps it was not even quite an 'adventure'. Nevertheless, the question: What was achieved at this high cost? – retains its full force. Have the dazzling promises which the Bolsheviks proclaimed on the eve of the Revolution been fulfilled?'

Before we answer the hypothetical opponent let us note that the question in and of itself is not new. On the contrary, it followed right at the heels of the October Revolution, since the day of its birth.

The French journalist, Claude Anet, who was in Petrograd during the Revolution, wrote as early as 27 October, 1917:

The maximalists (which was what the French called the Bolsheviks at that time) have seized power and the great day has come. At last, I say to myself, I shall behold the realisation of the socialist Eden which has been promised us for so many years ... Admirable adventure! A privileged position!

And so on and so forth. What sincere hatred was behind the ironical salutation! The very morning after the capture of the Winter Palace, the reactionary journalist hurried to register his claim for a ticket of admission to Eden. Fifteen years have passed since the Revolution. With all the greater absence of ceremony our enemies reveal their malicious joy over the fact that the land of the Soviets, even today, bears but little resemblance to a realm of general well-being. Why then the Revolution and why the sacrifice?

Permit me to express the opinion that the contradictions, difficulties, mistakes and insufficiency of the Soviet regime are no less familiar to me than to anyone. I, personally, have never concealed them, whether in speech or in writing. I have believed and I still believe that revolutionary politics as distinguished from conservative, cannot be built up on concealment. 'To speak out that which is' must be the highest principle of the workers' State.

But in criticism, as well as in creative activity, perspective is necessary. Subjectivism is a poor adviser, particularly in great questions. Periods of time must be commensurate with the tasks, and not with individual caprices. Fifteen years! How long is that in the life of one man! Within that period not a few of our generation were borne to their graves and those who remain have added innumerable grey hors. But these same fifteen years – what an insignificant period in the life of a people! Only a minute on the clock of history.

Capitalism required centuries to establish itself in the struggle against the Middle Ages, to raise the level of science and technique, to build railroads, to make use of electric current. And then? Then humanity was thrust by capitalism into the hell of wars and crises.

But Socialism is allowed by its enemies, that is, by the adherents of capitalism, only a decade and a half to install on earth Paradise, with all modern improvements. Such obligations were never assumed by us.

The processes of great changes must be measured by scales which are commensurate with them. I do not know if the Socialist society will resemble the biblical Paradise. I doubt it. But in the Soviet Union there is no Socialism as yet. The situation that prevails there is one of transition, full of contradictions, burdened with the heavy inheritance of the past and in addition is under the hostile pressure of the capitalistic states. The October Revolution has proclaimed the principles of the new society. The Soviet Republic has shown only the first stage of its realisation. Edison's first lamp was very bad. We must learn how to discern the future.

But the unhappiness that rains on living men! Do the results of the Revolution justify the sacrifice which it has caused? A fruitless question, rhetorical through and through; as if the processes of history admitted of a balance sheet accounting! We might just as well ask, in view of the difficulties and miseries of human existence, 'Does it pay to be born altogether?' To which Heine wrote: 'And the fool expects an answer' … Such melancholy reflections haven't hindered mankind from being born and from giving birth. Even in these days of unexampled world crisis, suicides fortunately constitute an unimportant percentage. But peoples never resort to suicide. When their burdens are intolerable they seek a way out through revolution.

Besides who are they who are indignant over the victims of the social upheaval? Most often those who have paved the way for the victims of the imperialist war, and have glorified or, at least, easily accommodated themselves to it. It is now our turn to ask, 'Has the war justified itself? What has it given us? What has it taught?'

The reactionary historian, Hippolyte Taine, in his eleven volume pamphlet against the great French Revolution describes, not without malicious joy, the sufferings of the French people in the years of the dictatorship of the Jacobins and afterward. The worst off were the lower classes of the cities, the plebeians, who as 'sansculottes' had given of their best for the Revolution. Now they or their wives stood in line throughout cold nights to return empty-handed to the extinguished family hearth. In the tenth year of the Revolution, Paris was poorer than before it began. Carefully selected, artificially pieced out facts serve Taine as Justification for his destructive verdict against the Revolution. Look, the plebeians wanted to be dictators and have precipitated themselves into misery!

It is hard to conceive of a more uninspired piece of moralising. First of all, if the Revolution precipitated the country into misery the blame lay principally on the ruling classes who drove the people to revolution. Second the great French Revolution did not exhaust itself in hungry lines before bakeries. The whole of modern France, in many respects the whole of modern civilisation, arose out of the bath of the French Revolution!

In the course of the Civil War in the United States in the 1860s of the past century, 50,000 men were killed. Can these sacrifices be justified?

From the standpoint of the American slaveholder and the ruling classes of Great Britain who marched with them – no! From the standpoint of the Negro or of the British working man – absolutely. And from the standpoint of the development of humanity as a whole there can be no doubt whatever. Out of the Civil War of the 1860s came the present United States with its unbounded practical initiative, its rationalised technique, its economic energy. On these achievements of Americanism, humanity will build the new society.

The October Revolution penetrated deeper than any of its predecessors into the Holy of Holies of society-into the property relations. So much the longer time is necessary to reveal the creative consequences of the Revolution in all spheres of life. But the general direction of the upheaval is already clear: the Soviet Republic has no reason whatever to bow its head before the capitalist accusers and speak the language of apology.

In order to appreciate the new regime from the standpoint of human development, one must first answer the question, 'How does social progress express itself and how can it be measured?'

The balance sheet of October

The deepest, the most objective and the most indisputable criterion says: progress can be measured by the growth of the productivity of social labour. From this angle the estimate of the October Revolution is already given by experience. The principle of socialistic organisation has for the first time in history shown its ability to record results in production unheard of in a short space of time.

The curve of the industrial development of Russia expressed in crude index numbers is as follows, taking 1913, the last year before the war as 100. The year 1920, the highest point of the civil war, is also the lowest point in industry – only 25, that is to say, a quarter of the pre-war production. In 1925 it rose to 75, that is, three-quarters of the pre-war production; in 1929 about 200, in 1932: 300, that is to say, three times as much as on the eve of the war.

The picture becomes even more striking in the light of the international index. From 1925 to 1932 the industrial production of Germany has diminished one and a half times, in America twice, in the Soviet Union it has increased fourfold. These figures speak for themselves.

I have no intention of denying or concealing the seamy side of the Soviet economy. The results of the industrial index are extraordinarily influenced by the unfavourable development of agriculture, that is to say, in the domain which essentially has not yet risen to Socialist methods, but at the same time had been led on the road to collectivisation with insufficient preparation, bureaucratically rather than technically and economically. This is a great question, which however goes beyond the limits of my lecture.

The index numbers cited require another important reservation. The indisputable and, in their way, splendid results of Soviet industrialisation demand a further economic checking-up from the stand point of the mutual adaptation of the various elements of the economy, their dynamic equilibrium and consequently their productive capacity. Here great difficulties and even set backs are inevitable. Socialism does not arise in its perfected form from the five-year Plan like Minerva from the head of Jupiter, or Venus from the foam of the sea. Before it are decades of persistent work, of mistakes, corrections, and reorganisation. Moreover, let us not forget that socialist construction in accordance with its very nature can only reach perfection on the international arena. But even the most favourable economic balance sheet of the results so far obtained could reveal only the incorrectness of the preliminary calculations, the faults of planning and errors of direction. It could in no way refute the empirically firmly established fact – the possibility, with the aid of socialist methods, of raising the productivity of collective labour to an unheard of height. This conquest, of world historical importance, cannot be taken away from us by anybody or anything.

After what has been said it is scarcely worthwhile to spend time on the complaints that the October Revolution has brought Russia to the downfall of its civilisation. That is the voice of the disquieted ruling houses and salons. The feudal bourgeois 'civilisation' overthrown by the proletarian upheaval was only barbarism with decorations *à la Talmi*. While it remained inaccessible to the Russian people, it brought little that was new to the treasury of mankind.

But even with respect to this civilisation, which is so bemoaned by the white émigrés, we must put the question more precisely – in what sense has it been destroyed? Only in one sense: the monopoly of a small minority in the treasures of civilisation has been done away with. But everything of cultural value in the old Russian civilisation has remained untouched. The 'Huns' of Bolshevism have shattered neither the conquests of the mind nor the creations of art. On the contrary, they carefully collected the monuments of human creativeness and arranged them in model order. The culture of the monarchy, the nobility and the bourgeoisie has now become the culture of the historic museums.

The people visit these museums eagerly. But they do not live in them. They learn. They construct. The fact alone that the October Revolution taught the Russian people, the dozens of peoples of Tsarist Russia, to read and write stands immeasurably higher than the whole former hot-house Russian civilisation.

The October Revolution has laid the foundations for a new civilisation which is designed, not for a select few, but for all. This is felt by the masses of the whole world. Hence their sympathy for the Soviet Union which is as passionate as once was their hatred for Tsarist Russia.

Human language is an irreplaceable instrument not only for giving names to events, but also for their valuation. By filtering out that which is accidental, episodic, artificial, it absorbs into itself that which is essential, characteristic, of full weight. Notice with what sensibility the languages of civilised nations have distinguished two epochs in the developments of Russia. The culture of the nobility brought into world currency such barbarisms as Tsar, Cossack, pogrom, nagaika. You know these words and what they mean. The October Revolution introduced into the language of the world such words as Bolshevik, Soviet, kolkhoz, Gosplan, piatileka. Here practical linguistics holds it historical Supreme Court!

The most profound meaning of the Revolution, but the hardest to submit to immediate measurement, consists in the fact that it forms and tempers the character of the people. The conception of the Russian people as slow, passive, melancholy, mystical, is widely spread and not accidental. It has its roots, in the past. But in Western countries up to the present time those far-reaching changes which have been introduced into the character of the people by the revolution, have not been sufficiently considered. Could it be otherwise?

Every man with experience of life can recall the picture of some youth that he has known, receptive, lyrical, all too susceptible, who later becomes suddenly under the influence of a powerful moral impetus, stronger, better balanced and hardly recognisable. In the developments of a whole nation, such moral transformations are wrought by the revolution.

The February insurrection against the autocracy, the struggle against the nobility, against the imperialist war, for peace, for land, for national equality, the October insurrection, the overthrow of the bourgeoisie and of those parties which supported it, or sought agreements with the bourgeoisie, three years of civil war on a front of 5,000 miles, the years of blockade, hunger, misery, and epidemics, the years of tense economic reconstruction, of new difficulties and renunciations-these make a hard but good school. A heavy hammer smashes glass, but forges steel. The hammer of the revolution is forging the steel of the people's character.

'Who will believe,' wrote a Tsarist general, Zalweski, with indignation shortly after the upheaval, 'that a porter or a watchman suddenly becomes a chief justice, a hospital attendant the director of the hospital, a barber an office-holder, a corporal a commander-in-chief, a day-worker a mayor, a locksmith the director of a factory?'

'Who will believe it?' But it had to be believed. They could do nothing else but believe it, when the corporals defeated the generals, when the mayor – the former day-worker – broke the resistance of the old bureaucracy, the wagon greaser put the transportation system into order, the locksmith as director put the industrial equipment into working condition. 'Who will believe it?' Let anyone only try not to believe it.

For an explanation of the extraordinary persistence which the masses of the people of the Soviet Union are showing throughout the years of the revolution, many foreign observers rely, in accord with ancient habit, on the 'passivity' of the Russian character. Gross anachronism! The revolutionary masses endure privations patiently but not passively. With their own hands they are creating a better future and are determined to create it at any cost. Let the enemy class only attempt to impose his will from outside on these patient masses! No, better, he should not try!

The revolution and its place in history

Let me now, in closing, attempt to ascertain the place of the October Revolution, not only in the history of Russia but in the history of the world. During the year of 1917, in a period of eight months, two historical curves intersect. The February upheaval – that belated echo of the great struggles which had been carried out in the past centuries on the territories of Holland, England, France, nearly all over Continental Europe – takes its place in the series of bourgeois revolutions. The October Revolution proclaimed and opened the domination of the proletariat. World capitalism suffered its first great defeat on the Russian territory. The chain broke at its weakest link. But it was the chain that broke, and not only the link.

Capitalism has outlived itself as a world system. It has ceased to fulfil its essential function: the raising of the level of human power and human wealth. Humanity cannot remain stagnant at the level which it has reached. Only a powerful increase in productive force and a sound, planned, that is, socialist organisation of production and distribution can assure humanity – all humanity – of a decent standard of life and at the same time give it the precious feeling of freedom with respect to its own economy. Freedom in two senses – first of all man will no longer be compelled to devote the greater part of his life to physical toil. Second, he will no longer be dependent on the laws of the market, that is, on the blind and obscure forces which work behind his back. He will build his economy freely, according to plan, with compass in hand. This time it is a question of subjecting the anatomy of society to the X-ray through and through, of disclosing all its secrets and subjecting all its functions to the reason and the will of collective humanity. In this sense, socialism must become a new step in the historical advance of mankind. Before our ancestor, who first armed himself with a stone axe, the whole of nature represented a conspiracy of secret and hostile forces. Since then, the natural sciences hand in hand with practical technology, have illuminated nature down to its most secret depths. By means of electrical energy, the physicist passes judgement on the nucleus of the atom. The hour is not far when science will easily solve the task of alchemists, and turn manure into gold and gold into manure. Where the demons and furies of nature once raged, now reigns over more courageously the industrious will of man.

But while he wrestled victoriously with nature, man built up his relations to order men blindly almost like the bee or the ant. Slowly and very haltingly he approached the problems of human society.

The Reformation represented the first victory of bourgeois individualism in a domain which had been ruled by dead tradition. From the church, critical thought went on to the State. Born in the struggle with absolutism and the medieval estates, the doctrine of the sovereignty of the people and of the rights of man and the citizen grew stronger. Thus arose the system of parliamentarianism. Critical thought penetrated into the domain of government administration. The political rationalism of democracy was the highest achievement of the revolutionary bourgeoisie.

But between nature and the state stands economic life. Technical science liberated man from the tyranny of the old elements – earth, water, fire and air – only to subject him to its own tyranny. Man ceased to be a slave to nature to become a slave to the machine, and, still worse, a slave to supply and demand. The present world crisis testifies in especially tragic fashion how man, who dives to the bottom of the ocean, who rise up to the stratosphere, who converses on invisible waves from the Antipodes, how this proud and daring ruler of nature remains a slave to the blind forces of his own economy. The historical task of our epoch consists in replacing the uncontrolled play of the market by reasonable planning, in disciplining the forces of production, compelling them to work together in harmony and obediently serve the needs of mankind. Only on this new social basis will man be able to stretch his weary limbs and – every man and every woman, not only a selected few – become a citizen with full power in the realm of thought.

The future of man

But this is not yet the end of the road. No, it is only the beginning. Man calls himself the crown of creation. He has a certain right to that claim. But who has asserted that present-day man is the last and highest representative of the species Homo Sapiens? No, physically as well as spiritually he is very far from perfection, prematurely born biologically, with feeble thought, and has not produced any new organic equilibrium.

It is true that humanity has more than once brought forth giants of thought and action, who tower over their contemporaries like summits in a chain of mountains. The human race has a right to be proud of its Aristotle, Shakespeare, Darwin, Beethoven, Goethe, Marx, Edison and Lenin. But why are they so rare? Above all, because almost without exception they came out of the middle and upper classes. Apart from rare exceptions, the sparks of genius in the suppressed depths of the people are choked before they can burst into flame. But also because the processes of creating, developing and educating a human being have been and remain essentially a matter of chance, not illuminated by theory and practice, not subjected to consciousness and will.

Anthropology, biology, physiology and psychology have accumulated mountains of material to raise up before mankind in their full scope the tasks of perfecting and developing body and spirit. Psycho-analysis, with the inspired hand of Sigmund Freud, has lifted the cover of the well which is poetically called the 'soul'. And what has been revealed? Our conscious thought is only a small part of the work of the dark psychic forces. Learned divers descend to the bottom of the ocean and there take photographs of mysterious fishes. Human thought, descending to the bottom of its own psychic sources must shed light on the most mysterious driving forces of the soul and subject them to reason and to will.

Once he has done with the anarchic forces of his own society man will set to work on himself, in the pestle and retort of the chemist. For the first time mankind will regard itself as raw material, or at best as a physical and psychic semi-finished product. Socialism will mean a leap from the realm of necessity into the realm of freedom in this sense also, that the man of today, with all his contradictions and lack of harmony, will open the road for a new and happier race.

Leon Trotsky
Copenhagen, 27 November 1932

Resistance Books and the IIRE are grateful to the Marxist Internet Archive for placing this text in the public domain. The online version is at: https://www.marxists.org/archive/trotsky/1932/11/oct.htm.

PEOPLE, PLACES, EVENTS AND ORGANIZATIONS

Anarchists: A revolutionary current, weakly organized but with an important tradition in Russia going back to the nineteenth century (Bakunin, Kropotkin). Having collaborated for a period of time with the Bolsheviks during the October revolution, the Anarchists turned again to opposition against the new power. Makhno was the best-known Anarchist leader during the revolution.

Antonov-Ovseenko, Vladimir (1884-1938): A member RSDLP in 1902 and then the Mensheviks. As an officer in the Tsarist army, he led a mutiny for which he was imprisoned. Antonov-Ovseenko was a member of the Mezhrayontsi, who joined the Bolsheviks in 1917. He was one of the leaders of the October insurrection, and became a Political Commissar for the Red Army during the civil war. He supported the opposition to Stalin, but later capitulated and was executed.

Austro-Marxism: An Austrian Marxist current, particularly prominent before the First World War. It counted among its representatives Max Adler, Rudolph Hilferding, Karl Renner, and Otto Bauer. It developed original theses on the national question and on workers councils. In 1918-1919, Austro-Marxism opposed the conquest of power by the socialist movement in the name of 'Austrian exceptionalism' and of the 'gradual revolution'.

Avksentiev, Nikolai (1878-1943): Leader of the SRs who supported the entrance of Russia into the war in 1914. Avksentiev became President of the Pan-Russian Soviet of Peasants after the February 1917 revolution, then Minister under Kerensky. He struggled against the Soviet regime from the moment of its formation, presiding over an anti-Bolshevik government in Ufa, then in Omsk.

Bakunin, Mikhail (1814-1876): Russian Anarchist revolutionary and an important member of the First International.

Bauer, Otto (1881-1938): Austro Marxist, leader of the left wing of the Austrian SP, important Marxist theoretician, and prominent figure in the Socialist International. Bauer defended the theory of 'gradual revolution' against the seizure of power in Austria during 1918-1919.

Bazarov, Vladimir (1874-1939): Menshevik Internationalist economist and former Bolshevik, Bazarov worked with the Economic Department of the Petrograd Soviet in 1917. He advocated 'state regulation' as an alternative to intervention in management by the factory committees.

Bebel, August (1840-1913): One of the principal founders of German social democracy. He was leader of the Second International where he was part of the centre-left.

Bernstein, Edward (1850-1932): Executor of Engels's estate, leader of German social democracy. He started an important theoretical controversy over 'revisionism' (meaning the revision, in a reformist direction, of Marxist conceptions) with his book, *Evolutionary Socialism.*

Bettelheim, Ernst (1889-1959): Hungarian communist, active in Austria where tried to organize in June 1919, an abortive, ultra-leftist attempt to seize power when confronted with the passivity of social democracy.

Blanqui, Auguste (1805-1881): French revolutionary of the nineteenth century, of communist inspiration, who spent more than 20 years of his life in prison for political activities. Blanqui was often criticized as an elitist revolutionary using conspiratorial methods because he wanted to conquer power based only on an activist minority, hence the term 'Blanquism'.

Brest-Litovsk Negotiations: Negotiations for a separate peace between the Soviet power and the Central Powers (above all Germany) which began in December 1917, and were concluded in March 1918. The Soviet regime was obliged to cede large and very rich territories, including the Ukraine. The Soviet government annulled this treaty — made meaningless by the defeat of Germany and by the Russian civil war — in November 1918. Brest-Litovsk is in in Byelorussia (formerly Poland).

Bolshevik: Russian word for 'majority,' the name of a current led by Lenin which divided the second congress of the RSDLP (1903). It was very much weakened by repression after the 1905 revolution. In 1912 it constituted itself as an independent party. It gained a new mass base in 1913-1914, in 1917, led the October revolution and in 1918 took the name of Communist Party.

Bukharin, Nikolai (1888-1938): Joined the Bolsheviks in 1906 and became a member of the Bolshevik Central Committee in 1917. Bukharin remained close to Lenin, although he clashed with him during the war on the national question and on the problem of the state. In 1918, he was opposed to signing the Treaty of Brest-Litovsk, creating the group of Left Communists. He defended of the NEP and was leader of the Communist International during the 1920s. He allied himself with Stalin from 1923 to 1927, went into opposition and then returned to supporting Stalin in 1929, but was murdered during the Moscow trials.

Central Executive Committee of Soviets of Workers' and Soldiers' Deputies: (Russian abbreviation TsIK) - Permanent leadership body elected by the First All-Russian Congress of Soviets of Workers' and Soldiers' Deputies in June 1917. It was dominated by moderate socialists until the Second Congress in October, when the Bolshevik gained a majority. The revolutionary constitution of January 1918 gave this Central Executive Committee the authority to legislate between sessions of the Congress of Soviets.

Central Soviet of Factory Committees (CS): Permanent leadership body of the Petrograd Factory Committees, elected at the First Conference of Factory Committees in May-June 1917. By contrast with the moderate-dominated Central Executive Committee of Soviets, the Central Soviet of Factory Committees was under strong Bolshevik influence from the beginning, as shown when the Bolshevik resolution won 335 out of 421 votes at the Conference of Factory Committees that elected it. After the July Days, Lenin thought for a time that the factory committees rather than the soviets might be the basis of a working-class insurrection.

Centrist: Unless otherwise specified, a current which vacillates between reform and revolution (and not a party of the 'centre,' between the right and the left in parliament).

Cheka: Political police of the Soviet regime. See Dzerzhinsky, Felix.

Chernov, Victor (1873-1952): Principal leader and theoretician of the SRs. Internationalist during the war, he returned to Russia after the February 1917 revolution. Chernov became Minister of Agriculture under Kerensky, leader of the right wing of the SRs during October 1917 and President of the Constituent Assembly. He opposed against soviet power, but threatened simultaneously by the Red Army and by Kolchak, he emigrated in 1921.

Chubar, Vlas (1891-1941): Ukrainian peasant who became a Bolshevik in 1907 and President of the Economic Council of the Ukraine from 1920 to 1922. Chubar joined the CC in 1921 and the Political Bureau in 1926. He disappeared during the Moscow Trials.

Civil War: The civil war began in October 1917. It was then generalized in 1918 by national and international counter-revolutionary forces trying to overthrow the Soviet power. The imperialist alliance included mainly Germany, France, Great Britain, the USA, Canada, and Japan. It ended in 1920-21 with the defeat of the counter-revolution.

Coalition government: Coalition between liberals and moderate socialist (Menshevik and Social Revolutionary) leaders of the Soviet. It was formed in May 1917 to bolster the flagging authority among workers and soldiers of the liberal Provisional Government of Prince Lvov set up after the February Revolution. Lvov continued to head the government until July, when Kerensky replaced him as Prime Minister. The Petrograd Soviet under Bolshevik leadership overthrew this coalition government in the revolution of November 1917.

Comintern: Third International.

Communist International: Third International.

Conciliators: Bolshevik current led by Rykov and V.P. Nogin. It struggled against the split in the RSDLP between Mensheviks and Bolsheviks — which took place after the defeat of the 1905-07 revolution and was formalized in 1912. The term is also used in other cases, for example to indicate the Bolsheviks who were ready to subordinate themselves to the bourgeois government that emerged after 1917, or those who wanted to reunite with the Mensheviks despite the split.

Congress of the Peoples of the East: The first Congress of the Peoples of the East met in Baku, Azerbaijan, in September 1920. It was attended by close to 2,000 delegates (of whom 55 were women ...), two-thirds of which were communists, coming from around 40 different nationalities.

Constituent Assembly: Assembly of elected representatives, established for the purpose of adopting a constitution. The necessity for a constituent assembly was imposed on Russia by the revolution of February 1917. When it finally convened after the revolution, as its members had been elected before the October revolution they did not reflect the experience of the revolution. It stood counterposed to the legitimate alternative authority of the Congress of Soviets. It was dissolved by the new revolutionary power in January 1918.

Cossack: A personal guard for the Tsar and a particularly feared mounted repressive force. The Cossacks furnished an important part of the White armies in the civil war of 1918-21. Many poor Cossacks also joined the Bolsheviks at the beginning of the revolution, and the anarchist armies, notably in the Ukraine.

Councils of Deputies: See Soviets.

'Czechoslovakians': Czech prisoners of war, armed by imperialism (under French command), and participating in the civil war against the Soviet power in Siberia during the summer of 1918. It was the revolt of the Czech

Legion on 25 May 1918, which marked the beginning of the generalized civil war.

Dan, Theodore (1871-1947): Leader of the Russian Social Democracy, spokesman for the Mensheviks from 1903. Dan was a pacifist during the war, joined the right wing of Menshevism in 1917 and opposed the October revolution. He went into exile in 1922.

Democratic-Centralist Opposition: An opposition group that arose at the 9th congress of the CP (1920) including Smirnov, Ossinsky, and Saparanov. It denounced extreme centralization and authoritarian methods.

Denikin, Anton (1872-1947): Russian general who led one of the counter-revolutionary army corps during the civil war (notably in the South in 1918). He emigrated in 1920.

Dzerzhinsky, Felix (1877-1926): Active in the Russian and Polish social democracy, he became a member of the Bolshevik CC from August 1917 until his death. Known for his personal integrity, Dzerzhinsky established the Cheka. He became President of the National Economic Council in 1924, and alternate member of the Political Bureau in 1924-25.

Ebert, Friedrich (1871-1925): Social democrat, leader of the SPD from 1913, and patriot during the First World War. Ebert contributed to the repression of the Spartakist insurrection (1919) and became Chancellor of the German Republic (1919-1925).

Engels, Friedrich (1820-1895): Principal collaborator of Karl Marx. He made his own contributions to the development of Marxist theory.

French Revolution: This refers to the bourgeois revolution of 1789-1815 and, more precisely, to its first, radical, years of 1789-1794. It ended with the dictatorship of Napoleon Bonaparte 1799-1815.

German Revolution: This refers to the revolutionary struggles, which occurred in Germany between 1918 and 1923.

Gorky, Maxim (1868-1936): Great Russian writer, sympathizer of the Bolsheviks and a friend of Lenin. In 1917, he hesitated in the face of the revolution. His journal, *Navy Zhizn* (New Life) was known for its internationalist, unified social-democratic outlook. Gorky critically supported the Bolsheviks in the 1920s. He capitulated in the end to Stalin.

Gotz, Abraham (1882-1940): Leader of the SRs, member of its right wing in 1917. As a partisan of Kerensky, he actively opposed the October Revolution. Arrested during the civil war, Gotz was condemned to death in 1922 but his sentence was commuted.

Groman, Vladimir (1874-1940): Menshevik economist and head of the Economic Department of the Petrograd Soviet during 1917. He advocated 'state regulation' of industry.

International, First: International Workingmen's Association (1864-1876), founded primarily by Marx and Engels.

International, Second: Socialist International. Broad workers international founded in 1889 which split in 1914 when the majority of its leaders capitulated in the face of imperialist pressures and renounced the fight against war. It was reconstituted on a reformist basis in 1923.

International, Third: Communist International, founded in 1919 on a revolutionary basis. It was transformed during the 1920s and 1930s into a diplomatic instrument in the hands of the Stalinist Soviet bureaucracy. Formally dissolved in 1943, it was replaced by the Cominform.

International, Fourth: Founded in 1938 on a revolutionary basis by, most significantly, Leon Trotsky. It continued the tradition of the anti-Stalinist Left Opposition.

Jaurès, Jean (1859-1914): Academic, journalist, deputy, and one of the main representatives of French humanist socialism. He was assassinated because he opposed the First World War and defended pacifist positions.

July Days: The armed worker and soldier demonstrations on 3-4 July 1917 to pressure the moderate leaders of the Central Executive Committee of Soviets to take power. Despite attempts by the Bolsheviks to hold them back, they took on a semi-insurrectional character. The coalition government responded with repression against the labour movement and the Bolsheviks, beginning a period of reaction that lasted for several weeks, until the defeat of Kornilov's attempted coup.

Kadet: 'Constitutionalist-democratic' current, which in 1917 became the principal bourgeois party. It formed the first provisional government after the overthrow of the Tsar in February 1917.

Kamenev, Lev (1885-1936): Joined the Russian Social Democracy in 1901. Kamenev opposed the orientation of Lenin in April 1917, and the decision for an insurrection in October. He was a standard-bearer of the Conciliators. He resigned from the CC and was re-elected in 1918. He remained one of the principal leaders of the CPSU — and also of the CI — during the 1920s. Allied with Stalin against the opposition from 1923 to 1925, Kamenev went into opposition from 1925-27 but capitulated in 1928. He was murdered during the Moscow Trials.

Kamkov, Katz (1885-1938): Leader of the left SRs, supporter the October revolution and an alliance with the Bolsheviks in 1917. Kamkov denounced the treaty of Brest-Litovsk as treacherous and was one of the organizers of the July 1918 assassination of Mirbach, the German ambassador in Petrograd. That event was one of the elements in the 'left SR uprising', which was designed to provoke a renewal of the war with Germany. He died in prison.

Kautsky, Karl (1854-1938): Collaborator with Engels and executor of his estate. He was one of the main theorists of German social democracy and of the Second International before the First World War (during which he was part of the centre-left), becoming a reformist.

Kerensky, Alexander (1881-1970): Socialist lawyer who, in 1917, was one of the main leaders of the 'workers' current. He became Minister of Justice in March 1917, then Minister of War. As Head of the provisional government in July 1917, Kerensky became an ally of the bourgeoisie and repressed the revolutionary movement. He emigrated to England, then to France and the United States.

Kollontai, Alexandra (1872-1952): Russian revolutionary and Member of the RSDLP in 1899. An Internationalist during the war, she joined the Bolsheviks in 1915, and entered into spokeswoman for the Workers' Opposition in 1920-22. Under Stalin, she did not play any political role and retired to diplomatic activity. She was one of the principal leaders and theorists of Marxist feminism.

Kolchak, Alexander (1874-1920): A vice-admiral who tried to unify the White armies under his 'supreme command' during the civil war. He installed bloody military dictatorships in the territories under his control. He was shot after being captured in Siberia.

Konovalov, Alexander (1875-1948): Kadet industrialist and banker, Minister of Trade and Industry in the Provisional Government. Konovalov resigned from the coalition government in late May 1917 in protest against economic 'anarchy', and was replaced by the engineer Pal'chinskii. He became Deputy Prime Minister in September 1917, and in that capacity in November surrendered to the Soviet on behalf of the Provisional Government.

Kornilov, Lavr (1870-1918): Career Russian officer, Commander in Chief during July 1917, he tried to organize a coup d'état in August. He formed a 'voluntary army' during the civil war.

Kronstadt revolt: Events of March 1921 when the military garrison of Kronstadt, an island-fortress in the Baltic near Petrograd, rebelled against the Soviet government under the slogan "Soviets with Bolsheviks" and the demand for the restoration of free commerce. Negotiations having failed, the Red Army crushed the rebellion.

Kropotkin, Peter (1842-1921): Russian revolutionary Anarchist, former prince, officer, explorer, and scholar. Active in Switzerland, France, and England, he returned to Russia in 1917. Kropotkin's writings have had a wide influence.

Kun, Bela (1885-1937): Hungarian revolutionary who became a Bolshevik while a prisoner of war in Russia. He was head of the Hungarian Soviet Republic in 1919. Leader of the CI, Bela Kun supported Stalin but was murdered in the Stalin purges.

Larin, Lou (1882-1932): Larin was a leader of the Menshevik Liquidator faction. Internationalist during the war, he joined the Bolshevik party in the summer of 1917. Larin was one of the Bolshevik 'comrades on the right' who shrank from direct economic confrontation with the bourgeoisie, but later defended 'war communism'. He capitulated to Stalin in 1926.

Left Communist Opposition: Opposition group formed by Bukharin, Radek, and Uritsky at the beginning of 1918 around the question of signing the Treaty of Brest-Litovsk. It proposed a programme for a combined struggle of communists 'against concessions', in pursuit of a defensive revolutionary war, for the extension of nationalizations, for centralized control in the economic sphere, and for the reinforcement of Soviet power at the rank and file level.

Left Opposition: Anti-Stalinist opposition (anti-bureaucratic), also called 'Bolshevik-Leninists'. Formed in 1923 within the CPSU, inspired in particular by Trotsky. Gave birth in 1929 to the International Left Opposition and in 1938 to the Fourth International.

Lenin, Vladimir (1870-1924): One of the main representatives of the second generation of Russian Marxists. Joined a Marxist circle in early 1890s, polemicized with Populism and 'legal Marxism'. Leader of the Bolsheviks from 1903, Lenin was the ideological spokesperson for the left in the Second International, the best-known leader of the October 1917 Russian Revolution, of the CPSU, and of the Third International, until his death.

Liebknecht, Karl (1871-1919): German Social Democratic revolutionary. Distinguished for his anti-militarist activity and being Internationalist during World War I. Liebknecht was imprisoned and then liberated in 1918 as a result of the revolution. Founder of the German Communist Party, he was assassinated with Rosa Luxemburg in January 1919 by reactionary forces.

Liquidationism: Referring to Liquidators, a wing of the Mensheviks who, after the defeat of the 1905-1907 Russian Revolution wanted to dissolve the underground apparatus of the party and pursue only legal activity.

Lozovsky, Salomon (1878-1952): Joined the RSDLP in 1901 and the Bolsheviks in 1903. Lozovsky became Conciliator, and in 1917 supported a coalition with the Mensheviks. Leader of the textile workers union, he became President of the International of Red Trade Unions from 1921 to 1937. He was purged in 1949.

Lunacharsky, Anatole (1875-1933): Art and literary critic, activist from 1892 and a Bolshevik in 1903. Lunacharsky moved away from Lenin in 1908 and became a Menshevik. He was an Internationalist during the war, joined the Mezhrayontsi, which joined the Bolshevik party in 1917. He was Peoples Commissar for Education from October 1917 to 1929.

Luxemburg, Rosa (1870-1919): Polish revolutionary and Marxist theorist. She played an important role in the struggle against reformism in the German social democracy. Luxemburg was known for her studies of imperialism and the critiques which she formulated with regard to Leninism (on the question of the party, as well as, during the Russian revolution, on the agrarian question and democracy). As an Internationalist during the war, she was imprisoned. Liberated in 1918, she was assassinated with Karl Liebknecht in January 1919 by reactionary forces.

Makhno, Nestor (1889-1934): Ukrainian Anarchist. Makhno organized a peasant and Cossack army in the southern Ukraine after the October revolution, which was allied with the Red army against Denikin (1919) and Wrangel (1920). This alliance broke up after the defeat of the White armies. He took refuge in Romania (1921), then in Paris.

Martov, Julius (1873-1923): Leader of the RSDLP, a friend of Lenin, ideological leader of the Menshevik current from 1903. Martov was Internationalist during the war, and a 'Centrist' on the question of the socialist revolution and taking power in October 1917. He developed a critique of the Soviet regime during the civil war and left Russia in 1920.

Martynov, Aleksandr (1865-1935): joined the RSDLP in 1889, a leader of the Menshevik Liquidators after 1905, and an Internationalist during the war. Martynov was part of the left wing of the Mensheviks in 1917. He joined the CP in 1925 and worked in the CI until his death.

Marx, Karl (1818-1883): Theoretician, militant of the communist workers movement, and founder of the First International. Marx formulated, with Engels, the foundations of historical materialism (Marxism). Marx and

Engels stressed the revolutionary (that is to say anti-reformist) content of their outlook. They foresaw the possibility that Russia, given the conditions at the end of the nineteenth century, might make a direct transition to socialism without passing through an historic stage of capitalist development. The realisation of this possibility would depend on the course of the national and international class struggle. They stood opposed to mechanistic interpretations of their theories and to unilinear conceptions of world history and human society.

Maximalists: Ultra-left split from the SRs.

Mechanists: A term that designates a current of materialist thought which overly simplifies interactions, especially between diverse social factors, in order to define a rigid chain of cause and effect. It's analysis of society neglects, in particular, the historical dimension. The Mechanists found their inspiration in the natural sciences of the eighteenth century, which utilized many comparisons with machines in particular with the internal workings of a clock.

Menshevik: The Russian term for 'minority.' A current of 'revolutionaries of the right', constituted in 1903 within the RSDLP and opposed to Bolshevism. During the First World War, the Mensheviks divided between an Internationalist current (Martov) and another, anti-German and favourable to military intervention (including Plekhanov). It divided in 1917 between a class-collaborationist wing, the majority (Dan, Lieber, Tseretelli) and a left split-off (Martov, Martynov). The Mensheviks opposed the October 1917 revolution.

Menshevik Defensists: Right wing of the social-democratic Menshevik Party. The Defensists advocated an alliance with liberal elements of the bourgeoisie as a necessary condition for the bourgeois-democratic revolution and rejected a break with the Allies during the First World War. They opposed the October Revolution, arguing that socialist forces in Russia were too weak and that it would lead to disaster.

Menshevik Internationalists: Left wing of the social-democratic Menshevik Party, including Martov and Martynov. They rejected the positions of the Menshevik Defensists as well as those of the Bolsheviks on soviet power. They advocated a coalition government of the socialist parties, but refused to join the coalition formed by the Bolsheviks and Left Social Revolutionaries after November 1917. Their most prominent leader was Martov.

Mezhrayontsi: The 'interdistrict' (or 'intercraft') committees. The organization came together mostly in 1917, with revolutionary cadres who did not align with either of the two main factions of Russian social democracy, among them Trotsky. It joined the Bolshevik party in July 1917.

Military-Industrial Committees: Committees formed at the initiative of the Tsarist government in 1915 in order to coordinate industrialists' (and later workers') mobilization for the war effort. They became a focal point for liberal opposition. In 1917 they then defended capital against the factory committees.

Miliukov, Pavel (1859-1943): Russian political figure. Founder of the Kadet party, he tried to save the monarchy in February 1917. Miliukov became Minister of Foreign Affairs in the provisional government, and political councillor to the White general Denikin during the civil war.

Milyutin, Vladimir (1859-1943): Economist who joined RSDLP in 1908, and became a Bolshevik in 1910. Partisan of a coalition government, he opposed the October insurrection. Milyutin became Commissar of Agriculture after the October revolution. He disappeared during the Stalin purges.

Moscow Trials: Succession of political trials organized in 1936-1938 in the USSR. During these trials the most bizarre accusations were presented against the majority of communist cadres who led the October revolution, asserting that they had always been counter-revolutionaries. These trials aimed at the physical elimination, from the CPSU and from the state, of all potential opposition to the faction led by Stalin. They constituted one of the central features of Stalin's purges.

NEP: 'New Economic Policy' put into operation in 1921. It represented a profound break with the command economy of war communism. It included the liberalization of the market and peasant production, favoured the development of small private industry and tried to attract foreign capital investment.

Nogin, Victor (1878-1924): Member of the RSDLP from 1898 and Bolshevik in from 1903. Nogin was a Conciliator in 1910, opposing the split with the Mensheviks. Elected to the CC in April 1917, Nogin was a partisan of a coalition government, and was appointed People's Commissar for Industry. He was denounced after his death as an 'enemy of the people' during the Stalin purges.

Ossinsky, Valerian (1887-1933): Bolshevik from 1907, Ossinsky was President of the National Economic Council in 1918, ideological leader of the Left Communists, and member of the CC in 1921-1930. Arrested during the Moscow trials, he then disappeared during the purges.

Pal'chinskii, Peter (1875-1929): Engineer who became acting Minister of Trade and Industry in the coalition government after Konovalov's resignation in May 1917, advocating the 'unloading' Petrograd. Pal'chinskii was Kerensky's governor-general of Petrograd during Kornilov's attempted coup at the end of August and helped organize the defence of the Winter Palace against the October insurrection. Later, he worked with the new Soviet authorities and was executed in 1929.

People's Commissar: Member of the Soviet government, charged with a specific function (e.g., Commissar of Labour).

Plekhanov, George (1856-1937): Russian intellectual and philosopher, part of the first generation of RSDLP cadre, he introduced Marxism to Russia. Plekhanov was a Menshevik leader from 1904. He adopted a chauvinist position during the First World War, and opposed the October 1917 revolution which he considered to be historically premature.

Pogrom: Anti-Semitic movement, often officially promoted, marked by looting and massacres.

Popular Socialist: See Workerists.

Populism: Principal revolutionary current in nineteenth-century Russia. It represented Russian socialism from 1848 to 1881, and included diverse movements and orientations (including both rural and urban organizing, propaganda, and assassination attempts against high government officials and the Tsar). Russian Marxism waged a battle against these perspectives (Plekhanov, Lenin). But this current had an impact on the entire Russian revolutionary tradition and, in particular, gave birth to the Social-Revolutionary Party.

Provisional Government: One of the governments between the revolution of February 1917 and the constitution of the RSFSR in January 1918. After the October Revolution in 1917, it had the name 'Provisional Government of the Workers and Peasants.'

Putilov Shipyard: Part of a giant factory in Petrograd employing over 30,000 workers. Initially a Social Revolutionary stronghold, it was a centre of Bolshevik activity from the spring of 1917 onwards, particularly during the July Days and the resistance to the Kornilov coup in August.

Radek, Karl (1885-1939): Active in the Polish, German and the Russian social democracy. He was an Internationalist during the war and joined the Bolshevik Party in 1917. Radek was close to Lenin despite disagreement on the national question. Appointed Vice-Commissar of Foreign Affairs in the Soviet government in 1918, he participated in the negotiations at Brest-Litovsk. He was opposed Stalin and died in prison.

Reed, John: Radical US journalist who reported on the Mexican and Russian revolutions. He wrote a famous account of the October revolution called *Ten Days That Shook the World,* and became a founder of the US Communist movement before dying in Russia and being buried by the Kremlin wall.

Russian Social Democratic Labour Party (RSDLP): Founded in 1898 (but temporarily destroyed by repression). It brought together all of the Russian revolutionary currents which claimed to be Marxist. It divided in 1903 between two main factions, Bolsheviks (led by Lenin) and Mensheviks (led by Martov). Temporarily reunified by the revolution of 1905, it then split into two parties in 1912 — giving birth in particular to the Bolshevik Party — although the local units remained united until 1917. Many independent personalities — including Trotsky — joined the Bolshevik party in 1917. It became the CPSU in 1918.

Russian Soviet Federal Socialist Republic (RSFSR): Founded in January 1918 by the Fifth All-Russian Congress of Soviets.

Russo-Japanese War: War waged in 1904-1905 between the Tsarist regime and Japan for possession of the easternmost territories. The Tsarist army, (and especially navy) was battered. The Russian defeat contributed to the 1905 revolution. The Japanese victory had a big impact in the Orient: it was the first time that an Asiatic power gained the upper hand over a Western empire.

Russo-Polish War: The war between the Soviet Red Army and the Polish government in May-September 1920. The Soviet intervention, instead of acting in alliance with a revolutionary movement in Poland, provoked a nationalist-defensive reflex. It ended in the retreat of the Red Army.

Ryabushinksii, Pavel (1871-1924): Banker and textile manufacturer. He was famous in 1917 for his prediction at a conference of industrialists that the 'bony hand of hunger' would seize the workers by the throat if they did not renounce their radicalism.

Ryazanov, David (1870-1938): Russian Marxist historian and militant socialist. Ryazanov refused to choose between the main factions of the RSDLP. He was an Internationalist during the war, and joined the Mezhrayontsi, which adhered to the Bolshevik party in 1917. He argued for collaboration with the Mensheviks after October. He founded the Marx-Engels Institute, which he headed until 1930. He disappeared during the Stalin purges.

Rykov, Alexis (1881-1938): Joined the RSDLP in 1901 and became a Bolshevik in 1903. He opposed Lenin's orientation to the 1905 revolution and became a Conciliator in 1910. Rykov was appointed Commissar of the Interior in 1917, and joined the Political Bureau from 1923 to 1929. In 1928, he joined Bukharin in opposition to Stalin. He was murdered during the Moscow Trials.

Shliapnikov, Alexander (1883-1937): Metalworker, member of the RSDLP in 1899, and of the Bolsheviks in 1903. Shliapnikov was Commissar of Labour after the October revolution, favoured a coalition government, and was elected to the Central Committee in 1918. Member of the Workers Opposition, he opposed Stalinism, but then capitulated. He was murdered during the Stalin purges.

Social Democrat: Today this term designates the current to which the reformist and socialist democratic parties belong. Before the First World War it referred to the Marxist current as a whole, including its more revolutionary elements (e.g., Lenin who was then a Russian social democrat).

United Internationalist Social Democrats: A small revolutionary group in 1917, influenced by the journal published by Maxim Gorky.

Schmidt, V.: Bolshevik worker and a leader of the Metalworkers' Union. He would become People's Commissar of Labour after the October revolution.

Skobelev, Matvey (1885-1938): Leader of the Menshevik group in the pre-revolutionary Duma (parliament) who became Minister of Labour in the coalition government in May 1917. He strongly opposed the interference by the factory committees in the management of industry.

Skrypnik, Mykola (1872-1933): Bolshevik and a leader of the factory committee movement. He became a leader of the Ukrainian Communist Party and opposed Russification. Skrypnik committed suicide in 1933 after failing to hinder Stalin's purge of the Ukrainian party.

Social Revolutionary (SR): Party that belonged to the Second International. Officially constituted in 1902, the SR was the continuation of the movement called 'populist' in the nineteenth century. Although dominant within the peasant movement, it also had roots in the large urban enterprises. Participated, after the February 1917 revolution, in the process of class collaboration with the provisional bourgeois government. It divided during the summer between a left revolutionary current, which grew in strength (Spiridinova, Kamkov), and a right reformist one which grew weaker (Chemov, Gotz). The right wing engaged from the start in a fight against the October revolution. The left wing participated in the Soviet government until the Treaty of Brest-Litovsk was signed, which it denounced as treacherous. It turned against the Bolsheviks and organized, in July of 1918, the 'uprising of the Left SRs'.

Socialist International: Second International.

Soviet: Russian term for 'council' for the structures of self-organization that appeared during the revolution of 1905 then re-emerged in 1917 (the councils of workers, peasants, and soldiers). They had both a territorial and pyramidal structure (with the possibility of recalling officials from top to bottom), as well as including the factory councils. They formed the skeleton of a new revolutionary state in 1917 and the institutional framework of socialist democracy. They lost their vitality during the civil war and were gutted of all truly representative content and of all power by the Stalinist bureaucracy.

SPD: The German Social Democratic party founded in 1891 which included the tradition of the Social-Democratic Workers Party (going back to 1875) through a fusion of the Marxist currents and the Lassalleans. It was represented most notably by Kautsky. The SPD became, until the First World War, the main party of the Second International. In 1914, a majority of its leaders capitulated to the interest of their own imperialist power and accepted the participation of Germany in the war. Having become reformist, the party participated in the repression of the German revolution of 1918-1923.

Spiridonova, Maria (18827-1941?): Militant SR, sentenced to twelve years in prison for shooting a general responsible for the massacre of peasants in 1906. Spiridonova was a leader of the Left SRs, an Internationalist, and supported a coalition with the Bolsheviks. She denounced the signing of the Treaty of Brest-Litovsk and prepared the 'uprising of the Left SRs' in July 1918. She disappeared during the Stalin purges.

Stalin, Joseph (1879-1953): Joined the RSDLP in 1898 and the Bolsheviks in 1903. Long-time revolutionary cadre aligned with the Leninist wing of the party. He was active underground in the Caucasus. Arrested he was deported to Siberia during the war. Conciliationist with regard to the provisional government in February 1917, but he realigned himself with Lenin's position in April. Elected to the CC, then appointed Commissar for Nationalities from 1919 to 1923, Stalin became Secretary of the CC in 1922. He strongly opposed Lenin in 1922-1923 on the nationalities question and on the internal party regime. Stalin became, from 1924 and up until his death, the main leader of the CPSU and of the Soviet state. He organized the great purges of the 1930s, and personified the process of bureaucratic degeneration suffered by the Soviet regime.

Sukhanov, Nicolai (1882-1940): Menshevik Internationalist journalist. He was a leader of the Central Executive Committee of Soviets and a member of the Economic Department of the Petrograd Soviet. Sukhanov later wrote a seven-volume memoir on the revolution. Murdered by Stalin's police in 1940.

Sverdlov, Yakov (1885-1919): Chairman of the Bolshevik Central Committee and key party organizer. After the October revolution, Sverdlov became president of the Central Executive Committee of Soviets, but died during the civil war.

Teodorovich, Ivan (1876-1938): Peasant, Social Democrat in 1898, became a Bolshevik in 1903. He was elected to the CC in April 1917, was a Conciliationist in April and November. Teodorovich became Commissar for Supplies after the October revolution, and then Secretary of the Peasant's International in 1928. He disappeared during the Stalin purges.

'Thermidor': This term originally referred to a political counter-revolution during the French revolution of 1789-1815. By analogy, the 'Soviet Thermidor' described the Stalinist counter-revolution which murdered socialist democracy and instituted a bureaucratic dictatorship, without re-establishing capitalism in the USSR.

'Three Whales': Pillars of the Bolshevik programme before 1917: a democratic republic, the eight-hour day, and land reform.

Trotsky, Leon (1879-1940): Social Democrat in 1896, Trotsky was one of the main participants in the 1905 revolution. A member of the RSDLP, he looked for a compromise between the Mensheviks and the Bolsheviks in 1910-1912 and opposed Lenin. Internationalist during the war, he broke definitively with the Mensheviks in 1914 and joined the Bolshevik party in 1917. Trotsky was one of the main leaders of the Russian revolution. He headed of the Soviet delegation to the negotiations of Brest-Litovsk, and was the head of the Red Army during the civil war. Trotsky opposed Stalin and the process of bureaucratization in the regime after the death of Lenin. Stalin forced him into exile. He founded the Fourth International in 1938, and was assassinated by Stalin's agents in Mexico.

Trudovik: See Workerist.

Tseretelli, Irakli (1881-1959): Georgian Menshevik who became a central figure in the coalition government. A former deputy in the Tsarist Duma (parliament) and a distinguished orator, Tseretelli was Minister of Posts and Telegraph, then Minister of Interior, and a leader of the Central Executive Committee of the Soviets until November 1917.

Two-and-a-half International: 'International of Vienna,' founded in 1921 by Centrist socialists who vacillated between the second and third internationals. It joined the reformist international in 1923.

Union of Soviet Socialist Republics (USSR): Created in 1923. Formally dissolved in 1991, it was replaced by a temporary Confederation of Independent States (CIS).

Uritsky, Moise (1873-1918): Social-Democratic activist during the 1890s, and a leader of the 1905 revolution. Uritsky was member of the Mezhrayontsi in 1917, and was elected to the Bolshevik CC. in July 1917. Head of the Cheka in Petrograd, he was assassinated by an SR.

Volodarsky V. (1891-1918): Member of the Jewish Marxist organization, the Bund. Volodarsky joined the Bolshevik Party in 1917 and was People's Commissar for Information in 1918. He was assassinated by a SR.

War Communism: Name given to the political-economic orientation adopted during the period of the civil war (1918-1921), characterized by its egalitarian spirit, a radical program of nationalization, and exceptional measures—such as the forcible requisition of food from the peasants.

'Whites': Term usually used to indicate the counter-revolutionaries, in opposition to the 'Reds'.

Workerists: Also called Trudoviks or Popular Socialists. Petit-bourgeois current based on the peasant radicalization during the revolution of 1905. The Workerists participated in the pseudo-parliaments of 1906-1914. When confronted with revolution, it expressed the conservative uneasiness of the petit-bourgeoisie in the provinces. In 1917, it was led by Kerensky.

Workers Opposition: Opposition group within the CP, formed in the autumn of 1920 by Shliapnikov and Kollontai, which argued for the control of production by the trade unions, the purging of non-workers from the party, and a return to the principle of electing officials. The Workers Opposition opposed Lenin, and especially Trotsky, during the trade union debate.

Wrangel, Piotr (1878-1928): Russian general. One of the main leaders of the White army during the civil war, he assisted, then replaced by Denikin, and set up a counter-revolutionary government supported by France. Wrangel was defeated in 1920.

Yudenich, Nikolai (1862-1933): White general who led an attack against Petrograd in 1919 with the support of Britain.

Zenzinov, Vladimir (1880-1953): Leading SR he supported the Russian war effort. As a leader of the SR party, he defended anti-Bolshevik positions in

February 1917. Zenzinov was aligned with the right of the party and joined the anti-Soviet government in Ufa during the civil war.

Zinoviev, Gregory (1883-1936): Joined the Social Democrats in 1900. Zinoviev was close to Lenin during his period of exile. In October 1917, he opposed the decision to launch an insurrection, and later was a partisan of coalition government. Zinoviev became one of the main leaders of the new regime. Secretary of the CI from 1919 to 1927, he allied with Stalin against the opposition from 1923 to 1925, then went into opposition from 1925-27 but capitulated in 1928. He was murdered after the Moscow Trials.

BIBLIOGRAPHY

Much has been written about the Russian Revolution. In this bibliography we only include some of the publications in English that are available and that have been referred to in this book. Where publications are available online, a URL has been provided.

Abramovich, Raphael R., *The Soviet Revolution 1917-1939*, New York, International Universities Press, 1962.

Acton, Edward, Vladimir Iu. Cherniaev, William G. Rosenberg, eds., *Critical Companion to the Russian Revolution 1914-1921*, Bloomington, IN, University of Indiana Press, 1997.

Allen, Barabara, *Alexander Shlyapnikov, 1885-1937: Life of an Old Bolshevik*, Chicago, Haymarket Books, 2016.

Avrich, Paul, ed., *The Anarchists in the Russian Revolution*, Ithaca, Cornell University Press, 1973.

_____, *The Russian Anarchists*, Oakland, CA, AK Press, 2005.

Beatty, Bessie, *The Red Heart of Russia*, New York, The Century Co., 1918.

Bettelheim, Charles, *Class Struggles in the USSR, First Period: 1917-1923*, New York, Monthly Review Press, New York, 1976.

Brinton, Maurice, *The Bolsheviks and Workers' Control. 1917-1921: The State and Counter-revolution*, London, Solidarity, 1970; https://www.marxists.org/archive/brinton/1970/workers-control/.

Bryant, Louise, *Six Months in Red Russia*, London, The Journeyman Press, 1982.

Carr, E.H., *A History of Soviet Russia*, 14 vols., London, Macmillan, 1950-1978.

_____, *The Russian Revolution from Lenin to Stalin, 1917-1929*, London, Macmillan, 1979.

Chamberlin, William H., *The Russian Revolution 1917-1921*, 2 vols., Princeton, NJ, Princeton University Press, 1987.

Clements, Barbara Evans, *Bolshevik Women*, Cambridge, UK, Cambridge University Press, 1997.

Cohen, Stephen, *Bukharin and the Bolshevik Revolution: A Political Biography, 1888-1938*, New York, Oxford University Press, 1980.

Dan, Theodore, *The Origins of Bolshevism*, New York, Schocken Books , 1970.

Daniels, Robert V., *The Conscience of the Revolution: Communist Opposition in Soviet Russia*, New York, Simon and Schuster, 1969.

_____, *Red October: The Bolshevik Revolution of 1917*, New York, Charles Scribners Sons, 1967.

Deutscher, Isaac, *Soviet Trade Unions: Their Place in Soviet Labour Policy*, Oxford, UK, Oxford University Press, 1950; https://www.marxists.org/archive/deutscher/1950/soviet-trade-unions/index.htm.

_____, *The Prophet: The Life of Leon Trotsky*, London, Verso, 2015.

Dune, Eduard M., *Notes of a Red Guard,* Urbana, IL, University of Illinois Press, 1993.

Farber Samuel, *Before Stalinism: The Rise and Fall of Soviet Democracy*, London, Verso, 1990.

Ferro, Marc, *October 1917: A Social History of the Russian Revolution*, London, Routledge, 1980.

Figes, Orlando, *A People's Tragedy: A History of the Russian Revolution*, New York, Viking Press, 1996.

Fitzpatrick, Sheila, *The Russian Revolution*, Second Edition, New York, Oxford University Press, 1994.

Gorky, Maxim, *Untimely Thoughts: Essays on Revolution - Culture and the Bolsheviks, 1917-1918,* New Haven, Yale University Press, 1995.

Haimson, Leopold, ed., *The Mensheviks*, Chicago, University of Chicago, 1974.

Haupt, Georges and Jean-Jacques Marie, *Makers of the Russian Revolution: Biographies of Bolshevik Leaders*, Ithaca, NY, Cornell University Press, 1974.

Ilyin-Zhenevsky, A.F., *The Bolsheviks in Power Reminiscences of the Year 1918*, London, New Park, 1984.

James, C.L.R., *World Revolution 1917-1936: The Rise and Fall of the Communist International*, New York, Pioneer Publishers, 1937.

Kaiser, Daniel H., ed., *The Workers' Revolution in Russia. 1917 - The View from Below*, Cambridge, Cambridge University Press, 1987.

Koenker, Diane, *Moscow Workers and the 1917 Revolution*, Princeton, Princeton University Press, 1981.

Kochan, Lionel, *Russia in Revolution*, London, Paladin, 1970.

Kollontai, Alexandra, *The Workers' Opposition;* https://www.marxists.org/archive/kollonta/1921/workers-opposition/.

_____, *Selected Writings*, London, Alison & Busby, 1977.

Krausz, Tamás, *Reconstructing Lenin, An Intellectual Biography*, New York, Monthly Review Press, 2015.

Krupskaya, Nadezhda, *Reminiscences of Lenin*, New York, International Publishers, 1970; https://www.marxists.org/archive/krupskaya/works/rol/index.htm

Lapidus, Gail Warshofsky, *Women in Soviet Society: Equality, Development, and Social Change*, Berkeley, CA, University of California Press, 1978.

Le Blanc, Paul, *Workers and Revolution: A Comparative Study of Bolshevik Russia and Sandinista Nicaragua*, Ph.D. dissertation, University of Pittsburgh, 1989.

_____, *Lenin and the Revolutionary Party*, Chicago, Haymarket Books, 2015.

_____, *Leon Trotsky*, London, Reaktion Books, 2015.

Left Opposition, *Documents of the 1923 Opposition*, London, New Park, 1975; https://www.marxists.org/history/etol/document/ilo/1923-lo/.

Lenin, V.I., *Collected Works*, Moscow, Progress Publishers, 1960-1970. Available on-line at https://www.marxists.org/archive/lenin/works/index.htm

_____, *Revolution, Democracy, Socialism: Selected Writings*, ed. by Paul Le Blanc, London, Pluto Press, 2008.

Lewin, Moshe, *Lenin's Last Struggle*, Ann Arbor, University of Michigan Press, 2005.

_____, *The Making of the Soviet System: Essays in the Social History of Interwar Russia*, New York, The New Press, 1994.

Liebman, Marcel, *Leninism under Lenin*, London, Merlin Press, 2010.

Lih, Lars, *Lenin*, London, Reaktion Books, 2011.

_____, *Lenin Rediscovered*, Chicago, Haymarket Books, 2008.

Lincoln, W. Bruce, *In War's Dark Shadow*, New York, Simon and Schuster, 1983.

_____, *Passage Through Armageddon*, New York, Simon and Schuster, 1986.

_____, *Red Victory*, New York, Simon and Schuster, 1989.

Lunacharsky, Anatoly, *Revolutionary Silhouettes*, London, Allen Lane-Penguin, 1967; https://www.marxists.org/archive/lunachar/works/silhouet/.

Luxemburg, Rosa, *Rosa Luxemburg Speaks*, ed. Mary-Alice Waters, New York, Pathfinder Press, 1970.

Mandel, David, *The Petrograd Workers and the Fall of the Old Regime*, New York, St. Martin's, 1983.

_____, *The Petrograd Workers and the Soviet Seizure of Power*, London, Macmillan, 1984. http://classiques.uqac.ca/contemporains/mandel_mark_david/petrograd_workers_Soviet_power/mandel_petrograd_workers_t2.pdf.

Mandel, Ernest, *Power and Money – A Marxist Theory of Bureaucracy*, London, Verso, 1992.

_____, 'The Place of Marxism in History', *Notebooks for Study and Research* No 1, IIRE, Amsterdam, 1986; http://www.iire.org/images/stories/notebooks/placeofmarxisminhistory.pdf

_____, *Trotsky*, London, Verso, 1980.

Medvedev, Roy, *Let History Judge: The Origins and Consequences of Stalinism*, New York, Columbia University Press, 1989.

_____, *The October Revolution*, New York, Columbia University Press, 1979.

Mitchell, David, *Red Mirage*, London, Macmillan, 1970.

Moynahan, Brian, *Comrades: 1917 – Russia in Revolution*, Boston, Little, Brown and Co., 1991.

Murphy, Kevin, *Revolution and Counter-Revolution: Class Struggle in a Moscow Metal Factory*, Chicago, Haymarket Books, 2007.

Nimtz, August, *Lenin's Electoral Strategy, From Marx and Engels Through the Revolution of 1905: The Ballot or the Streets – or Both*, New York, Palgrave Macmillan, 2014.

_____, *Lenin's Electoral Strategy, From 1907 to the October Revolution of 1917: The Ballot or the Streets – or Both*, New York, Palgrave Macmillan, 2014.

Pipes, Richard, *The Russian Revolution,* New York, Vintage Books, 1990.

Porter, Cathy, *Alexandra Kollontai,* Updated Edition, London, Merlin Press, 2013.

Rabinowitch, Alexander, *The Bolsheviks Come to Power: The Revolution of 1917 in Petrograd,* Chicago, Haymarket Books, 2009.

_____, *The Bolsheviks in Power: The First Year of Soviet Rule in Petrograd,* Bloomington, IN, Indiana University Press, 2007.

Reed, John, *Ten Days that Shook the World,* New York, Dover, 2006; https://www.marxists.org/archive/reed/1919/10days/10days/index.htm

Rees, John, 'In Defence of October', *International Socialism,* No 52, London, 1991.

Remington, Thomas F., *Building Socialism in Soviet Russia,* University of Pittsburgh Press, 1984; http://digital.library.pitt.edu/cgi-bin/t/text/text-idx?c=pittpress;cc=pittpress;view=toc;idno=31735057896064.

Riddell, John (ed.), *Lenin's Struggle for a Revolutionary International. Documents: 1917-1916, The Preparatory Years,* New York, Monad Press, 1984.

Samary, Catharine, *Plan, Market and Democracy,* NSR no. 7/8, IIRE, Amsterdam, 1988; https://fileserver.iire.org/nsr/NSR7.pdf.

Shapiro, Leonard, *The Communist Party of the Soviet Union.* London: Eyre & Spottiswoode, 1970.

_____, *The Russian Revolution of 1917 - The Origins of Modern Communism,* New York, Basic Books, 1984.

Shliapnikov, Alexander, *On the Eve of 1917,* London, Allison & Busby, 1982; https://www.marxists.org/archive/shliapnikov/1923/eve1917/index.html.

Serge, Victor, *Year One of the Revolution,* Chicago, Haymarket, 2015.

_____, *Destiny of a Revolution,* London, 1937.

_____, *Memoirs of a Revolutionary,* New York, New York Review of Books, 2012.

_____, *Revolution in Danger, Writings from Russia, 1919–1921,* Chicago, Haymarket, 2015.

Smith, Steven A., *Red Petrograd, Revolution in the Factories, 1917-18,* Cambridge, Cambridge University Press, 1985.

_____, *The Russian Revolution, A Very Short Introduction,* Oxford, Oxford University Press, 2002.

Sukhanov, Nicholas, *The Russian Revolution 1917 – A Personal Record*, Princeton, Princeton University, 1984.

Suny, Ronald G., *The Soviet Experiment: Russia, the USSR, and the Successor States*, New York, Oxford University Press, 2010.

_____,'Toward a Social History of the October Revolution,' *American Historical Review*, February 1983, pp. 31-53.

Trotsky, Leon, *History of the Russian Revolution*, Chicago, Haymarket, 2007.

_____, *The Revolution Betrayed*, New York, Dover, 2004.

_____, *1905*, London, Well Red Publications, 2005; https://www.marxists.org/archive/trotsky/1907/1905/.

_____, *The First Five Years of the Communist International*, 2 vols., New York, Pathfinder Press, New York.

_____, *My Life - An Attempt at an Autobiography*, London, Well Red Publications, 2004.

_____, *Permanent Revolution and Results and Prospects*, London, Resistance Books, 2011.

_____, *Writings from Exile, Selected Writings*, ed. by Kunal Chattopadhyay and Paul Le Blanc, London, Pluto Press, 2012.

Robert C. Tucker, *Stalin as Revolutionary: 1879-1929*, New York, W.W. Norton & Company, 1988.

_____, *Stalin in Power: The Revolution from Above, 1928-1941*, New York, W. W. Norton & Company, 1990.

Wade, Rex A., *The Russian Revolution, 1917*, New York, Cambridge University Press, 2000.

Williams, Albert Rhys, *Through the Russian Revolution*, New York, Boni and Liveright, 1921.

Zinoviev, Gregory: *History of the Bolshevik Party*, London, New Park, 1973; https://www.marxists.org/archive/zinoviev/works/history/ch01.htm.

ABOUT RESISTANCE BOOKS AND THE IIRE

Resistance Books

Resistance Books is the publishing arm of Socialist Resistance. Resistance Books publishes books independently, and also jointly with Merlin Press, the International Institute for Research and Education in Amsterdam. Further information about Resistance Books, including a full list of titles available and how to order them, can be obtained at www.resistancebooks. org.

To contact Resistance Books:
Email: info@resistancebooks.org;
Website: www.resistancebooks.org;
Post: Resistance Books, PO Box 62732, London, SW2 9GQ.

Socialist Resistance is a revolutionary Marxist, internationalist, ecosocialist and feminist organisation. Analysis and news from Socialist Resistance can be read online at www.socialistresistance.org or by purchasing its quarterly magazine.

To contact Socialist Resistance, email contact@socialistresistance.org or write to Socialist Resistance, PO Box 62732, London, SW2 9GQ.

Socialist Resistance is a member of the Fourth International, whose online magazine, *International Viewpoint*, is available at www. internationalviewpoint.org.

The International Institute for Research and Education

The IIRE is a centre for the development of critical thought and the exchange of experiences and ideas between people engaged in their struggles. Since 1982, when the Institute opened in Amsterdam, its main activity has been the organisation of courses for progressive forces. The seminars, courses and study groups deal with all subjects related to the emancipation of the oppressed and exploited around the world. It has welcomed participants from across the world, most of them from developing countries. The IIRE provides activists and academics opportunities for research and education in three locations: Amsterdam, Islamabad and Manila.

The IIRE publishes *Notebooks for Study and Research*, which focus on contemporary political debates, as well as themes of historical and theoretical importance. The *Notebooks* have appeared in several languages besides English and French. All the *Notebooks* are available by going to http://iire.org/en/resources/notebooks-for-study-and-research.html. Other publications and audio files of the events held at the IIRE are available in several languages and can be freely downloaded from www.iire.org.

To contact the International Institute for Research and Education:
Email: iire@iire.org
Website: www.iire.org
Phone: 00 31 20 671 7263
Post: International Institute for Research and Education,
Lombokstraat 40, Amsterdam, 1094 AL, The Netherlands

ALSO AVAILABLE FROM THE MERLIN PRESS

GREEN CAPITALISM: WHY IT CAN'T WORK
by Daniel Tanuro

What should be done to resolve the climate crisis? Tanuro argues that government measures - eco-taxes, commodification of natural resources, and carbon trading - do not tackle the drive for profit. Evidence from the Intergovernmental Panel on Climate Change and other sources demonstrates the impossibility of a sustainable 'green capitalism'.
Climate degradation comes with the "natural" functioning of capitalism - a system based on the accumulation of capital (in particular the functioning of the energy system required by this accumulation process). An "emancipatory project" to overcome the impending crisis needs to recognize natural constraints and aim for a fundamental redefinition of social wealth.

'an important contribution to the fight against climate change and for ecosocialism. Tanuro isn't just a writer, he's a leading environmental activist, and it shows - he provides a wealth of concrete information and analysis that we can actually use in the struggle against capitalist ecocide.' *Climate & Capitalism*

A lucid and rigorous demonstration that climate change cannot be overcome unless capitalism is overcome. The scourge of humanity is also the scourge of nature. This is a great achievement: putting forth the necessary contours of the direction that must be taken if we are to be equal to the greatest challenge ever faced by humankind. Joel Kovel, author *The Enemy of Nature*

The climate crisis is at a critical moment while millions despair that no action is being taken. The difficulties our "world leaders" have in taking meaningful action do not spring out of nowhere but from their refusal to understand that this crisis is the consequence of the globalised, neoliberal economic system. This book argues that we cannot simply green our current society, but that we need a more thorough, more fundamental social transformation. We also need to ensure that the struggle for a better world has built into its DNA the pursuit of an ecologically sustainable society.
Natalie Bennett, leader of the Green Party of England and Wales

This is probably the most important book I have ever read and reviewed. It is no exaggeration to say that on the response to its argument depends nothing less than the very survival of the planet on which we have our being.
Michael Barratt Brown, *Spokesman* #123

ISBN 978-0-85036-646-4 paperback
Published by Merlin Press in association with Resistance Books and IIRE

CHINA'S RISE: STRENGTH AND FRAGILITY
Au Loong Yu
With contributions from Bai Ruixue, Bruno Jetin & Pierre Rousset

Au Loong Yu provides the most thorough account of the extent and nature of the transformation of the Chinese state into authoritarian capitalism. This book is essential reading for all those who seek to understand and grasp the dynamics of Chinese-style capitalism and working class resistance to the despotic system.
Immanuel Ness, Brooklyn College, Editor: International Encyclopedia of Revolution and Protest, 1500 to the Present.

This collection of essays on China brings a rare and much needed perspective to the literature on the rising star of the global economy. Most are authored by Chinese Marxist critics of the regime. This "insider" Marxist perspective translates into a discussion of issues rarely covered in the existing literature, including a special focus on the workers movement. Very useful.
Gilbert Achcar, Professor at the School of Oriental and African Studies, London

A collection of lucid and enlightening essays. Au Loong Yu leaves no doubt that China has become capitalist to the fullest extent - with the party bureaucracy as the new bourgeoisie. This leads to old and new contradictions, not to the end of history.
Bodo Zeuner, Professor in political science, Berlin

A fascinating analysis of contemporary struggles in China situated in a rich theoretical overview of Maoism and class relations, as well as the country's position in the international system. A powerful and provocative challenge to many misconceptions on the Left that deserves to be widely read and debated.
Adam Hanieh, School of Oriental and African Studies; editorial board member of the journal Historical Materialism.

. 'a very important addition to the growing literature about Chinese workers today'
Socialist Review.

'Au Loong Yu's book is the best one currently available on modern China and the first one that socialists should turn to for insight when workers in that country inevitably resume their resistance in the future.' Counterfire
326 pages, graphs and tables

ISBN 978-0-85036-637-2

Issue 54 of the IIRE Notebooks for Study and Research
Published by Merlin Press in association with Resistance Books and IIRE

1956: JOHN SAVILLE, E P THOMPSON AND THE REASONER
Edited by Paul Flewers and John McIlroy

1956 was a year of political drama. It saw the Anglo-French seizure of the Suez Canal, Nikita Khrushchev's Secret Speech denouncing Stalin, unrest across Eastern Europe and the Russian invasion of Hungary.

This book discusses the convulsions which enveloped the Communist Party of Great Britain in the aftermath of Khrushchev's revelations. It reprints the text of The Reasoner for the first time in 60 years. It tells the story of this dissident journal and its editiors: John Saville and E.P. Thompson. The Reasoner proved critical in organising opposition to Stalinism in the Communist Party.

- Original essays explore how the events of 1956 came about, their impact on British Communism and the political thinking of Saville and Thompson.
- The editors have provided detailed notes on each issue and a selection of documents from both the party leadership and its opponents.

Meticulously evidenced, thought-provoking and iconoclastic, this text is essential reading for all those seeking to understand British Communism and the politics of Marxism in the seconf half of the twentieth century.

ISBN 978-0-85036-726-3

SOCIALIST REGISTER 2017: RETHINKING REVOLUTION
Edited by Leo Panitch and Greg Albo

Since its inception in 1964, the Socialist Register has been concerned to interrogate the shifting meaning of, and prospects for, revolutionary ruptures from capitalism. This always involved looking forward more thank back, seeking both to transcend the legacy of 'October 1917' and to understand its effects – both positive and negative – on political, intellectual and cultural life.

This 53rd volume of the Socialist Register considers trajectories of radical politics in various regions in the face of neoliberal austerity and capitalist crises. It examines the processes at work in the remaking of the socialist movement today, and what they entail for reviving the prospects for revolutionary transformations that would lead to genuine democratization of state, economy and society.

These essays address:

- The legacy of the Russian and Chinese revolutions
- The salience of the concept of the revolutionary party
- The question of agency – of working classes and other oppressed groups
- The immense ecological challenge for revolutionary politics
- The significance of Sanders and Corbyn for radical movements and parties
- Experiences of left governments, from Venezuela and Bolivia to Greece
- Revolutionary prospects, from Québec to South Africa
- Revolutionary vision, including its artistic expression, in the 21st century

Contributors: Pierre Beaudet, Patrick Bond, Robert Cavooris, Jodi Dean, Fabien Escalona, Sam Gindin, Andreas Malm, Walter Benn Michaels, August H Nimtz, Bryan D Palmer, Leo Panitch, Adolph Reed Jr, Joan Sangster, David Schwartzman, Steve Striffler, Hilary Wainwright, Wang Hui, Slavoj Žižek, A W Zurbrugg

Published in paperback in Canada by Fernwood Publishing and the USA by Monthly Review Press, and in paperback in the UK and the rest of the world and hardback in all territories by The Merlin Press

www.merlinpress.co.uk